MW01470139

Cultural Capital and Black Education

African American Communities and the Funding of Black Schooling, 1865 to the Present

A volume in
Research on African American Education
Series Editors: Carol Camp Yeakey and Ronald D. Henderson

Cultural Capital and Black Education

African American Communities and the Funding of Black Schooling, 1865 to the Present

Edited by

V.P. Franklin
Teachers College, Columbia University

and

Carter Julian Savage
Boys & Girls Clubs of America

INFORMATION AGE
PUBLISHING

80 Mason Street • Greenwich, Connecticut 06830 • www.infoagepub.com

Library of Congress Cataloging-in-Publication Data

Cultural capital and Black education : African American communities and
the funding of Black schooling, 1865 to the present / edited by V.P.
Franklin and Carter Julian Savage.
    p. cm. – (Research on African American education)
  Includes bibliographical references.
  ISBN 1-59311-040-5 (pbk.) – ISBN 1-59311-041-3 (hardcover)
  1. African American schools–Finance. 2. Segregation in
education–Economic aspects–United States. 3. Educational
equalization–United States. I. Franklin, V. P. (Vincent P.), 1947- II.
Savage, Carter Julian. III. Series.
  LC2707.C85 2004
  371.829'96073–dc22

                                             2004020281

Printed in the United States of America

ACKNOWLEDGEMENT

Earlier versions of six chapters in this volume were originally published in *The Journal of African American History*, vol. 88, Spring 2002. The editors would like to acknowledge the officers and staff of the Association for the Study of African American Life and History, the publisher of *The Journal of African American History*, for its support for this volume. The Editorial Office for *The Journal of African American History* (JAAH) is located at the Institute for Urban and Minority Education (IUME), Teachers College, Columbia University. We would also like to acknowledge the support of Professor Edmund Gordon and IUME staff, especially Paula Russell and JAAH Editorial Assistants Edward D. Collins and Steven Zemke, in the production of this volume.

CONTENTS

FOREWORD

We are most pleased to welcome *Cultural Capital and Black Education: African American Communities and the Funding of Black Schooling, 1865 to the Present*, as the second volume in our book series, Research on African American Education. Good history always tells a story and in so doing, provides a way of looking backward as a vehicle for moving forward. What makes this volume so unique is its examination of the role of African Americans in providing the financial and other material resources for public and private schools established in black communities in the United States, from the antebellum era to the 1990s. Recognizing the value of literacy and schooling for themselves and their children, literacy and formal schooling became closely associated with freedom, with liberty, with emancipation, no matter how impoverished formerly enslaved African Americans were. The insightful chapters in this volume build upon the aforementioned themes and provide sound historical background for understanding the obstacles African Americans had to overcome. To say that this excellent volume is unique is an understatement, for what *Cultural Capital and Black Education: African American Communities and the Funding of Black Schooling, 1850 to the Present* provides is a historical lens to understand sacrifices made in African Americans' quest for literacy and formal schooling. More importantly, this volume provides us with lessons learned as a pathway to a greater understanding of just how much more remains to be accomplished as we move into the 21st century.

—Carol Camp Yeakey
Ronald D. Henderson

INTRODUCTION

V.P. Franklin

In June 1876, when Reverend Daniel Payne stepped down after serving for 20 years as president of Wilberforce University, the first institution of higher learning founded by African Americans in the United States, he felt great pride in what he had accomplished. Under his administration the university had become solvent, and through the African Methodist Episcopal (AME) Church, the largest black-controlled religious denomination in the mid-19th century, he had raised over $92,000 in funds to support the educational enterprise. Through the annual "Education Sunday" collections and fundraising activities by hundreds of AME congregations throughout the country, Wilberforce University and the numerous other AME-sponsored educational institutions and programs received financial support essential for their maintenance and advancement. *Cultural Capital and Black Education: African American Communities and the Funding of Black Schooling, 1850 to the Present* examines the role of African Americans in providing financial and other material resources for public and private schools established in black communities in the United States from the antebellum era to the 1990s.

Over the last three decades there have been regular reports in books, magazines, and newspapers describing the precarious financial conditions for urban public school systems with a majority of African American and other nonwhite students. Urban public schools are dependent upon the state legislators and local politicians for their funding and as these school systems became majority black, there has been a greater unwillingness to

Cultural Capital and Black Education, pages xi–xx
Copyright © 2004 by Information Age Publishing
All rights of reproduction in any form reserved.

make sure that the educational expenditures are comparable for students in urban and suburban, rich and poor school districts. The failure of the state and local judges to mandate the equalization of funding for students in urban and suburban public school districts has meant that public school administrators in financially strapped urban school systems, many of whom are African Americans, have eliminated many academic programs, such as art, music, science, and math programs, and most extracurricular activities. The result has been high levels of academic failure, as measured by newly mandated standardized tests, and consistently high dropout rates, particularly among African Americans and other children of color in financially depressed urban public school systems.[1]

The failure of state and local officials to provide equal or even adequate funding for separate black or predominantly black public schools is not a new development in the history of African American education in the United States. In the period from the end of the Civil War to the Supreme Court's *Brown v. Board of Education* decision in 1954, outlawing of legal segregation in public education, white legislators in most of the southern states (and many northern states) refused to utilize public expenditures to ensure the equalization of funding for black and white public schooling. In fact, W.E.B. Du Bois, in the Atlanta University Studies devoted to *The Negro Common School* (1901) and *The Common School and the Negro American* (1911), pointed out that African Americans in most southern states were paying more in public taxation than they were receiving in state and local funding for separate black public schools. As a result of this situation, in the period from 1890 to 1910, southern black taxpayers were in effect providing the funds for the public schooling of white children. White state officials consistently refused to supply adequate funding for black public education until they felt threatened by the possibility of court-mandated public school desegregation in the late 1940s and early 1950s.[2]

As a result of the discriminatory funding practices of white state officials, African American children throughout the country attended inadequately funded public schools from the Reconstruction era to the 1960s. Many times the resources needed for basic instruction, including blackboards, pencils, books, chairs, desks, even land and the buildings, had to be supplied by members of the local black communities. In many instances, white public school officials were only willing to provide funds for the salary of a black elementary school teacher, who was paid much less than a similarly qualified white teacher. Everything else needed for the instruction of black children had to be supplied by African Americans in the local black communities. Historian James D. Anderson, in *The Education of Blacks in the South, 1861–1935* (1988), pointed out that "since the end of the Reconstruction era, black southerners had adapted to a structure of oppressive education by practicing *double taxation*. They had no choice but to pay both direct and indirect taxes for public education. Southern public school authorities diverted school taxes largely to the development of white public education. Blacks then resorted to making private contributions to finance public schools, in effect taxing themselves a second time. Then, to have their privately financed schools recognized and even partially supported by state and local school authorities, black southerners had to deed to the state their contributions of money, land and school equipment."[3] The chapters in *Cultural Capital and Black Education* not only confirm Anderson's findings for the southern states from Reconstruction to the 1930s, but also document the contributions of African Americans to their own schooling in northern states in the antebellum period and in the southern states through the 1940s and 1950s.

One of the major reasons why often impoverished African Americans were willing to subject themselves to "double taxation" was because they recognized the value of literacy and schooling for themselves and their children. The desire for literacy and formal education became a "core value" in the African American cultural value system as a result of the experience of enslavement (with its prohibition of education) and legalized oppression and discrimination in the United States. For formerly enslaved African Americans and their descendents, literacy and formal schooling was closely associated with "freedom," which they were willing to make great sacrifices to obtain.[4]

While individual African Americans benefited from the educational programs provided by the state philanthropic groups, the establishment of public and private educational institutions in many parts of the country was the result of the collective efforts of the African American community. In recent scholarship on the economic value of formal schooling, several researchers have used the term "cultural capital" to refer to the financial advantages that accrue to certain social classes due to the higher levels of education and their ability to influence popular styles and tastes in artistic and cultural arenas. For example, social theorist Pierre Bourdieu argued that wealthy capitalists, such as the owners of music companies, movie studios, art galleries, and media outlets, are able to profit financially from being in a position to create "hype" and determine how middle- and working-class children and adults spend their money for entertainment or other recreational activities. According to Bourdieu, these corporate capitalists possess "cultural capital," which becomes a resource for increasing their corporate profits. Bourdieu, Michael Apple, and other social theorists have emphasized cultural capital in the form of educational credentials possessed by members of the upper and middle classes, which become economic resources for individual economic advancement. Highly educated individuals possess various amounts of cultural capital, the unschooled do not.[5]

Recent researchers on the development of African American educational, charitable, and economic institutions have found that these "business enterprises" were dependent on both "social capital" and *collective* forms of "cultural capital." Under the capitalist system, for any business enterprise to succeed it must have "financial capital," or money to pay for raw materials and labor; "physical capital" in the form of land, machines, and other types of equipment; and "human capital," in the form of the skills and expertise of the workers and managers. More recently, economists and other social scientists have come to recognize the importance of "social capital" for the success of business enterprises. Robert Putnam, Francis Fukuyama, Glenn Loury, and others have argued that social capital, in the form of family networks and labor, community and neighborhood groups, social and fraternal organizations, and voluntary associations, has served as an important resource for the successful functioning of many business enterprises.[6]

When we examine the formation and development of many black banks, orphanages, settlement houses, homes for the aged, and especially educational institutions, we see that these came about as results of collective efforts of the members of African American social and fraternal groups, women's clubs and organizations, and religious denominations. African Americans mobilized their collective resources to establish social and cultural institutions that would benefit not just individuals, but the entire group.[7]

The contributors to *Cultural Capital and Black Education* argue that when a particular business enterprise, such as the opening of a school or college, is considered important for the social or cultural development of the entire group, that institution or enterprise could also draw upon collective "cultural capital." Cultural capital is defined here as the sense of group consciousness and collective identity that serves as an economic resource for the financial and material support of business enterprises that are aimed at the advancement of an entire group. Historically, one of the most important economic undertakings for African Americans, Jewish Americans, Roman Catholics, and women in the United States was the opening of institutions of higher education. Wilberforce University, Yeshiva University, Notre Dame University, Vassar College, and other private colleges and universities founded by specific cultural or religious groups drew upon cultural capital as an important resource. The members of these groups (and others) were willing to donate money, energy, time, and other resources to support these "business enterprises" because these institutions were perceived as beneficial to the entire group. When we examine the history of black elementary, secondary, and higher education, we find that the use of cultural capital as a collective resource helps explain why these educational institutions were founded and supported by members of the local and national black communities. These schools, colleges, and universities were seen as important for the advancement of African Americans collectively in the United States, and thus the members of the community were willing to provide various types of support to insure their schools' success.

The chapters in *Cultural Capital and Black Education* demonstrate that "cultural capital" in various forms became a major resource historically for the funding of African American schools and other educational activities and programs. African Americans were willing to contribute their time, energies, and financial and material resources to support these educational institutions because they knew they were important for the advancement of African Americans as a group. Adah Ward Randolph, in her chapter "Owning, Controlling, and Building upon Cultural Capital: The Albany Enterprise Academy and Black Education in Southeast Ohio, 1863–1886," describes the efforts and sacrifices made by African Americans in southwest Ohio to support an educational institution that would prepare black youths for careers in business, industry, and education. In 1866 Thomas Jefferson Ferguson, the principal of Albany Enterprise Academy, made it clear that the purpose of the school was to demonstrate that "the colored man [and woman] can be made to contribute largely to the advancement of [their] own elevation, and to become ultimately not only self sustaining and self reliant, but a prop and guardian of democratic principles...."

In his chapter, "'I Must Learn Now or Not At All': Social and Cultural Capital in the Educational Initiatives of Formerly Enslaved African Americans in Mississippi, 1862–1869," Christopher M. Span documents the efforts to establish schools and other educational institutions during and immediately after the Civil War. In Vicksburg, Natchez, Meridian, and other cities and towns, and on numerous plantations throughout the state, African Americans used their own meager resources to open schools because "illiterate men and women, young and old, wanted to learn, and semiliterate or literate friends and relatives wanted to teach them." A northern observer of these educational activities reported in 1864 that in Columbus, Mississippi, and throughout the state, formerly enslaved African Americans "show a commendable spirit of independence and desire to provide for themselves.... Many of them working as laborers are willing to pay a one-dollar tuition per month for their children's education."

In my chapter, "Cultural Capital and Black Higher Education: The AME Colleges and Universities as Collective Economic Enterprises, 1865–1910," I describe how cultural capital was used by Bishop Daniel Payne and the other AME ministers and educators to support their educational institutions. Viewing these colleges and universities as significant economic undertakings, the chapter explains why the members of AME churches locally and nationally were willing to make the great sacrifices necessary to support financially these institutions of higher education. The AME leadership's commitment to providing an "educated clergy" for the hundreds of congregations organized following the Civil War meant that theological seminaries as well as colleges and universities had to be established. At the same time, these institutions of higher learning also provided the training and courses of study needed for black men and women who would serve as the teachers in the expanding number of public school systems established in various parts of the United States in the late 19th and early 20th centuries. Cultural capital generated by members of the AME church was used to address the pressing educational needs of African Americans that were not being met by state and federal agencies or white philanthropic foundations during that era.

Carter Julian Savage documents the importance of cultural capital in the support of the all-black school in rural Franklin, Tennessee, between 1890 and 1967. The school was opened in the late 1880s as Claiborne's Institute, but was subsequently renamed the Franklin Colored School, Franklin Training School, and finally Natchez High School. Although the school was eventually incorporated into the local public school system, throughout its long history as an all-black educational institution, it embodied "cultural capital and African American agency" in Tennessee.

In "'Sister Laborers': African American Women, Cultural Capital, and Educational Philanthropy, 1865–1970," Betty Collier-Thomas argues that it was African American women's sense of "group consciousness," informed by considerations of race, gender, and class, that prompted them to join together and assume the responsibility of using their human resources to support collective economic and philanthropic activities. These women generated the cultural capital required for social and economic programs to advance African Americans in general, and African American women in particular. Collier-Thomas examines the organized philanthropic activities of African American women's clubs and social and religious organizations and finds that "black women raised funds to support orphanages, homes for the aged, and, most importantly, facilities for young black women, not merely to allow them to survive, but to demonstrate that now that we are free, we can…take care of our own."

The chapter by Richard M. Breaux builds upon the work of Betty Collier-Thomas. In "Maintaining a Home for Girls: The Iowa Federation of Colored Women's Clubs at the University of Iowa, 1919–1950," Richard Breaux describes the history and development of "Sue Brown Hall" for African American women who were denied access to campus housing at this midwestern state university. Through the financial support provided by the black club women, the Federation Home was established, and the residents understood the importance of these collective efforts on their behalf. In a 1923 letter to the clubwomen, the students expressed their "hearty appreciation for the faithful work that you have done and are doing now" in maintaining the Federation Home. The sacrifices made by the club women inspired these students to use their education for the collective benefit of the entire African American community.

In addition to documenting the material resources provided by the members of African American communities to support educational institutions and housing for black students, the studies by Peggy B. Gill and Monica A. White also emphasize the commitment to academic excellence among African American educators in separate black schools as a form of cultural capital important for the success of African American educational efforts. In the chapter, "Community, Commitment, and African American Education: The Jackson School of Smith County Texas, 1925–1954," Gill describes the establishment of a "county training school" in rural east Texas with financial support from the local African American community and Rosenwald Fund. The Jackson School became the center of cultural activities for the African American community. Through extensive oral interviews with former students and teachers, Gill documents the role of the school in the lives of individuals in the community and describes "the evolution of shared values, assumptions, beliefs, and knowledge. These shared meanings and experiences became common possessions and the source of the community's cultural capital." The former teachers at the Jackson School described the fundraising activities that took place in the community to support the students' extracurricular activities, and emphasized the collective efforts to make sure that "no child is left behind."

In her chapter, "Paradise Lost? Teachers' Perspectives on the Use of Cultural Capital in the Segregated Schools of New Orleans," Monica White contrasts the educational practices in all-black schools before and after the legal desegregation of the public school system. Before public school desegregation in the 1960s, black teachers in New Orleans considered themselves leaders in the community and role models for the children and viewed their commitment to black public education as a calling and vocation. In interviews, former teachers emphasized their personal responsibility for the academic success of their students, and their willingness to be accountable to parents and the community for the professional services they provided. In contrast, many teachers in the 1990s considered themselves outsiders who were detached from the local school community, and were responsible primarily for the transmission of knowledge and information required for state-mandated systems of standardized testing. Given the high rates of academic failure for black students being taught by black teachers in the 1990s, White concludes that in the era before public school desegregation, cultural capital in the form of the personal and professional commitments of black teachers to their students was an important resource for academic achievement and success.

What are the important lessons that we can learn from these studies of the history of cultural capital and African American education? One of the most disturbing and persistent characteristics of the public schooling made available to African American children in the United States has been the inadequacy of the funding. From the antebellum era when the first "common schools" were opened in the northern states, the public education made available to African American students was separate and unequal. Providing equal and adequate schools for African American children was generally viewed as a threat to white supremacy, and white taxpayers then and now refuse to support public schooling that would allow African Americans to advance from their subordinate position in this society. Individual African Americans were provided the opportunity to receive the same types and levels of schooling as whites, but the denial of access to public and private schooling for African Americans as a group became a cornerstone in the structure of white racial oppression and domination.

Enslaved and oppressed African Americans clearly understood that "knowledge is power" and made extraordinary efforts to provide and support schools for themselves and their children throughout the 19th century and first half of the 20th century. With the Supreme Court's *Brown* decision and the federal government's efforts in the 1950s and 1960s to insure African American children's access to all publicly supported schools, many African Americans came to believe that they would no longer have to use their own resources to provide excellent, or even adequate, public or private schooling for their children. However, over the last 50 years, it has become increasingly clear this is not the case.

In the final chapter, "Social Capital, Cultural Capital, and the Challenge of African American Education in the 21st Century," I point out that in the past, education in general, and schooling in particular, was important for African Americans in providing viable answers to the question, "Why are we here?" There are those who have argued that African Americans need schooling in order to compete and to eventually become "integrated" into the dominant institutions in American society. This integrationist perspective focuses on the importance of education for African Americans to be considered first-class citizens and to ensure that they are on the road to parity with European and other ethnic groups in the United States. Other African American leaders and spokespersons have argued that African Americans' role in the United States and the world is to serve as a model for other oppressed people. The advancement of U.S. African Americans "from slavery to freedom" and their struggle against unjust racial discrimination and oppression has inspired movements for social change throughout the world. However, at the beginning of the 21st century, the AIDS epidemic, the disproportionate incarceration rates for African Americans, and the persistent underfunding of public school systems with large numbers of African American and other minority students are among the most significant threats to their future prospects. In advocating the formation of an "African American Council on Education," organizations and leaders are called upon to mobilize the collective resources in the local and national black community—cultural capital—to improve the quality of schooling made available to African American children to prepare them as contributing citizens to American society and leaders in the African world. Thus, the answer to the question, "Why are we here?" provided in this chapter, and addressed indirectly by the contributors to this volume, is, "We are here to protect our children and prepare them for the positions they will occupy in the world in the 21st century." Cultural capital will be an important resource in preparing African American children to fulfill their destiny, and to provide them with the knowledge needed to answer the even more important question, "Why am *I* here?"

NOTES

1. Carl L. Bankston and Stephen J. Caldes, "Majority African American Schools and the Perpetuation of Injustice: The Influence of Defacto Segregation on Academic Achievement," *Social Forces* 72 (1996): 534–555; and *A Troubled Dream: The Promise and Failure of School Desegregation in Louisiana* (Nashville, TN, 2002); Pat Wingert, "Urban Schools Play Anxious Numbers Game," *Newsweek* (31 December–7 January 2002): 99. For a detailed analysis of the financial and academic inadequacies of urban public schools for African American children and suggestions for reform, see Janice E. Hale, *Learning While Black: Creating Educational Excellence for African American Children* (Baltimore, MD, 2001), 37–93.

2. W.E.B. Du Bois, ed., *The Negro Common School* (Atlanta, GA, 1901), 77–91; and *The Common School and the Negro American* (Atlanta, GA, 1911), 7–8.

3. James D. Anderson, *The Education of Blacks in the South, 1862–1935* (Chapel Hill, NC, 1988), 156.

4. V.P. Franklin, *Black Self-Determination: A Cultural History of African American Resistance* (Brooklyn, NY, 1992), 147–185.

5. Pierre Bourdieu, *Distinction: A Social Critique of the Judgment of Taste* (Cambridge, MA, 1984), 225–228; Pierre Bourdieu and J. C. Passaron, *Reproduction in Education Society and Culture* (London, 1977), 71–106. See also Bourdieu, *The Field of Cultural Production: Essays on Art and Literature* (New York, 1993), 43–45, 99–104; Michael W. Apple, *Cultural Politics and Education* (New York, 1996), 22–24; and *Education the "Right" Way: Markets, Standards, God, and Inequality* (New York, 2001), 73–82.

6. Robert D. Putnam, "Bowling Alone: America's Declining Social Capital," *Current* 373 (June 1995): 3–4; "The Prosperous Community: Social Capital and Economic Growth," *Current* 356 (October 1993): 4–9; and *Bowling Alone: The Collapse and Revival of American Community* (New York, 2000); Francis Fukuyama, "Social Capital and the Global Economy," *Foreign Affairs* 74 (September-October 1995): 89–103; and *Trust: The Social Virtues and the*

Creation of Prosperity (New York, 1995); Glenn Loury, "New Dividends through Social Capital," *Black Enterprise* 15 (July 1985): 36–37; Frank Fratoe, "Social Capital and Black Business Owners," *Review of Black Political Economy* 14 (Spring 1988): 33–50.

7. John Sibley Butler, *Entrepreneurship and Self-Help Among Black Americans: A Reconsideration of Race and Economics* (Albany, NY, 1991); James B. Stewart, "Toward a Broader Involvement of Black Economists in Discussions of Race and Public Policy: A Plea for the Reconceptualization of Race and Power in Economic Theory," *Review of Black Political Economy* 23 (Winter 1995): 13–35; Bettye Collier-Thomas, "'The Relief Corps of Heaven': Black Women as Philanthropists," in *Philanthropy in Communities of Color: Traditions and Challenges*, ed. Piers C. Rogers (Indianapolis, IN), 25–39.

CHAPTER 1

"I MUST LEARN NOW OR NOT AT ALL"

Social and Cultural Capital in the Educational Initiatives of Formerly Enslaved African Americans in Mississippi, 1862–1869

Christopher M. Span

Before the Civil War there wasn't a free school in the state, but under the Reconstruction government, we built them in every county. . . . We paid to have every child, Negro and white, schooled equally. Today, they've cut down on the educational program, and discriminated against the Negro children, so that out of every educational dollar, the Negro child gets only 30 cents.

—George Washington Albright, *The Daily Worker* (1937)

In June 1937, at the age of 91, an ex-slave from Holly Spring, Mississippi, by the name of George Washington Albright was interviewed by the *Daily Worker* regarding his legislative and educational activities during and after the Civil War.[1] Albright proffered the above statement and his intentions seemed unmistakable. Cognizant of Mississippi blacks' existing educational opportunities and their extremely vulnerable and denigrated status, he

Cultural Capital and Black Education, pages 1–13
Copyright © 2004 by Information Age Publishing
All rights of reproduction in any form reserved.

wanted to inform the public of the important contributions African Americans—in particular former slaves—played in the establishment of the state's first comprehensive public school system. Albright knew firsthand that the status of African Americans in the years immediately after slavery and in contemporary Jim Crow Mississippi was markedly different. Prior to the end of the Reconstruction era and the rise of state-sanctioned segregation, Mississippi blacks—despite the overwhelming majority being former slaves—viewed freedom optimistically and had rights that extended beyond second-class citizenship. For nearly a decade after the war they voted, became landowners, determined and negotiated their working conditions, and were leaders and contributors in their local communities, regions, and the entire state.

As an active agent in promoting education in postwar Mississippi, Albright recalled the principal public school initiatives he and the other black delegates elected to the state's 1868 constitutional convention wanted for Mississippi. The state's public schools were to be free, all-inclusive, and most importantly equitable, irrespective of the child's sex, race, class, or previous condition of servitude.[2] In attempting to achieve this aim, Albright was convinced that his generation—through their determination, appreciation of the value of education, and limited resources—collectively laid the groundwork for the rise of universal public schooling in postwar Mississippi. They provided the financial and "sweat equity" for the establishment and continuation of the first schools, served as teachers, solicited northern-born teachers to migrate to Mississippi, and pressured state legislators to consider their educational ambitions and needs as new citizens. During the war Albright, himself barely literate, served as one of the first teachers of formerly enslaved African Americans in Mississippi. As the war commenced, his first class was taught under a shade tree, then in an abandoned barn, and thereafter in a church. "The state had no teachers," contended Albright, "until we brought in teachers from the North, men and women, white and Negro."[3] To Albright, this generation of formerly enslaved African Americans was not a powerless citizenry forced to accept the status quo as were their descendants in Jim Crow Mississippi. On the contrary, they were an empowered and contributing force not just in their own educational pursuits, but in the advancement of universal education for all children in postbellum Mississippi.

The editors of the *Daily Worker* virtually dismissed Albright's recollections of his and his entire generation's pro-active stance in the first decade after slavery. While the communist editors thought his commentary to be quite animated, they questioned the accuracy of Albright's memories, especially regarding the legislative and educational impact former slaves had on the state's postbellum political economy.[4] However, Albright's retrospection concerning public education in Mississippi—despite his occasional misnomers—was sharply accurate and epitomized W. E. B. Du Bois's assertion that "public education for all at public expense was, in the South, a Negro idea."[5]

Contemporary scholarship indicates that both during and after the Civil War, opportunities for schooling African Americans throughout the South arose primarily from the initial efforts and enthusiasm of African Americans themselves.[6] This was especially true in Mississippi. Prior to the end of the war, before the concerted arrival of northern religious or freedmen aid organizations, such as the American Missionary Association or the Freedmen's Bureau, African Americans in Mississippi initiated the process of organizing schools wherever possible, and educating themselves. As early as 1862, free, freed, fugitive, and enslaved African Americans established churches and schoolhouses for individual and collective improvement on abandoned property throughout the state. Barely literate former slaves and the state's few literate or semiliterate free blacks served as these schools' first teachers, and previously enslaved African Americans—young and old, male and female—were their initial pupils. Fortunately, these combined grassroots initiatives served as the catalyst for Mississippi's first tax-supported comprehensive public school system.

For the historian of African American education, particular questions arise pertaining to the collective educational goals of formerly enslaved African Americans in general, and in Mississippi in particular. For example, from where did this motivation stem, and was it in fact a collective sentiment? What practical or tangible goals did this oppressed people envision for their acquired learning? What purposes would it serve in their new lives as free people? Despite being the majority in the state's population, how did an impoverished, overwhelmingly illiterate, and extremely vulnerable group of former slaves establish a system of grassroots schools for themselves and their children? To rephrase the question: What concrete measures did formerly enslaved African Americans in Mississippi establish to perpetuate their culturally defined love and appreciation of learning? Contemporary theorists of social capital and cultural capital offer an insightful perspective for the historian of African American education to consider when addressing these questions. These concepts have several advantages. They center the researcher's questions on the cultural attributes of the group studied, for instance, what the group valued, relied upon, and practiced at a particular place and time. For the sake of this research, this emphasis allows us to better understand the influence Mississippi former slaves' culture, group consciousness, and resources had on their educational development.

Social capital, according to historian V. P. Franklin, is defined as "the network of social organizations, cultural institutions, voluntary civic associations, family and kinship groups in a community that assist in the development of an economic enterprise."[7] Cultural capital refers to "the sense of group consciousness that is utilized as a resource in the development of collective economic enterprises."[8] While the earliest educational initiatives of formerly enslaved African Americans have not been viewed as an "economic enterprise," grassroots black schooling, its establishment, and its perpetuation during this time period required more than group consciousness or a collective appreciation for learning. In reality, it required material, financial, and human resources to start and ensure a prolonged and successful outcome. Such considerations typified the earliest educational initiatives of African Americans in Mississippi as they rallied around their groups' past and present experiences, collective desire for learning, and limited resources to successfully establish a system of grassroots schools for themselves and their children.

In Reconstruction Mississippi, formerly enslaved African Americans valued very highly the idea of being educated, and this sentiment served as an invaluable resource in their earliest educational initiatives. Between 1862 and 1869, this collective group consciousness served as the primary resource or cultural capital needed to begin and sustain their grassroots educational enterprises. Education—or at least some degree of literacy—was a paramount goal and invaluable acquisition for Mississippi's black masses. Whereas poor whites, according to W. E. B. Du Bois, viewed "formal schooling" as a "luxury connected to wealth" and did not demand an opportunity to acquire it, African Americans in Mississippi, both during and after slavery, demanded schooling, connecting it with freedom, autonomy, and self-determination.[9] It is highly likely that the prohibition against "learning to read and write in the old slave codes," as suggested by Mississippi historian Vernon Lane Wharton, had a great deal to do with former slaves' adamant determination toward acquiring literacy.[10] However, this prohibition was not alone in motivating former slaves in Mississippi to pursue the rudiments of learning. As a skill, literacy had numerous social purposes and was central to African Americans' definitions of freedom, progress, success, and self-identity, and their views on the nature of citizenship. Acquiring any amount of education in slavery's aftermath represented a dual advancement to Mississippi's black community. It represented a step toward shedding an imposed "slave" status and obtaining greater freedom as prospective citizens. Accordingly, countless African Americans purposely sought schooling and literacy, viewing them as the foundations for self-improvement and one means for attaining social and economic parity in the state's evolving postbellum political economy.

The primary motivation for black Mississippians' educational enthusiasm stemmed from their beliefs about what being literate represented in their daily interactions, opportunities, and livelihood. As historians Janet Duitsman Cornelius, Thomas Webber, and V. P. Franklin have documented, African Americans' profound respect for education and its potential usefulness existed for generations during enslavement.[11] Upon emancipation, African Americans valued literacy for a number of very practical reasons, such as being able to the read the Bible and teach it to the young, understand their legal rights, negotiate labor contracts, and buy or lease land. The testimonies of formerly enslaved African Americans in Mississippi confirm this assessment. When asked by her teacher why she wanted to learn to read, an unnamed 85-year-old woman from Vicksburg, who was a former slave, sincerely replied, "I must learn now or not at all . . . so I can read the Bible and teach the young."[12] Similarly, in Natchez another elder former slave was convinced that learning to read and write would help him establish his own business. When his educational motives were questioned, he informed his teacher, "I wants to learn to cipher so I can do business."[13] These everyday expectations served as the principal reasons those formerly enslaved gave for desiring literacy.

However, education was perceived as more than a means of personal and professional improvement. White state officials' hostile and/or disinterested treatment of African Americans in Mississippi before and after the war quickly reinforced their belief that being literate was one of several pragmatic and necessary strategies to deal with these negative circumstances. Nothing exemplified these conditions more than the labor contracts offered by the state's landowning gentry. Mississippi planters used their political and economic leverage to induce the state legislature to pass a number of laws to explicitly control how the freedpeople in Mississippi could express their newly won freedom. "Black codes" defined the legal "rights" of the state's former slaves and free blacks. They determined African Americans' rights to acquire and own property, marry, file lawsuits, testify in court decisions involving members of their own race, and establish contractual arrangements. All of these activities necessitated some degree of literacy. Yet, Mississippi's black codes also served as a legal stratagem to reinforce and perpetuate the landowning gentry's supremacy and control over African Americans' economic, political, and social opportunities. Overall, black codes protected the interests of Mississippi's landowners and defined African Americans as a permanent underclass. In 1865, when Mississippi's black codes went into effect, even a rudimentary education served as a useful possession and practical means of self-protection.[14]

African Americans in Mississippi viewed education as an absolute necessity to protect them in their new status as free people. Landless, vulnerable, illiterate, and victimized by unscrupulous politicians and landowners, most African Americans in Mississippi had to create strategies to challenge their subjugated and precarious condition. For example, black Mississippians established various organizations and committees, such as the African Benevolent Association and masonic lodges, to promote their general interests and concerns. Economically, many migrated to other counties in search of better working conditions. Some fled to Union camps and worked closely with the army and northern-born migrants to extend their employment options. As a group, they refused to accept repressive labor contracts. In 1868, when black males gained the franchise in the state, they, like southern black males elsewhere, formed "Loyal Leagues" and other partisan organizations to ensure that their political interests were met.[15] Educationally, black Mississippians built, maintained, and taught in schools established for themselves and their children. These postbellum initiatives, which evolved from the cultural values and expectations of black Mississippians, were created to address their overall social, political, and economic concerns. Moreover, like George Washington Albright, most African Americans in Mississippi understood that their individual circumstances were invariably tied to the fortunes of the group.

Finally, and perhaps more importantly, Mississippi freedpeople's collective desire for education became the cultural capital needed to erect the first schools for themselves, their children, and fellow citizens in Mississippi. One former slave's remark exemplified this notion when he proudly declared that building a "school-house would be the first proof of *our* independence" (emphasis added).[16] Embedded in this statement was the drive, initiative, and determination that "provided the grassroots foundation for the educational activities of Northern missionary societies and the Freedmen's Bureau" upon their arrival in the state in 1863.[17]

BLACK EDUCATIONAL INITIATIVES
IN POSTBELLUM MISSISSIPPI

The truth that formerly enslaved African Americans utilized their own social and cultural capital for their educational advancement after emancipation is most evident in their activities between 1862 and 1869. Throughout the state, black Mississippians, through their own initiatives and resources, built schools and collected and spent their own funds for specific educational purposes they saw as essential to their overall advancement. At the close of the Civil War, for example, freedpeople in Natchez raised about $40 per month over a 2-year period to support their schools and to pay teachers' salaries.[18] In Raymond, Mississippi, a group of former slaves collectively purchased a plot of land and erected a building to function as both a schoolhouse and church.[19] African Americans in Grenada built a church that also served as a schoolhouse. And despite their impoverished condition, they paid the "board and washing costs" for the town's two northern-born teachers.[20] In Vicksburg, Natchez, and Meridian, African Americans taxed themselves and formed all-black boards of directors that oversaw the erection of a number of schoolhouses and churches. In Vicksburg, for example, Hiram Revels led such a board, and the members were responsible for assessing and collecting the funds to be used for schools.[21] At the same time, African Americans in these cities organized a variety of political, social, and religious organizations, including the African Benevolent Association, Masonic lodges, Loyal Leagues, and several African Methodist Episcopal churches.[22]

There were equally impressive examples of social and cultural capital in action on the secluded cotton plantations of Mississippi. On these abandoned plantations, well before the end of the war, black Mississippians converted parts of the "big house" into their own private schoolhouses. By 1864, these educational initiatives had become commonplace and arriving northern missionaries and Union officials discovered that large numbers of former slaves had already begun to learn to read and write. These schools were virtually independent, relying only on the resources—usually a Bible, a few books or primers, and teachers—gathered by the African Americans attending or teaching in the schools. James Yeatman, the sanitary commissioner appointed by the St. Louis–based Western Sanitary Commission to the Mississippi Valley, encountered several of these independent black schools as he moved through the countryside documenting the general health conditions for the state's wartime inhabitants. "There is at [the] Groshon's plantation," remarked Yeatman, "a school of about forty to fifty students, young and old, taught by Rosa Anna, a colored girl."[23] Up the road on the Savage plantation, a local black man conducted a school for at least 30 pupils.[24] On the Goodrich plantation, Yeatman continued, a former slave known as "Uncle Jack" taught a school with over 80 students. "William McCuthehen, a colored man," identified by Yeatman, "commenced a school on the Currie place" and taught at least 60 students.[25]

Great enthusiasm for learning and sharing knowledge epitomized these early black schools. Illiterate men and women, young and old, wanted to learn, and semiliterate or literate friends and relatives wanted to teach them. This was precisely how George Washington Albright began his school; and the activities there were supported by the cultural capital provided by local African Americans. After picking up the rudiments of learning from his semiliterate mother during slavery, Albright's first objective as a free person was to establish a school. For Albright and many others who started their own educational institutions, pedagogical training, makeshift classrooms, and the limited financial and material resources were secondary concerns. With imagination, resourcefulness, and some degree of flexibility in what constituted a "school" or a "teacher," the freedpeople in Mississippi relied on their collective desire and respect for learning and made good use of whatever resources were available.

As political conditions stabilized in Mississippi and more northern-based missionaries came southward to work with the freedpeople, local African Americans coordinated their educational efforts and programs with those provided by these agencies. For instance, in Natchez, Mississippi, former slaves and free blacks combined their efforts with those of the American Missionary Association. Most noteworthy was Mrs. Lily Grandison, a former slave who "had taught among her fellow slaves for many years by night and stealth" prior to emancipation because the formal instruction of slaves was strictly forbidden.[26] Once emancipated, Mrs. Grandison became one of "three native black female teachers" to open a school. Even in the midst of the wartime disorder, she charged students a $1–$2 monthly tuition.[27] The same was true of Josephine Nicks, a free black native of Natchez. She also maintained a small private school both during and immediately after the Civil War, but like Lily Grandison, combined her independent efforts— very likely for financial reasons—with the educational activities of the American Missionary Association.

Some black Mississippians were unwilling to give up their educational institutions or relinquish their autonomy to the northern-based agencies in postwar Mississippi. For example, in 1867 there were at least ten private black schools in Natchez, Mississippi, and at least five in Vicksburg. Unlike those of Nicks and Grandison, these schools remained independent institutions.[28] Upon his arrival, Joseph Warren, the acting educational superintendent of the Freedmen's Bureau, acknowledged the existence of at least ten additional private black schools outside the cities of Natchez and Vicksburg, some with pupils numbering in the hundreds.[29] These schools, Warren confirmed, were established and controlled by the local black residents.

> A school with a colored teacher can be found at Aberdeen. At Canton, one or two schools have been established [for] some time. At Brandon an interesting school of nearly 40 scholars was being taught by a young colored woman [who migrated] from Mobile [Alabama]. At Forrest, a colored sergeant was teaching a small number of scholars. At Meridian two schools were in operation taught by colored men . . . each with about 30 scholars. At Columbus 3 colored schools are in operation taught by colored men poorly qualified with a total of about 100 scholars . . . [and] an evening school is taught by a colored man at Corinth.[30]

Still the primary, and often underestimated, form of cultural capital that the freedpeople provided for their educational institutions was money. In the years during and after the Civil War, black schools in Mississippi survived on tuition and financial contributions from Mississippi's African Americans. Despite their landless and poverty-stricken status, the great majority of Mississippi's freedpeople willingly contributed to their group's overall educational development. As one northern emissary noted in Columbus, Mississippi, "they show a commendable spirit of independence and desire to provide for themselves. . . . Many of them working as laborers are willing to pay a one-dollar tuition per month for their children's education."[31] "By the advice of the more intelligent of the colored people," Vicksburg's black residents agreed to charge tuition of 60 cents per month per pupil to defray some of the educational costs.[32] At that same time, they decided to tax themselves to ensure that public education was available to black children in the city.

Black militiamen and day laborers, mostly transient workers in the early years, also contributed to the cause of black education. Many used their first salaries to clothe, feed, house, and educate themselves, their families, and the most destitute among them.[33] Between 1863 and 1865, a number of African Americans in Mississippi—with some assistance from the Union Army—leased plots of land on confiscated or abandoned plantations and were very successful in harvesting cotton and corn for themselves and for a small profit. Former slaves Granville Green, Tom Taylor, Luke Johnson, Solomon Richardson, and many others produced hundreds of bails of cotton purchased by the government and northern industry and used the remainder to clothe dependent freedpeople and their children in Union camps and refugee asylums.[34]

In many instances, the financial contributions to educational activities by the freedpeople in Mississippi were not always monetary. Throughout the state, many paid their teachers in food, clothing, laundry, local transportation, and shelter when resentful and antagonistic white Mississippians refused to accept their patronage or assist these educators in their activities on behalf of the former slaves. Moreover, most of the labor needed for the building of these schools was provided by the freedpeople. Throughout the state these forms of material and physical assistance were essential, but traditionally have gone unrecognized as significant financial contributions to the advancement of black education in the region. Such cultural capital offered by the freedpeople in Mississippi assisted in paying the travel, housing, and material needs of the teachers who taught in their schools. Simultaneously, it demonstrated the self-determinist attitudes and practices of black Mississippians in pursuit of social and economic advancement.

Black Mississippians' financial contributions provided a significant proportion of the funds for establishing a network of local educational institutions. Historian Clifford Ganus, Jr., calculated that the reported tuition paid by Mississippi's freedpeople between August 1866 and June 1870 was $23,976.10, or almost $6,000 a year.[35] This contribution amounted to almost 34 percent, or one-third, of the total known revenue collected and expended for educational activities sponsored by the Freedmen's Bureau and various missionary societies in Mississippi during that period. Equally important, this reported monetary contribution was not inclusive of the time, energy, and resources that Mississippi freedpeople provided, or the additional funds contributed to the growing number of relatively independent and private black schools in the state.

Adding to the significance of such contributions was the fact that these collective efforts were sustained at a time when few African Americans were receiving a living wage and the state suffered two years of devastating crop failures. During the crop failure in 1866–67, black farm workers went unpaid for their labors, and most were displaced from the plantations where they had worked all year.[36] At the same time, working people in the black community were taxed by the state's local authorities to assist in the care of dependent freedpeople. The 1867 Freedmen's Pauper Tax Law, as it was known, was a modified extension of one of the abandoned 1865–66 black codes. It authorized the Board of Police of each county to levy a poll tax on "each and every freedmen, free Negro, and Mulatto between the ages of eighteen and sixty not to exceed one dollar annually."[37] No such tax was found for the state's white residents; even for the care of dependent or disabled Confederate veterans or their families. In some counties the Freedmen's Pauper Tax amounted to as much as $20,000 or as little as $5,000 per year. However, as historian William Leon Wood revealed, "much discrimination was practiced at collection intervals and instead of providing a livelihood for destitute blacks," the funds were used to enrich corrupt civil authorities.[38]

CONCLUSION

In retrospect, the testimony of George Washington Albright regarding black Mississippians' contributions to the state's first comprehensive public school system was indeed accurate. The combined enthusiasm, activities, and contributions of the state's freedpeople both during and after the war were the catalyst for the establishment of public schools in Mississippi. Enthusiasm for literacy and learning was firmly rooted in the African American cultural value system, and this cultural appreciation for education served as an invaluable resource—the cultural capital—for the establishment of the first black schools in the state. African Americans in Mississippi clearly understood that an education would be important for social mobility and individual and collective improvement. Schools served as the institution to promote these interests, and would assist the former slaves in becoming citizens. Black Mississippians' regard for learning was so great that it manifested itself in various ways in the early postbellum years. Most former slaves able to obtain some degree of learning worked with the northern-based educational agencies operating in the state. A significant minority independently began private schools that were opened on abandoned plantations. Through their own efforts or with the help of others, black Mississippians utilized their skills and meager resources to create a system of grassroots schools for themselves and their families in the years during and immediately after the Civil War.

NOTES

1. George Washington Albright's narrative can be found in George P. Rawick's compilation of WPA interviews with formerly enslaved African Americans. It was reprinted from the *Daily Worker*, June 18, 1937. The *Daily Worker* was an East Coast weekly newspaper for the American Communist Party. George P. Rawick, *The American Slave: A Composite Autobiography* (New Haven, 1977), 8–19, quote on 16–17.

2. Ibid.

3. Ibid.

4. Ibid. The interviewer and the editors appeared to have had some difficulty understanding Albright—"Hollis Springs" should be Holly Springs, for example. There is no way of telling whether the interviewer's difficulty or Albright's memory was the problem where the narrative incorrectly reports the number of black delegates to the Mississippi Constitutional Convention of 1868. Albright's written statement declares that 74 out of 100 delegates of the 1868 constitutional convention were black. However, only 17 of the 100 delegates were black. The editors also assumed that Albright exaggerated the number of schools in Marshall County. Albright states that blacks built 40 schools in Marshall County, which, according to the 1870–71 superintendent's annual report, is nearly accurate. The superintendent's report affirms that 39 schools were available to blacks in Marshall County in the inaugural year of public schooling in Mississippi. See *Annual Report of the Superintendent of Public Education of the State of Mississippi for the Year Ending December, 1871* (Jackson, Miss., 1872), 124–131.

5. W. E. B. Du Bois, *Black Reconstruction in America: An Essay toward a History of the Part in Which Black Folk Played in the Attempt to Reconstruct Democracy in America, 1860–1880* (New York, 1935), 641.

6. Extensive scholarship details the educational motivations of African Americans during the Reconstruction era. Most notable are: James D. Anderson, *The Education of Blacks in the South, 1860–1935* (Chapel Hill, 1988), 4–16; Ronald Butchart, *Northern Schools, Southern Blacks, and Reconstruction* (Westport, Conn., 1980); Eric Foner, *Reconstruction: America's Unfinished Revolution, 1863–1877* (New York, 1988), 96–102; Jacqueline Jones, *Soldiers of Light and Love: Northern Teachers and Georgia Blacks, 1865–1873* (Chapel Hill, 1980); Robert C. Morris, *Reading, 'Riting, and Reconstruction: The Education of Freedmen in the South, 1862–1870* (Chicago, 1981); Randy Sparks, "'The White People's Arms Are Longer than Ours': Education and the American Missionary Association in Reconstruction Mississippi," *Journal of Mississippi History* 54 (no. 1, 1992): 1–27.

7.   V. P. Franklin, "Cultural Capital and Black Higher Education: The AME Colleges and Universities as Collective Economic Enterprises, 1856–1910" in this volume.

8.   Ibid., 38.

9.   Du Bois, *Black Reconstruction*, 640.

10.   Vernon Lane Wharton, *The Negro in Mississippi, 1865–1890* (New York, 1947), 45.

11.   Janet Duitsman Cornelius, *When I Can Read My Title Clearly: Literacy, Slavery, and Religion in the Antebellum South* (Columbia, SC, 1991); V. P. Franklin, *Black Self-Determination: A Cultural History of African American Resistance* (Brooklyn, NY, 1992); Thomas Webber, *Deep Like Rivers: Education in the Slave Quarter Community, 1831–1865* (New York, 1978).

12.   James E. Yeatman, *A Report on the Condition of the Freedmen in Mississippi* (St. Louis, 1864), 3.

13.   Foner, *Reconstruction: America's Unfinished Revolution*, 97.

14.   Donald Nieman, "The Freedmen's Bureau and the Mississippi Black Code," *The Journal of Mississippi History* 40 (1978): 91–118, 93–94; David Sansing, "The Failure of Johnsonian Reconstruction in Mississippi, 1865–1866," *The Journal of Mississippi History* 34 (1972): 373–390, 378–387.

15.   James T. Currie, *Vicksburg and Her Plantations, 1863–1870* (Jackson, Miss., 1980), 178–203.

16.   John Dennett, *The South As It Is: 1865–1866* (New York, 1965), 304.

17.   Anderson, *The Education of Blacks in the South*, 15.

18.   Sparks, "The White Folks Arms Are Longer than Ours'," 3.

19.   Clifford Ganus Jr., "The Freedmen's Bureau in Mississippi," Ph.D. diss., Tulane University, June 1953, 301.

20.   Sparks, "The White Folks Arms Are Longer than Ours'," 3.

21.   Colonel Samuel Thomas, "Special Order No. 231," *Vicksburg Journal* (September 7, 1865); William Leon Woods, "Travail of Freedom: Mississippi Blacks, 1862–1870," Ph.D. diss., Princeton University, 1979, 168.

22.   Du Bois, *Black Reconstruction*, 646–647; Sparks, "The White Folks Arms Are Longer than Ours'," 3; Wharton, *The Negro in Mississippi*, 45–46, 243–256; Foner, *Reconstruction: America's Unfinished Revolution*, 98; Ganus Jr., "The Freedmen's Bureau in Mississippi," 301–303.

23.   Yeatman, *A Report on the Conditions of the Freedmen in Mississippi*, 11.

24.   Ibid.

25.   Ibid.

26.   Sparks, "The White Folks Arms Are No Longer than Ours'," 2. See also the American Missionary Association Archives microfilmed records for Mississippi at the Amistad Research Center, Tulane University, New Orleans, Louisiana.

27.   Sparks, "The White Folks Arms Are No Longer than Ours'," 3.

28.   For a discussion of the conflicting educational values between former Mississippi slaves and the various northern-based freedmen aid and religious organizations in postwar Mississippi, see Christopher M. Span, "Alternative Pedagogy: The Rise of the Private Black Academy in Early Postbellum Mississippi, 1862–1870," in *Chartered Schools: Two Hundred Years of Independent*

Academies, 1727–1925, ed. Nancy Beadie and Kim Tolley (New York, 2002), 211–227.

29. Joseph Warren to Stuart Eldridge, November 15, 1865, BRFAL, Miss., RG 105. Bureau of Refugees, Freedmen, and Abandoned Lands, Mississippi, Records Group 105. Manuscripts obtained from the Mississippi Department of Archives and History.

30. Ibid.

31. *Statistics of the Operations of the Executive Board of Friends' Association of Philadelphia and its Vicinity, for the Relief of Colored Freedmen, As Presented to a Public Meeting of Friends, Held at Arch Street Meeting House, Philadelphia, 1st Month 19th, 1864* (Philadelphia, PA, 1864), 20.

32. Ibid., 21.

33. Yeatman, *A Report on the Conditions of the Freedmen in Mississippi,* 16–18.

34. Ibid., 14.

35. Ganus, "The Freedmen's Bureau in Mississippi," 392–393. This total was aggregated from an appendix table of Ganus's. Bureau and missionary aid collected in this same time span was approximately $47,857.14. The total amount collected, inclusive of known freedmen contributions, was $71,833.24.

36. Ibid., 311.

37. Wood, "Travail of Freedom," 147.

38. Ibid.

CHAPTER 2

OWNING, CONTROLLING, AND BUILDING UPON CULTURAL CAPITAL

The Albany Enterprise Academy and Black Education in Southeast Ohio, 1863–1886

Adah Ward Randolph

To this end we have established ALBANY ENTERPRISE ACADEMY, to be owned and controlled by colored persons. . . .

—Constitution of the Albany Enterprise Academy (1864, p. 5)

Doxey Wilkinson described education as "a dependent, inter-acting unit of the whole culture. Indeed, it lies at the heart of the culture, and necessarily reflects the contending values which there prevail."[1] In the United States, free and enslaved African Americans sought education through legal and extralegal means throughout the 19th century, and recognized that formal schooling was an essential part of cultural development and vital to securing their freedom. The primary question for many African Americans was how and where to obtain an education.

Cultural Capital and Black Education, pages 15–33
Copyright © 2004 by Information Age Publishing

V. P. Franklin has pointed out that cultural capital and social capital can be important elements in bringing about "community revitalization."[2] "From the early nineteenth century, black mutual benefit societies and social and fraternal organizations sponsored business enterprises that were collectively owned and provided much needed social services to members of the black community."[3] Within this context, cultural capital is "the sense of group consciousness and collective identity that serves as an economic resource to support collective economic or philanthropic efforts."[4] As a culturally aware group, cultural capital assists African Americans in defining their "collective identity," while "complex social networks" help to create and maintain economic resources to support collective advancement.[5] Cultural capital grew out of the sense of responsibility and supported collective philanthropic or charitable efforts that "became the backbone for social and economic development."[6] It represented "a deep race consciousness" and clear understanding of what it means to be African American.[7] This consciousness also served as a vehicle for other programs for "racial uplift" and was essential to the creation and support of their community.

In the 19th century, "free" African Americans in northern states such as Ohio had their rights of citizenship circumscribed by "black laws." Yet African Americans sought to establish viable institutions, including schools. Why did free African Americans establish separate educational institutions, particularly in northern states such as Ohio? What resources did they use? What were the purposes of these educational institutions? Who led such efforts? This chapter describes the efforts of free African Americans in southeast Ohio to pursue educational advancement using their social and cultural capital.

STATE LAW AND BLACK EDUCATION IN OHIO

In 1804, state legislators passed "black laws" limiting free blacks' participation in social, economic, political, and educational institutions in Ohio. The laws resulted from the discord among Ohio whites over the advancing antislavery movement, the state's entrance into the Union without slavery, and differences among whites over the place of Africans in American society. In Ohio, racial beliefs, opinions, and attitudes were often divided along geographical lines. Race relations in southeast Ohio, because of its close proximity to slave states Kentucky and Virginia, typified these divisions.

The Ohio constitution of 1803 called for the establishment of common schools, but they did not begin to appear until 1825. White sentiment against the inclusion of African Americans in common schooling was evident in an 1827 editorial in the *Ohio State Journal*. "If we enlighten their [African Americans'] minds by education, what a new world of misery does open to their view. Knowledge would open their eyes to their present degraded state—their incapacity of enjoying the rights of citizenship, or of being received into the social interests of the whites as friends. They would be rendered uneasy with their condition, and, seeing no hopes of improvement, would harbor designs unfriendly to the peace and permanency of our institutions."[8] This writer was more concerned that whites would lose, the "peace and permanency of our institutions," than that African Americans should have the potential advantages of education. If African Americans were to be educated in Ohio, it would not be in white "public institutions."

The Ohio legislators passed its educational black law in 1829, excluding all black youth "from participation in the public school systems in Ohio."[9] Property tax monies for the support of public schools were to be returned to African American taxpayers. Mutual benefit societies and private religious associations maintained "colored schools" in Cincinnati, Columbus, Cleveland, and the southern counties of Ohio. According to historian Carter G. Woodson, school tax funds "received from free blacks were supposed to be given to them for the establishment of their schools." However, "no help came from the cities and the state before 1849 when the legislature passed a law authorizing the establishment of schools for children of color at public expense."[10] During the antebellum era, free African Americans in Ohio, particularly in the southeast section of the state, were concerned about their brothers and sisters in chains and were active in the antislavery movement. However, they were also concerned about educating their own children and given their exclusion from public schools, set out to construct their own institutions. Social and cultural capital was important in the creation of these black schools.

CONNECTING COMMUNITIES THROUGH CULTURAL AND SOCIAL CAPITAL

Whereas, we a portion of the free colored citizens of the State of Ohio, believing that the time has come for us to define our views and positions in regard to our political, social, educational and religious elevation, . . . to direct our current attention to the education of our youth. . . .

—Convention of the Colored Citizens of Gallia County,
Frederick Douglass' Paper (1852, p. 1)

African Americans were barred from the public schools throughout Ohio, and in the southeast region, black settlement was opposed by whites, who sent many petitions to the state legislature calling for African Americans' exclusion.[11] Despite the strong opposition to their settlement, African Americans, whether free blacks or fugitive slaves, continued to migrate to Ohio; most lived in urban areas such as Columbus and Cincinnati, while some settled in the rural areas. In Gallipolis, Ohio, the black residents established a private school after 1835, and paid a teacher $50 each quarter.[12] Gallipolis, a river town, and Albany, Ohio, were both stops on the Underground Railroad, the secret escape route for those fleeing enslavement.[13]

African Americans who gathered in Gallipolis in 1851 to protest the Fugitive Slave Law used the occasion to strengthen and promote the advancement of the African American community. During the five-day meeting, they created a "Declaration of Sentiments" calling for "the immediate and unconditional repeal of the [1850] Fugitive Slave Law." They resolved that every community represented "establish a well regulated Sabbath School in their midst" to strengthen the "social circle, based upon the principles of true morality." They further supported education in their communities by recommending continual "patronage and support" of the Albany Manual Labor Academy because it allowed African Americans to enroll. These African Americans had a "social circle" that began with their settlement in the state, their collective antislavery work, the Underground Railroad, and the establishment of churches and schools.[14]

According to Carter G. Woodson, black Ohioans began creating schools in the early 1830s, and by 1835, 25 such institutions existed in "Logan, Clark, Columbiana, Guernsey, Jefferson, Highland, Brown, Darke, Shelby, Green, Miami, Warren, Scioto, Gallia, Ross, and Muskingum counties.[15] In 1850 the life-threatening provisions in the new fugitive slave law for "free" African Americans led to the calling of a "black state convention" where local black leaders from all over Ohio met to protest and to plan alternative strategies, such as emigration to Canada, and joining African American refugees fleeing from legalized oppression in the United States.[16] Called to protest the injustice of the Fugitive Slave Law, this public forum also examined other ways African Americans in Ohio could overcome oppression. One such way was to establish educational institutions for black youth in rural communities. African Americans in Gallipolis and throughout Ohio had established private schools as early as the 1830s, and at this convention, they were of "the opinion that the Albany Manual Labor Academy richly deserves our patronage and support; therefore . . . we recommend it to our people in this part of the State."[17]

In 1847, a school that was the precursor of the Albany Manual Labor Academy was opened in Lee township in Albany, Ohio, by the Lewis family. William Lewis, a graduate of Oberlin College, his wife Eliza, and William's sister, Lamira, who had originally begun to teach students in her father's home, opened the Lewis Academy. Originally from Connecticut, the family had moved to Oberlin in the 1830s. In 1850, the academy, shifting from individual ownership to a joint stock company, was renamed the Albany Manual Labor Academy. Shares were sold for $25 each.[18] The name change reflected a unique aspect of the school—students and teachers both performed manual labor to help defray the costs and expenses of the new institution. In order to promote "the highest physical, as well as mental development, to cultivate habits of industry, and insure a sound constitution, and to render labor respectable, it is indispensable that we combine labor with study, in all our educational arrangements. This is essential also, to counteract a spirit of aristocracy, that is abound in the earth, or pride of caste, that looks upon labor as degrading."[19]

Another distinction in the early history of the Albany Manual Labor Academy was that it admitted African Americans and women. According to the academy's 1850 constitution,

> No person of good moral character, who is not a slaveholder either in practice or principle, shall be denied the privilege of being a stockholder in the institution; no one shall be rendered ineligible to office, or refused admittance as a student, on terms of perfect equality, on account of caste, color, or place of nativity. . . . None are invited, who are unwilling to conform to the rules of the institution, in respect to moral deportment, application to study, the performance of a certain amount of labor, and in according cheerfully to the colored man, all the rights of a common humanity.[20]

The academy hosted the "Christian anti-slavery meetings" organized by the Lewis family, who were closely associated with the liberal ideals of Oberlin College.[21] Additionally, the academy was connected to the Western Home and Missionary Society, which sought to spread the "pure gospel" at home and abroad, and was also involved in antislavery endeavors. The black state convention in southeast Ohio viewed the academy as an institution where African Americans could freely pursue "mechanical, agricultural and professional pursuits."[22]

By 1851, Albany Academy was offering primary and secondary courses of study. The primary curriculum included courses in orthography, reading, writing, composition, geography, and arithmetic. The secondary department, a three-year course, provided courses in orthography, reading, writing, arithmetic, grammar (including the study of poetry), geography using maps and globes, and the histories of Greece, Rome, England, and the United States. Drawing, painting, and languages were also taught, as well as chemistry, philosophy, and mathematics. The academy provided African Americans an opportunity to learn not just reading, writing, and arithmetic, but also advanced subjects in preparation for college admission.[23]

Albany Manual Labor Academy became Albany Manual Labor University in 1853 when it received its charter from Ohio. Unfortunately, in 1862, increasing debt, the inability to raise funds to pay the mortgage, and the outbreak of the Civil War caused the school's property to be sold at sheriff's sales. The Christian Church purchased the property and established Franklin College, which did not admit African Americans. In response,

African Americans in southeast Ohio sought to build their own educational institution. The Albany Enterprise Academy was the result of the collective effort of African Americans from all over Ohio and outside the state. An example of cultural and social capital at work in the establishment of schools for African Americans, it represented the collective consciousness of black Ohioians.

ALBANY ENTERPRISE ACADEMY

We have established ALBANY ENTERPRISE ACADEMY, . . . to demonstrate the capacity of colored men to originate and successfully manage such a school. . . [24]

—Constitution of the Albany Enterprise Academy (1864, p. 5)

According to the 1850 Census, in Lee Township where Albany is located, there were four black citizens. By 1860, Lee Township listed 174 black residents. The establishment of Albany Manual Labor University, which enrolled black students, and the links to Gallipolis, Athens, and Albany for fugitive slaves, helps to explain the growth of the black population.[25]

In *North of Slavery: The Negro in the Free States, 1790–1860* (1961), Leon F. Litwack maintained that by 1860, "nearly every northern state had provided for a Negro public school system."[26] However, African Americans' access to public education varied across Ohio, and black leaders complained that black children in southern Ohio were not even provided "an ordinary English education."[27] In fact, in small rural towns such as Gallipolis and Oxford, African Americans did not gain access to public education until after the Civil War.[28] By 1864, newspaper advertisements began to appear for the Albany Enterprise Academy, created to educate black youth in southern Ohio and beyond. The founders of the Albany Enterprise Academy raised funds from its black stockholders, from philanthropic and governmental organizations, through the activity of soliciting agents, and through newspaper solicitations. The constitution indicated that,

> Adjacent to this part of the State are portions of Virginia and of Kentucky, where no opportunity is afforded for an education of any sort. This destitution of educational facilities was in some degree remedied by the Albany Manual Labor School, at which institution colored youths were for a number of years received and educated. The insolvency of that school and its consequent sale, to parties who refused admission to colored students, had rendered it necessary for the colored people to establish a school, in which their youths could be trained for [teaching] and the higher business pursuits.[29]

In the local newspapers in Amesville, Ohio, on June 20, 1864, and in Marietta, Ohio, on July 2, 1864, well-respected white ministers described the origins and circumstances of the Albany Enterprise Academy. Reverend Charles Merwin, pastor of the Presbyterian Church in Amesville, contended that,

> From a personal and particular examination on the spot, I have no doubt that the effort thus far conducted by the colored people, to found an institution for their own benefit, and which shall not be liable to be wrested from them, has been as successful as the most sanguine friends of the enterprise could expect, and that it is entirely worthy of the confidence and generous co-operation of the friends of education and of the colored race. The enterprise has the confidence and cordial sympathy of the enlightened and virtuous community where it is situated, with the exception of a few individuals who object to the institution because it is under the control of people of color, and who though impotent for evil at home may possibly injure the cause abroad.

> It is earnestly to be hoped that all the means necessary to complete this very important enterprise will be generously given, until the long oppressed race shall have a fair opportunity of asserting their claim to a standing among the enlightened, intelligent and cultivated of mankind.[30]

Reverend Merwin supported the school, and recommended that others assist it as well.

Reverend Thomas Wickes, of the Congregational Church in Marietta, Ohio, also agreed with Reverend Merwin. In his editorial on July 2, 1864, Reverend Wickes concluded that "an enterprise eminently worthy of patronage and encouragement, promising to be a success, and a blessing for those whose benefit it has been founded. As such we cordially commend it to the sympathy and aid of the liberal minded and benevolent."[31] I. W. Andrews, president of Marietta College, also encouraged the work at the Enterprise Academy. In his editorial Reverend Merwin revealed that he had been "requested by some friends and patrons of the Albany Enterprise Academy, a School for the colored people, to visit that Institution, I would hereby state that I have endeavored faithfully to perform the duty assigned to me, and that I find the effort to build up a permanent school of the kind designated, in successful progress."[32] Reverend Merwin indicated that "the undertaking is nearly free from debt, and I doubt not has been as well and economically conducted as any similar enterprise."[33] These three influential white leaders solicited support for Enterprise Academy from white citizens, who did provide philanthropic support for the institution. For example, Thomas and Isaac Carleton of Syracuse, Meigs County, were among the largest donors, giving $3,000.[34] Other white patrons donated smaller amounts.[35] However, before these funds were secured, the institution was already close to completion.

According to one account, "On November 20, 1863, a site of about twenty acres was purchased on the north edge of town. By the following June, a two-story brick building, thirty by forty-eight feet, was nearing completion."[36] In 1863, Jonathan Cable, the former soliciting agent of Albany Manual Labor University, received the consent of the shareholders, particularly Lyman Chase, and signed over the remainder of the endowment fund to Albany Enterprise Academy.[37] This allowed the institution to be built on land previously occupied by Albany Manual Labor University. Other white patrons donated land as well, but these were not the only resources acquired for the school.[38] The Freedman's Bureau provided the institution with a $2,000 loan. And members of the black community, the teachers, and the black stockholders also supported the Enterprise Academy financially. After the stockholders' meeting, they held a picnic to foster fellowship between the institution and the black community.[39]

According to Reverend Merwin, at its beginning the institution, often referred to as Enterprise Academy, was practically "debt free." By September 1864, Albany Enterprise Academy had resources totaling $5,000. All the stockholders were members of various African American communities and each contributed $25 to the endeavor. Enterprise Academy used the labor of the students and teachers to defray some of the expenses of the institution.

Although Ivan Tribe, a local historian, suggested that Albany Enterprise Academy offered only "minimal education," the school's officers sought to train teachers and students interested in "the higher business pursuits."[40] The officers were from all over southern Ohio, and included Peter H. Clark of Cincinnati (president), John H. Williams of Chillicothe, Reverend G. W. Bryant of Xenia, D. E. Asbury of Harmar, Reverend Richard De Baptiste of Chicago, and W. P. Brooks of St. Louis, Missouri (all vice presidents).[41] A complex social network was formed to ensure the development of Albany Enterprise Academy. In addition to funds provided by the black stockholders, a general agent, John T. Berry, was employed to travel throughout Ohio and elsewhere to secure funding for the institution. The members of Berry's family migrated to Albany from Oberlin in 1856 to secure schooling for their children.[42]

Enterprise Academy's president Peter H. Clark had been involved in community mobilization for black education for many years. Clark was a member of the black convention movement, a Republican, and belonged to Cincinnati's growing black middle class. He was one of the first black teachers in Cincinnati, and later was superintendent of Cincinnati's all-black schools and principal of Gaines High School.[43] As president of Albany Enterprise Academy and as a teacher in Cincinnati, Clark understood the need for competent black teachers and business professionals. Clark believed in and worked for the enfranchisement of African Americans in Ohio, and Albany Enterprise Academy represented the future of black education and advancement in the state. The constitution for the academy also revealed that the founders were using cultural capital to promote black self-determination in the field of education.[44]

> To this end we have established the Albany Enterprise Academy, to *be owned and controlled by colored persons* [emphasis added], though its benefits are open to all. In thus restricting the ownership of the school to colored persons, we are actuated by no narrow prejudice, no desire to build up the wall of caste, which we sincerely hope is crumbling to ruin, but we desire to demonstrate the capacity of colored men to originate and successfully manage such a school, believing that such a demonstration will afford an argument in favor of the colored man which none can gainsay.[45]

The struggle to establish and control the governance of the all-black schools in Cincinnati influenced this document.[46] To ensure control over the management of the school, Albany Enterprise Academy was owned and operated by African Americans for African Americans. Clark and others used their own funds to develop the Albany Enterprise Academy, just as they had done in establishing all-black schools in Cincinnati.[47] Moreover, they were connected to other independent black institutions such as Avery College in Pittsburgh.[48]

According to the constitution, "the object of the institution . . . is to furnish a sound Christian and Literacy education, to all persons of good moral character, who may wish to avail themselves of its privileges, and particularly to colored youths."[49] Reverend Merwin observed during his visit that the "school embraces the various ages from small children to full grown men and women, and the various hues from the most sable to those of the fairest complexions."[50] During the 1863–1864 school year, three terms were held and 78 pupils were taught by four teachers.[51] Miss Joanna L. Gee taught two terms, and Mrs. M. J. Cooper was her assistant. Miss Julia F. Triplett taught during the final term. Triplett's assistant was Miss A. D. Goings. Reverend John R. Bowles, former chaplain of the 55th Massachusetts Volunteers and "a gentlemen [with] well-known ability and experience as an educator," was appointed principal. The trustees felt "under his care it will enter upon a course of extended usefulness, and justify the favors its numerous friends have shown it." As noted earlier, one such friend was Isaac Carleton of Syracuse in Meigs County, Ohio, who "donated a tract of land in Illinois, containing 160 acres, the value of which exceeds $2,500."[52] Thomas J. Ferguson and Cornelius Berry served as agents during the 1863–1864 school year.[53] Ferguson, originally an agent and trustee, eventually became principal and left an indelible mark on the school.

THOMAS JEFFERSON FERGUSON
AND ALBANY ENTERPRISE ACADEMY

*Progress is the watchword of the universe. Governments, arts and sciences are
all progressive. Man himself is progressive, and all connected with him must keep
pace with his moral and intellectual organization.*

—T. J. Ferguson, *Negro Education: The Hope of the Race* (1866, p. 3)

According to June Purcell Guild in *Black Laws of Virginia* (1936), "the
Negro in Old Dominion, whether indentured servant, slave, free person of
color or citizen has always been an enormously disadvantaged human
being."[54] Thomas Jefferson Ferguson was born in Essex County, Virginia, on
September 15, 1830, just a year before Nat Turner's insurrection in Henrico
County.[55] Charles William Dabney in *Universal Education in the South, From the
Beginning to 1900, Volume I* (1936), contends that before "1830 the people of
the South were not actively opposed to the literary training of their slaves.
Following the Nat Turner insurrection and the agitation of the abolitionists,
considerable oppression sprung up, which gave rise to the legislation for-
bidding the literary training of slaves."[56] It is possible that Ferguson's family
migrated from Virginia to Ohio when free blacks were excluded from the
common schools.[57]

In 1859, Ferguson is listed as a student in the Collegiate Department at
Albany Manual Labor University. University records lists Cincinnati as his
home residence.[58] Another student listed was James Monroe Trotter, who
became Recorder of Deeds in Washington, D.C. under President Grover
Cleveland. At Albany Manual Labor University, Ferguson and Trotter were
exposed to the ideas of radical abolitionists who wanted the overthrow of
slavery with its "tyranny and oppression."[59] After graduation, Ferguson
taught in the segregated public schools of Albany and Middleport, Ohio,
and Parkersburg, West Virginia.[60] According to historian Carter G. Woodson, Ferguson was involved after 1866 with Reconstruction politics and
worked for "the enlargement of freedom and opportunity for his race."[61]
He was known in the area for his public speaking. In March 1859, Ferguson purchased land in the village of Albany.[62] In 1867, Ferguson married
Elmira Wilson from Parkersburg, West Virginia, who was ten years his junior, and together, they had nine children. Ferguson's son, Ralph Waldo
Emerson Ferguson would eventually publish *Waldo's Diadem*, the Albany
black newspaper.[63] When Ferguson came to Albany Manual Labor University to be molded by "the principles of justice,"[64] he believed that education
was the key to African American advancement.

In *Negro Education: The Hope of the Race*, published in 1866, Ferguson
argued that "much as we may desire that all the avenues of wealth and
honor were open to him in common with his white fellow-citizens, we can-

not deny but that his education—the general enlightenment of the whole mass of colored people in the country—is the most desirable and the most conducive to his elevation and prosperity."[65] Ferguson had been involved in politics, but believed that "the elevation of the human race should not be a political question with any party."[66] In the United States, the "reconstruction of the nation's race relations was limited."[67] Ferguson understood the limitations on black rights, but included copies of the Emancipation Proclamation, the Thirteenth Amendment, and the 1866 Civil Rights Bill in this pamphlet. Ferguson believed education was more than just "preparation for life," but "for living as full citizens." He declared that "education proper, has a higher and more sacred meaning. As all actions have their distinct parts, education too as an active operation has its distinct parts. To be educated, is to have all those powers of body and soul drawn out and cultivated which enable man to fill with dignity and ability his appointed sphere in the great economy of life."[68]

In the short pamphlet, Ferguson explained how some African Americans had advanced despite oppression, and he encouraged freed people to pursue schooling. Finally, Ferguson discussed the need for teachers for all-black schools. Ferguson sought to "show that the general diffusion of knowledge will be beneficial to the white man, the colored man, and the country at large; that a plan has been presented by which the colored man can be made to contribute largely to the advancement of his own elevation, and to become ultimately not only self sustaining and self reliant, but a prop and guardian of democratic principles; that the susceptibility of the race having been blunted by oppression, they need help in the first stages of their progress as free men and citizens."[69] Although Ferguson appealed to all Americans, he particularly wanted African American teachers to be in the vanguard of black advancement. Ferguson expected teachers to use social and cultural capital to support the development of the entire race.[70] Ferguson sought competent and trained black educators for black schools and in 1861 helped to organize the Ohio Colored Teachers' Association. As principal and trustee of Albany Enterprise Academy, Ferguson hired black teachers because he believed they had a role in uplifting their race, and many of his students became teachers in other Ohio communities.[71]

In 1870, the Fifteenth Amendment granted African American men the right to vote.[72] However, whites in Ohio still viewed African Americans as members of an "inferior race."[73] Many African Americans refuted charges of mental inferiority by receiving formal schooling and professional training. Consequently, Albany Enterprise Academy grew. In 1870, through solicitations and funds raised from its fruit farm, a girls dormitory was built. With its furnishings, it cost $5,000, $2,000 of which was provided by the Freedman's Bureau. The new girls dormitory contained a "kitchen, dining room, pantry, washroom, cellar, and coal room" and was completed in

1871.[74] Boys lived with private families. Students came from the Albany area and from as far as Kentucky and West Virginia.[75] By 1871 Ferguson had become president of the Board of Trustees of the Albany Enterprise Academy, and his major objective for the school remained the same: "to prepare [black youth as] teachers or educators of their race or to fill with honor other useful positions in society."[76] The curriculum consisted of primary and secondary courses of study. "In the Primary department, instruction is given in the elementary principles of reading, writing, spelling, mental arithmetic, primary geography, and primary grammar."[77] In the secondary or "academic" department, "more instruction is given in reading, writing, spelling, practical and higher arithmetic, higher geography, grammar and analysis of the English language, algebra, geometry, book keeping, natural, moral and mental philosophy, anatomy, chemistry, astronomy, history, thus furnishing a complete scientific course of instruction."[78]

In 1871, 31 males and 33 females were enrolled, and Reverend A. G. Binga was the principal. The school term consisted of three quarters covering 42 weeks. Primary and secondary or "academic" students' tuition was $3.50 and $5.00 per term. The fee for boarding students was $1.25 per week. By 1811, thirty-nine of Enterprise Academy graduates had already become teachers in Ohio and other schools throughout the country. The 1871 report listed other goals.

> At present, we propose to confine ourselves to teaching the branches heretofore named, but it is our hope that the time is not far distant when our Academy will develop into a first class College, where those of our race, who choose can qualify themselves as completely as at any Institution of Learning in the West. The prospect now is, that we will have a large number of Students at the opening of our Fall Term, and to provide for this, our board propose[s] to secure the services of the best teachers possible. We are now negotiating with Rev. T. J. Ferguson, and Rev. J. R. Bowles, whose services we hope to obtain.[79]

Ferguson, president of the trustee board, also became a full-time teacher at Enterprise Academy in 1871. William Sanders Scarborough, future president of Wilberforce University, also taught there during this period.[80] Ferguson believed the staff was the critical component in producing exemplary graduates and excellent teachers.

The 1871 Albany Enterprise catalogue listed John J. Sparrow as a student from Martinsville, Ohio. In 1874, Sparrow became the second black male on the teaching staff of the all-black Loving School in Columbus, Ohio.[81] During Sparrows's first term, the Loving School, which had opened in 1871, had its most successful year. The Visiting Committee, which was comprised of leading black men in Columbus, indicated that "we are much pleased . . . with the thorough knowledge that the teachers have of the course of instruction relative to their grades."[82] As noted earlier, some have reported that Enterprise Academy provided a rudimentary curriculum. However, Sparrow's appointment at Loving undermines that assertion. In order to teach in Columbus, teachers had to pass the School Board's Examinations and possess a teaching certificate as well as letters declaring their moral character.[83] Sparrow would not have been hired in Columbus if he had not been fully qualified.

Enterprise Academy's mission was to "establish a school, in which their youths could be trained for teachers and the higher business pursuits."[84] Their graduates in turn would assist in the advancement of African Americans collectively. Enterprise Academy produced exemplary graduates such as Olivia Davidson, a teacher and fundraiser for Tuskegee Institute, and Booker T. Washington's second wife; Andrew Jackson Davidson, for many years the only black lawyer in Athens, Ohio; and Edwin C. Berry, who developed the well-known Berry Hotel in Athens, Ohio. Milton M. Holland, Congressional Medal of Honor recipient for service at the Battle of Bull Run, a graduate of Howard University Law School in 1872, and the founder of the Alpha Insurance Company in Washington, D.C., also attended Enterprise Academy.[85] Despite such successes, Enterprise Academy remained open only until 1886. In the 1870s, the institution had seen its greatest growth with "enrollments in excess of one hundred students."[86] However, enrollment declined in the late 1870s, and remained low in the 1880s.

As African Americans in Ohio pushed to secure their civil rights through legal means, those in Albany relocated to more prosperous parts of the state such as Columbus where they were beginning to enter the public schools. In Columbus, they agitated for and secured the all-black Loving School. However, by 1881, the school was razed, and black children attended mixed public schools in Columbus and in 1887 the legislators repealed the law calling for segregated schools. The black movement from private to public schools was occurring all over Ohio during this period.[87] Consequently, many black parents were less likely to send their children to private institutions such as Albany Enterprise Academy.

On September 24, 1885, a fire of suspicious origin destroyed the dormitory, and Albany Enterprise Academy never recovered from the loss. As early as 1864, Reverend Merwin had revealed that "a few individuals . . . object to the institution because it is under the control of people of color."[88] Moreover, in 1885, Thomas Ferguson was in poor health, and the school in financial difficulty. In the 1885 November edition of *Waldo's Diadem*, Ralph Waldo Emerson Ferguson reported that even though a "complete academic course of study" was available at Enterprise Academy, our "buildings are much in need of repair and money is required to establish Industrial Dept. Our little fruit farm is doing well and paying something to the institution."[89] In the "Items of Interest" section, Ferguson reported on the "grand success" of the school at Middleport headed by his sister, Luella.[90] Enterprise Academy had used cultural capital to further the education of African Americans in surrounding communities through its graduates. However, despite the efforts of its supporters, Albany Enterprise Academy still needed funds. In 1886, when T. J. Ferguson resigned due to ill health, Albany Enterprise Academy closed its doors. During its existence, no students had "ever been denied admittance" even when they could not pay their tuition.[91] It had survived as an institution built upon cultural capital for more than 20 years.

On March 30, 1887, Thomas Ferguson died. Ferguson had been a pioneer in many areas. He was the first black member of the Albany City Council (1872), served as president of the Mass Convention of Colored Voters in Athens County (1879), and became the first black to serve on a jury in Athens County (1880). His greatest achievement, however, was training hundreds of African American students and teachers at the Albany Enterprise Academy.

CONCLUSION

In response to the passage of the black laws in Ohio, African Americans established their own private schools. One such institution in southeast Ohio, Albany Enterprise Academy, was collectively "owned and controlled" by African Americans using cultural capital. For African Americans in the 19th century, education was a vehicle for advancement. Before Albany Enterprise Academy closed in 1886, it produced graduates who would become as Ferguson had envisioned, "teachers of their people" and youth who succeeded at "higher pursuits." Graduates taught in Gallipolis and other cities and towns throughout the state and elsewhere. When African Americans were allowed to enroll in Albany Manual Labor University, they contributed to that school. When it was replaced by Franklin College, African Americans were excluded so they decided to open their own school. The vision of Peter H. Clark, Thomas Jefferson Ferguson, and other black citizens, along with support from sympathetic whites, and cultural capital from the African American community were necessary elements for the establishment of Albany Enterprise Academy, a significant contributor to the education of African Americans in southeast Ohio between 1863 and 1886.

NOTES

1. Doxey Wilkinson, as quoted in Carter G. Woodson, *The Education of the Negro Prior to 1861* (1919; reprinted Salem, NH, 1991), i.

2. V. P. Franklin, "Social Capital, Cultural Capital, and Empowerment Zones: A Strategy for Economic and Community Development," in *The State of Black Philadelphia: Economic Power—Leveling the Playing Field* (Philadelphia, 1998), 19.

3. Ibid., 21.

4. Bettye Collier-Thomas, "The 'Relief Corps of Heaven': Black Women As Philanthropists," in Pier C. Rogers, ed., *Philanthropy in Communities of Color: Traditions and Challenges* (Indianapolis, IN, 2001), 26.

5. Ibid., 26; Franklin, "Social Capital, Cultural Capital, and Empowerment Zones," 20.

6. Collier-Thomas, "The 'Relief Corps of Heaven,'" 28.

7. Ibid., 28–29.

8. Frederick A. McGinnis, *The Education of Negroes in Ohio* (Blanchester, OH, 1962), 11–12; Frank U. Quillin, *The Color Line in Ohio* (New York, ([1913] 1969), 48.

9. Mame Charlotte Mason, "The Policy of the Segregation of the Negro in the Public Schools of Ohio, Indiana, and Illinois" (Master's thesis, University of Chicago, 1917), 14; *Laws of Ohio 32: 37; Quillin, "The Color Line in Ohio," The Ohio State Journal (March 5, 1829)*; also see Adah Ward, "The African American Struggle for Education in Columbus, Ohio: 1803–1913" (Master's thesis, Ohio State University, 1992), Ch. 2, for a thorough understanding of the development of exclusionary educational laws in Ohio.

10. Carter G. Woodson, *The Education of the Negro Prior to 1861* (1919; reprinted Salem, NH, 1991), 327.

11. Wendell P. Dabney, *Cincinnati's Colored Citizens: Historical, Sociological and Biographical* (Cincinnati, OH, 1926); *David A. Gerber, Black Ohio and the Color Line: 1860–1915* (Urbana, IL, 1976); Ward, "The African American Struggle for Education in Columbus," Ch. 2; Woodson, *The Education of the Negro*, 328.

12. Woodson, *The Education of the Negro*, 244.

13. Wilbur H. Siebert, *The Mysteries of Ohio's Underground Railroads* (Columbus, OH, 1951), 97–98.

14. Frederick Douglass' Paper, January 1, 1852, 3.

15. Woodson, *The Education of the Negro*, 243–244.

16. Frederick Douglass' Paper, January 1, 1852, 3.

17. Woodson, *The Education of the Negro, 243–244, 277; Frederick Douglass' Paper, January 1, 1852, 3*.

18. *The Constitution of the Albany Manual Labor Academy, with the Minutes and Proceedings of the First Annual Meeting of the Stockholders 1850* (Cincinnati, OH, 1851), 3; Ivan M. Tribe, "Rise and Decline of Private Academies in Albany, Ohio," *Ohio History* 78 (no. 3, 1969): 188–201.

19. *The Constitution of the Albany Manual Labor Academy, 1850*, 3.

20. Ibid., 7.

21. Ibid., 10.

22. Ibid., 13; *Frederick Douglass' Paper*, January 1, 1852, 3.

23. *Constitution of the Albany Manual Labor Academy, 1850*, 16.

24. *Constitution of Albany Enterprise Academy, 1864* (Cincinnati, OH, 1864), 5; Ohio University Archives File 101–6(4).

25.   One family that came to the area seeking an education for their children was the Davidsons. Eliza Brown Davidson, a widow and former attendant to General George Custer, settled in Albany. Her daughter Olivia, after attending Albany Enterprise Academy, would become a teacher at Tuskegee Institute, and later marry Booker T. Washington. *Athens Messenger, February 14, 1925*.

26.   Leon F. Litwack, *North of Slavery: The Negro in the Free States: 1790–1860 (Chicago, 1961), 121*.

27.   *Constitution of Albany Enterprise Academy, 1864*, 5.

28.   Adah Ward Randolph, "From Albany to Gallipolis: Black Education in Southeast Ohio, 1863–1951." Paper presented at the American Educational Research Association, April 2001; Kate Rousmaniere, "School Segregation in Oxford, Ohio: The Perry Gibson Case of 1887." Available from *http://www.users.muhio.edu/bransocl/edl204/OxfordDeseg.html*. (January 2003).

29.   *Constitution of Albany Enterprise Academy, 1864*, 5.

30.   Rev. Charles Merwin, "Albany School for Colored People," *Athens Messenger, June 20, 1864*. Pamphlet File Ohio University Archives.

31.   Ibid.

32.   Ibid.

33.   Ibid.

34.   Tribe, "Rise and Decline of Private Academies," 196.

35.   John T. Berry was the general agent for the academy and solicited funds from Merwin and others. Also, General Oliver O. Howard of the Freedman's Bureau, Morrison R. Waite who later became Chief Justice of the United States Supreme Court, and two area members of Congress, Rufus Dawes of Marietta and Eliakim H. Moore of Athens, supported the institution; ibid., 196–197.

36.   Tribe, "Rise and Decline of Private Academies," 197.

37.   Ibid.

38.   Each stockholder was vested by purchasing stock at $25 each. Initially, 17 stockholders invested in the academy. The stockholders were Peter H. Clark of Cincinnati; John H. Williams of Chillicothe, Ohio; Reverend G. W. Bryant of Xenia, Ohio; D. E. Asbury and G. W. Harison of Harmar, Ohio; Rev. Richard De Baptiste of Chicago; W. P. Brooks of St. Louis, Missouri; James Abrams of Chillicothe, Ohio; Woody Wiley, Jackson Wiley, P. Clary, Cornelius Berry, Henry Winston, and Richard Snow, all of Albany, Ohio; Reverend Rufus Conrad of Xenia, Ohio; and D. Norman of Goar P. O., Hocking County, Ohio; see Constitution of the Albany Enterprise Academy, 1864, 3. The Freedman's Bureau was the federal agency established to support the education and other activities for the freed people at the end of the Civil War. Hence, money was loaned to the private institution to support the education of freed people who would attend the institution; Tribe, "The Rise and Decline of Private Academies," 197.

39.   Tribe, "The Rise and Decline of Private Academies," 198.

40.   *Constitution of the Albany Enterprise Academy, 1864*, 5.

41.   The secretary was James Abrams of Chillicothe and the treasurer was Woody Wiley of Albany, Ohio. The trustees, primarily from Albany, were Jackson Wiley, P. Clay, Cornelius Berry, Henry Winston, Richard Snow, and Woody

Wiley. Other trustees were G. W. Harison of Harmar, Rev. Rufus Conrad of Xenia, and D. Norman of Hocking County.

42. C. H. Harris, "Dishwasher Founded Athens' Berry Hotel," *Athens Messenger,* July 8, 1953.

43. "Peter Humphries Clark," *Dictionary of American Negro Biography* (New York, 1982), 114–116.

44. According to Dabney in *Cincinnati's Colored Citizens: Historical, Sociological and Biographical* (1926), Clark was considered "Cincinnati's most famous colored citizen." Clark, a teacher in Cincinnati as early as 1849, "labored, after school hours, instructing advanced classes of young people and preparing teachers to maintain the supply demanded by the colored schools within a large radius of Cincinnati" (p. 107). According to David A. Gerber in *Black Ohio and the Color Line,* after attending the National Equal Rights League in Syracuse in 1864, Clark was elected president of the Ohio Equal Rights League in January 1865 (p. 35). Clark was involved in local and national politics and spoke of his relationship with Frederick Douglass, from whom he learned it was "never premature to demand justice" (p. 171). For information on the self-determinist activities of African Americans in Ohio and other northern states in the antebellum era, see V. P. Franklin, *Black Self-Determination: A Cultural History of African American Resistance* (Brooklyn, NY, 1992), 83–102.

45. *Constitution of the Albany Enterprise Academy, 1864,* 1.

46. Dabney, *Cincinnati's Colored Citizens,* 105–106.

47. The stockholders, particularly Clark, were concerned about the control of the institution because of the experiences of African Americans in Cincinnati's public schools. In Cincinnati, Clark had learned that even though the all-black school board was "in charge" of the all-black public schools, they did not control them. Consequently, the stockholders' goal was to maintain control of the academy through their own financial support and with the financial support of white patrons. The constitution stipulated that "no alteration or amendment shall at any time be made which will divert the property from its legitimate use as set forth in Article 2 of this Constitution, nor any which shall take the ownership of the institution from the colored people." The stockholders "moved to establish their own educational institutions and enlisted the support of abolitionists, some white philanthropists, and several state legislators." The Freedman's Bureau loaned $2,000 to the trustees. Lyman C. Chase, a member of the board of Albany Manual Labor University, forwarded its endowment to the trustees of Albany Enterprise Academy. During the 1863–1864 school year, "classes were already being conducted and forty-nine students were enrolled." Also, the stockholders' funds and funds secured by the general agent helped to complete the chapel. Hence, white philanthropists could provide financial support but they could not become stockholders of the institution. Albany Enterprise Academy would remain in the control of its black stockholders.

48. Russell Irvine, "Charles Avery and Avery's College, 1849–192: Pittsburgh Philanthropy." Paper presented at the History of Education Society, November 2, 2002. Personal communication with the author concerning monies used to support Albany Enterprise Academy by Avery.

49. *Constitution of the Albany Enterprise Academy, 1864,* 6.

50. *Athens Messenger,* June 30, 1864.

51. *Constitution of the Albany Enterprise Academy, 1864*, 9.

52. Ibid., 1–2.

53. "Notable African Americans of Southeastern Ohio," available from *Some Southeastern Ohio Afro-American Notables: Biographical Sketches*. Retrieved from: *http://www.seorf.ohiou.edu/xx057/notables.html*, 1998, 1.

54. June Purcell Guild, *Black Laws in Virginia: A Summary of the Legislative Acts of Virginia Concerning Negroes from Earliest Times to the Present (Richmond, VA, 1936)*, 12.

55. Ivan M. Tribe, "Albany, Ohio: The First Fifty Years of a Rural Midwestern Community" (Unpublished paper, 1980), 100. Copy located in the Athens Historical Society.

56. William Dabney, *Universal Education In the South: From the Beginning to 1900*, Volume 1 (Chapel Hill, NC, 1936), 437.

57. Luther P. Jackson, *Free Negro Labor and Property Holding in Virginia, 1830–1860* (New York, 1942), 19–26.

58. *Annual Catalogue of the Officers and Students of the Albany Manual Labor University, 1857–8 and 1858–9* (Athens, OH, 1859), 9.

59. *The Constitution of the Albany Manual Labor Academy, 1850*, 6.

60. *Albany Echo*, September 1876.

61. Tribe, "The Rise and Decline of Private Academies," 199.

62. Tribe, "Albany, Ohio: The First Fifty Years," 100.

63. Florence Brown, "Things I Remember and Things that have been Told to me about the Colored People of Albany" (Unpublished paper, 1955), 6. Athens Historical Society Vertical File-Albany.

64. *The Constitution of the Albany Manual Labor Academy, 1850*, 6.

65. T. J. Ferguson, *Negro Education: The Hope of the Race* (Marietta, OH, 1866), 4.

66. Ibid., Preface.

67. Gerber, *Black Ohio and the Color Line*, 26.

68. Ferguson, *Negro Education*, Preface.

69. Ibid.

70. Ferguson challenged black teachers to be well educated. He argued that experienced teachers were needed to teach the young. Ferguson pondered why if the Dutch, Irish, French, and others employed their own teachers, then why should not blacks? He contended that "qualifications being equal, the more intimate the teacher is with the manners and customs of a people, the more successful he must be among them as a teacher. Moreover, black teachers were good mentors, and teaching was the one profession that blacks "can as yet successfully engage." Hence, Ferguson realized the importance of black teachers' connection with their communities. Moreover, because they were black, these teachers would share a keen understanding of "race consciousness" and their role in preparing youth to be competent. Ferguson's philosophy coincides with that of current educational scholars, such as Jacqueline Jordan Irvine, whose research establishes the significance of cultural influences and educational success for black youth. See Jacqueline Jordan Irvine, "Beyond Role Models: An Examination of Cultural Influences on the Pedagogical Perspectives of Black Teachers," *Peabody Journal of Education* 4(1989): 243–275.

71. For example, John J. Sparrow, listed in the 1870–71 catalogue, became a teacher in Columbus, Ohio. See Ward, "The African American Struggle for Education," 53–54.

72. Gerber, *Black Ohio and the Color Line*, 41.

73. Litwack, *North of Slavery*, 103.

74. Florence Brown and Jane D. Daily, "The Enterprise Academy (Albany, Ohio)" (Unpublished paper, 1932), 2. Athens Historical Society Vertical File-Albany.

75. Tribe, "Albany, Ohio: First Fifty Years," 100.

76. *Catalogue of Albany Enterprise Academy for the Year 1870–1871* (Athens, OH, 1871), 2.

77. Ibid., 3.

78. Ibid., 4.

79. Ibid., 5.

80. Tribe, "The Rise and Decline of Private Academies," 199.

81. Ward, "The African American Struggle for Education," 53, 137; Catalogue of Albany Enterprise Academy for the Year 1870–1871, 4.

82. Ward, "The African American Struggle for Education," 53–54.

83. Ibid.,47.

84. *Constitution of the Albany Enterprise Academy, 1864*, 5.

85. Tribe, "Rise and Decline of Private Academies," 199–200; Brown, "Things I Remember," 4.

86. Tribe, "Albany, Ohio: First Fifty Years," 100; Tribe, "Rise and Decline of Private Academies," 199–200.

87. Ward, "The African American Struggle for Education"; Rousmaniere, "School Segregation in Oxford."

88. Rev. Charles Merwin, "Albany School for Colored People," *Athens Messenger,* June 20, 1864.

89. Brown & Daily, "The Enterprise Academy," 3.

90. *Waldo's Diadem,* Vol. 2, No. 3, November 1885, 44.

91. Ibid., 44.

CHAPTER 3

CULTURAL CAPITAL AND BLACK HIGHER EDUCATION

The AME Colleges and Universities as Collective Economic Enterprises, 1865–1910

V.P. Franklin

In the 19th century the opening of an institution of higher education was a formidable economic undertaking for any religious denomination. This was particularly the case for predominantly black denominations, such as the African Methodist Episcopal (AME) Church. Under the early leadership of Bishop Daniel Payne, however, the AME Church founded a number of institutions of higher education, beginning with Wilberforce University in 1856. These colleges and universities were established to provide an "educated ministry" for the AME congregations and to prepare an "educated leadership group" for the African population inside and outside the United States.

As economic enterprises, these institutions of higher learning could depend upon "financial" and "physical capital" from the denomination's General and Annual Conferences as well as "human capital" in the form of the educational skills and background of the teachers and administrators. More recently, economists and social scientists have emphasized the impor-

Cultural Capital and Black Education, pages 35–47
Copyright © 2004 by Information Age Publishing
All rights of reproduction in any form reserved.

tance of "social capital" for the success of economic enterprises, that is the network of social organizations, cultural institutions, voluntary civic associations, family, and kinship groups in a local community that assist in the development of economic enterprises. Entrepreneurs interested in starting small businesses or large industries need a social infrastructure within the community where the enterprise is located to supply resources for production, manufacture, and distribution. Even where there is sufficient financial capital, without the social and human capital in the form of managers and workers, technicians and salespersons, suppliers and distribution agents, there is little guarantee of economic success.[1]

CULTURAL CAPITAL AND ECONOMIC DEVELOPMENT

While the concept of social capital is extremely helpful in explaining the success or failure of economic enterprises, in trying to explain the history and development of collective black economic enterprises, we must employ the concept of cultural capital. In the non-Marxist context, cultural capital refers to "the sense of group consciousness" that is utilized as a resource in the development of collective economic enterprises. Many business enterprises started by black fraternal groups, mutual benefit societies, religious denominations, and other social and political organizations were created to meet a social or economic need in the African American community. They were supported by blacks outside the organizations' membership because these economic ventures were considered important in defining the "collective identity" of African Americans as a group.[2]

Penn State University economist James B. Stewart has pointed out that "the production of collective identity has value to members of a group and is a normal activity undertaken jointly by individuals and groups." In the case of African Americans there is a great deal of evidence that they gave financial support to economic enterprises that would advance the social development of the whole group, rather than individual capitalists. In these instances the sense of group consciousness became an important resource that was used for the collective social and economic development of African Americans in the United States locally and nationally.[3]

In examining the history of collective black economic and philanthropic activity, it becomes clear that to attract the support of groups and individuals outside the membership of the organizations sponsoring these economic enterprises, it was important for the social and cultural goals to be considered as important, or in some cases more important, than the economic objectives. It was not enough that business enterprises served a particular need in the black community. These businesses were attractive and generated widespread support because their customers understood that the profits were to be reinvested in the black community to assist in the social and economic development of African Americans as a group.[4]

When we examine the economic enterprises sponsored by black mutual benefit societies and fraternal organizations, such as the Prince Hall Masons, Knights of Pythias, Odd Fellows and Elks, we find that historically these businesses were able to "take advantage of a disadvantage." In other words, because of racial discrimination, African Americans were denied access to life insurance, funeral and death benefits, training and employment in certain trades, employment bureaus, hospitals, and other vital social services. It was the mutual benefit societies and fraternal groups that financed business enterprises to provide these services to black communities. For example, throughout the 19th and early 20th centuries, in towns and cities where public burial grounds for blacks were inadequate, black mutual benefit societies purchased cemeteries, which operated as business enterprises and were collectively owned by the organization. However, these cemeteries were not provided exclusively for their membership, but were open to all African Americans who had a need for them. In this instance the business could draw upon the cultural capital in the black community as well as the social capital among its membership. The profits could then be used to finance other social service enterprises within the community.[5]

This was also the case for the black cooperatives in the 19th and 20th centuries. "Colored farmers cooperatives" were started throughout the South as part of the Farmers Alliance or Populist Movement in the 1880s and 1890s. Southern black farmers were not allowed to join the Southern Farmers Alliance, but once the Colored Farmers National Alliance was formed in East Texas in 1886, African Americans organized their own cooperatives to sell their crops to specific merchants for set prices, and purchase large amounts of goods that were then sold to their members at wholesale prices. Although these cooperatives and "farm exchanges" were only short-lived (as was the case for those started by white farmers), the black farmers' cooperative enterprises laid the basis for the cooperative movement among African Americans.[6]

Cooperative enterprises founded by African Americans that adhered to the "Rochdale principles" were able to utilize cultural capital as an important resource. Under the Rochdale approach, profits from cooperative businesses were not only distributed quarterly among the membership, but also were reinvested in programs for the social development of the local community. The fact that the profits from the cooperatives were reinvested in the black community made this economic approach more attractive to those persons interested in fostering "community development." Rochdale-type cooperative enterprises among African Americans have a long history and were economically viable because they were able to utilize social and cultural capital as economic resources.[7]

One of the areas where social and cultural capital was most important was in the provision of schooling in the African American community. Social capital was important for the support of local elementary and secondary schools in northern and southern communities, particularly where there were few or no public schools available to African Americans. Throughout the 19th and into the 20th century, African American churches and other religious institutions opened Sunday schools, religious day schools, private religious academies, secondary schools, seminaries, and institutions of higher education. These activities demonstrated the strong cultural commitment to the African American cultural values of freedom, self-determination, and education and were able to utilize social and cultural capital.

EDUCATION AND THE AFRICAN METHODIST EPISCOPAL CHURCH

The opening of the Bethel African Church in Philadelphia in 1794 and the subsequent formation in 1816 of the African Methodist Episcopal Church as a separate religious denomination exemplify the core cultural values of the African American experience in the United States. Black Methodists who were made to feel unwelcome by white Methodists built their own churches to be "free and independent" of the control and interference of their white co-religionists. After the opening of Bethel African Church, the black Methodists resisted attempts by white Methodist ministers to control the religious practices and liturgy and even refused to allow them to preach in their church. In 1816, when the courts ruled that white Methodists had no right to control the activities in the African churches, black Methodists from Pennsylvania, New Jersey, Maryland, and Delaware came together to take control of their own destiny, and formed the first of many religious denominations in this country based on the cultural value of black self-determination. These black Christians believed that people of African descent must take responsibility for their survival and advancement in American society.[8]

Along with freedom, resistance, and self-determination, from their beginnings the AME congregations demonstrated a strong commitment to education in general, and schooling and literacy training in particular. Richard Allen opened a Sunday school and a day school in the Bethel African Church soon after it was opened in 1794. Reverend Daniel Coker, one of the founders of the AME denomination, opened the "African Bethel School" in Baltimore in 1816, and taught there until 1820 when he was sent to Liberia, West Africa, as a missionary where he remained until his death in 1856.[9] According to AME bishop and historian Daniel Alexander Payne, in 1833 the Ohio Annual Conference was the first to pass resolutions calling for the establishment of schools by the denomination. Ten years later the Baltimore Conference issued a similar call that was also taken up by the Philadelphia Conference and presented at the General Conference in May 1844. The General Conference accepted the resolution calling for the promotion of an "educated ministry" within the AME denomination.[10]

The first denominational educational enterprise was undertaken by the Ohio Conference in 1845 when the "Union Seminary" was opened in the basement of an AME Church in Columbus. Reverend J.M. Brown was the first principal and Frances Ellen Watkins (later Harper) was his assistant. A separate building was later constructed to house the school, which offered only elementary courses. However, after Wilberforce University was purchased by the denomination in 1863, the land and building in Columbus were sold, and the funds were donated to the new institution, which was to include a seminary for the training of AME ministers.[11]

Reverend (later Bishop) Daniel Payne became one of the outspoken proponents for an educated clergy within the AME denomination. He wholeheartedly endorsed the resolution passed by the General Conference in 1844, and published a series of essays in 1845 on "The Education of the Ministry." In his autobiography, *Recollections of Seventy Years*, first published in 1888, Bishop Payne described in detail the debates among the early church leaders over the opening of primary schools for its membership, and seminaries and institutions of higher education for the training of church and community leaders. More importantly, *Recollections of Seventy Years* provided a detailed account of the founding and purchase of Wilberforce University, the first AME institution of higher education. Payne's autobiography makes it clear that cultural capital was an important resource in the AME Church's acquisition of Wilberforce University in 1863. More recent research on the financing of Wilberforce and the other AME collegiate institutions opened between 1870 and 1910 has demonstrated that cultural capital was important for the economic survival and advancement of these schools throughout that period.

THE ECONOMIC FOUNDATIONS
FOR WILBERFORCE UNIVERSITY

The initial financial capital used in the opening of Wilberforce University was provided by the Cincinnati Conference of the (white) Methodist Episcopal Church. The school was opened in Tawana Springs, Ohio, in October 1856 as a charitable and philanthropic effort aimed at the free black population in the area. M.M. Gaddis was the first principal and Daniel Payne was one of the four African American trustees for the school. In his autobiography, Bishop Payne pointed out that the classes provided "elementary English studies; therefore the institution was improperly called a university. This error was not our error—it was that of our zealous white friends who projected it and took out the charter." Bishop Payne felt that "a more modest title would have been better suited to such a humble beginning" (p. 151). However, once the institution was purchased by the AME Church, the title "university" would be of assistance in raising money among the membership of the denomination because it was perceived as an enterprise undertaken for the advancement of the entire group.[12]

Mr. Gaddis was succeeded by J.K. Parker and Dr. Richard S. Rust, who were forced to close the school in June 1862 due to financial and other pressures associated with the outbreak of the Civil War. Then in March 1863 Reverend Payne attended a meeting of the trustees in which he was informed that the state of Ohio was interested in possibly purchasing the land and building to open an asylum. Reverend Payne discussed the possible purchase of the school by the AME denomination with several ministers, bishops, and lay leaders who agreed that he should express to the trustees the AME church's desire to buy the property "in the name of God, for the A.M.E. Church" (p. 153). At that time, Payne did not know where he would obtain the $2,500 down payment, not to mention the entire $10,000 total cost for the property. In *Recollections*, Payne declared that "when I made the bid for the property, I had not a ten-dollar bill at my command, but I had faith in God" (p. 153). Reverend Payne immediately set out on his fundraising campaign, and although several individuals donated sums of $50 to $100, the bulk of the $2,500 down payment came from collections taken up by the AME churches in the Ohio and Baltimore Conferences.

The remaining $7,500 was paid within 2 years; however, before it was paid off there was a devastating fire at the school on the day of President Abraham Lincoln's assassination (April 14, 1865) that destroyed the entire central building. Reverend Payne was away at the time, but upon his return, "as I stood and gazed on the ruins my heart ached, but my spirit soared to heaven, and as my faith laid hands upon the strong arm of the Almighty I said: 'From these ashes a nobler building shall arise!' My audacious faith had not been disappointed. The Omnipotent honored it, and there now stands a nobler building than the first" (p. 154).

When we examine the history of the financing of Wilberforce University, particularly between 1865 and 1910, we find that cultural capital was an important economic resource. While Bishop Payne, who served as president of the school from 1863 to 1876, was primarily interested in Wilberforce University providing an "educated clergy" for the AME Church, in actuality the school served a much broader purpose. From the beginning the school was coeducational, and eventually there were four courses of study: the classical, scientific, normal, and theological. Bishop Payne himself pointed out that of the 29 persons who graduated from Wilberforce University before 1877, only 11 were trained in theology. The majority of graduates of Wilberforce throughout the 19th century became educators who taught in black public and private elementary and secondary schools throughout the United States. This meant that as an economic enterprise, Wilberforce University was benefiting African Americans as a group, not just the AME denomination, and thus could utilize cultural capital as an economic resource in raising funds for the support of the institution.[13]

THE THIRD SUNDAY IN SEPTEMBER: EDUCATION DAY IN THE AME CHURCH

In 1876 the AME General Conference established the "Department of Education" and Reverend J.C. Embry was appointed the first "Commissioner of Education." The purpose of the new department was to oversee the establishment and maintenance of all educational institutions within the AME denomination. Provision was made for "local boards of education" to be elected by the annual conferences in each episcopal district. The Commissioner of Education oversaw these philathropic efforts, raised funds for the thirteen AME educational institutions in existence at that time, and forwarded the funds to the Financial Secretary of the General Conference for distribution to the various schools.[14]

A major reorganization of the Department of Education was carried by the 1884 General Conference and the chief education officer was designated the "Secretary of Education." In the period between 1884 and 1910, the Department served primarily as a conduit for funds from the General Conference to the individual schools. More importantly, it was at the 1884 General Conference that it was resolved to set aside one day each year for collections for AME educational institutions. The third Sunday in September came to be designated "Endowment Day," later "Education Day" in which members of AME congregations were asked to contribute at least one dollar for the various educational enterprises undertaken by the church. Significant advance notice was to be given for the annual education drive and on that Sunday sermons were to be devoted to that topic. Funds raised were initially donated directly to local AME schools by the presiding elders. Later, these funds were forwarded to the Financial Secretary of the General Conference for distribution to the various educational institutions.[15]

In the first Quadrennial Report by the Department of Education (1888) following the introduction of "Endowment Day" in all AME congregations, it was reported that there were fifteen educational institutions established through the denomination and four "prospective" schools. The property was valued at $405,950, with an indebtedness of $28,872. In the previous year's "Endowment Day" campaign (1887–88), $5,815 was raised, and $4,946 was distributed to the schools. The Quadrennial Reports to the General Conference by the Department of Education revealed a steady increase in the amount of financial support by the denomination for its educational institutions. For example, in the 1908–1912 quadrennium, the Education Day collection averaged $50,000. Throughout the period from 1876 to 1912, the vast majority of the financial contributions to AME schools came from the African American community in general, and the AME membership in particular.[16]

Specifically with regard to the financing of Wilberforce University, Joseph Turner McMillan in a recent study reported that although contributions were made by the State of Ohio, the American Missionary Association, and other nonblack institutions and organizations between 1865 and 1888, "the most consistent financial support for Wilberforce University came from the black community. Significantly, the members of the AME Church were committed to the mission of Wilberforce and continued to make sacrifices for the building of the institution. Perhaps the most faithful was the Ohio Conference, where Wilberforce was located, and the Baltimore Conference, [Reverend] Payne's last pastorate before he became a bishop" (156).

Beginning in 1888, Wilberforce University also received $5,000 in funds from the State of Ohio for the development of a "Combined Normal and Industrial Department." The appropriation of state funds for the support of educational programs at a separate black institution opened by a religious denomination was extremely controversial in 1888 for several reasons. Support for normal and agricultural training at a school controlled by a religious denomination was viewed by some as contrary to the constitutional provision for the "separation of church and state." And the opening of a state-supported educational program at a virtually all-black institution in a state that had just recently (1887) repealed its anti-black laws and guaranteed equal rights to the black population was viewed by some as a step backward toward legal segregation. However, because it was viewed as politically expedient by both Democrats and Republicans in the Ohio state legislature, the subsidy was approved and increased throughout the 1890s. The state appropriation increased to $17,425 by 1896 and was important for the support of faculty and students in the normal and industrial courses. Several buildings on campus were erected through state funding, and enrollment doubled as a result of the expansion in these two areas.[17]

The state appropriation continued to increase throughout the early decades of the 20th century, but there was constant friction between the state educational officials, the administrators, and trustees for the Normal and Agricultural department at Wilberforce, and the AME Church leaders at the university and throughout the state of Ohio. Finally, in 1948 the AME church severed the ties between Wilberforce University and the State of Ohio, leading to the creation of a new school, Central State University. However, before and after the receipt of state funds, Wilberforce University was able to utilize cultural capital as an economic resource because this educational institution was considered important to the collective identity and social advancement of the African American population in the United States.[18]

SUCCESSES AND FAILURES IN AME HIGHER EDUCATION

When we examine the history, development, and financial resources available to the other AME institutions of higher education, we find that they too had access to cultural capital as well as social capital from the local African American communities where these schools were located. Indeed, it was the overestimation of the amount of social capital in these local communities that led to the proliferation of AME colleges and universities. In some instances, however, the physical, human, social, cultural, and most critically, the financial capital was insufficient to sustain such a large economic enterprise as opening an institution of higher education. From the early 1880s Bishop Daniel Payne was well aware of these economic realities and issued several warnings to the membership. Following the 1884 General Conference, Bishop Payne published an article in the *AME Church Review* entitled, "Thoughts about the Past, the Present, and the Future of the AME Church," in which he commented negatively on the proliferation of schools and so-called colleges being opened by AME Conferences throughout the country. "Do not *fritter* away ten thousand dollars between different *would-be colleges*." "Concentrate that sum," Payne warned, "Yes concentrate ten times ten thousand upon one. By doing so you will make it strong."[19]

In his *History of the AME Church*, first published in 1891, Bishop Payne included the same admonition: "The founding of a college requires a great deal of forethought and preparation. This is true of those who command a deep, long and wide purse. Especially is this true of a people, or leaders of a people, who are poverty-stricken and unacquainted with enterprises that require large sums of money to secure success." He warned that "we should never be in haste to 'adopt a resolution' to found a college. Resolution costs nothing but thought," he warned, "but the establishment of an institution of learning worthy of the name college demands more than paper resolutions, which cost nothing but a sheet of paper, a pen, and a little ink."[20] Unfortunately, Bishop Payne's advice and warnings went completely unheeded by the various AME Conferences around the country and many of the schools opened between 1876 and 1900 were forced to close temporarily, move to other locations, or close permanently.

In the case of Edward Waters College, founded by the North Florida Conference in 1870, it was the combination of black and white philanthropy, the persistence of the Jacksonville black community, and able local leadership that allowed it to survive on its extremely shaky economic foundations. The situation for Paul Quinn College, founded in Austin by the Texas Conference in 1872 and later moved to East Waco, was only slightly better off than Edward Waters. The launching of the "Ten Cents a Brick" fundraising campaign among the Texas AME congregations was helpful in the beginning, but it was cultural capital in the form of a loan from the black fraternal group the Knights of Pythias that proved extremely important in the construction of Paul Quinn's main building, Johnson Hall.[21]

Shorter College, founded by the Arkansas, South Arkansas, and West Arkansas Annual Conferences in 1885, was forced to move from Little Rock to Arkadelphia in 1891 because the black community there promised more financial support. It was not enough to sustain the school, however, so it moved back to Little Rock in 1895. Fortunately, the philanthropic support from the Arkansas General Conference was enough to keep Shorter College open into the 20th century, but only as a junior college. Morris Brown College, founded by the North Georgia and Georgia Conferences in 1881, was initially on a firmer financial base than Shorter College, but it was forced to move several times within the city of Atlanta before finally locating in buildings formerly owned by Atlanta University. It was the successful fundraising campaigns and other philanthropic efforts supported by the Georgia black community that allowed Morris Brown College to survive its economically fragile beginnings.[22]

Allen University was founded in Cokebury, South Carolina, by the Columbia District Conference in 1870 and originally named "Payne Institute." In 1871 the control of the school was transferred to the South Carolina Conference and in 1880 it was moved to Columbia because it was considered a more centralized location and the name was changed to honor Richard Allen. Considered one of the most successful AME colleges due to the far-reaching philanthropic efforts of the South Carolina Conference, Allen University was the exception to the rule. Other AME colleges, and an even larger number of theological schools and institutes, founded in Mississippi, North Carolina, Oklahoma, Virginia, Louisiana, and Kansas did not survive to the end of the 20th century. Although some merged with larger and more economically viable institutions, many simply closed after years of struggle, just as Bishop Payne had predicted.[23]

CONCLUSION

The fact that the educational vision of people of African descent, newly freed and independent, sometimes extended beyond their financial realities should not be dismissed lightly, especially by a newer generation of African Americans at the beginning of the 21st century whose economic and financial realities extend far beyond their educational visions. Cultural capital, the sense of group consciousness and collective identity, was an extremely important economic resource in the numerous collective educational enterprises undertaken by the AME, the AME Zion, the Colored Methodist Episcopal, and the National Baptist denominations. Oftentimes, when financial capital was raised through charitable donations and campaigns that asked individuals to donate "a penny-a-brick"; and physical capital consisted of what materials they could lay their hands on to make chairs, desks, blackboards, and schoolhouses; when the human capital was the knowledge and techniques they had mastered at the workbench, in the stable or corral working beside skilled former slaves; and the social capital was their sense of community and the family and kinship networks that were based on mutual respect, obligations, expectations, and trust; these African Americans were able to make their educational dreams a reality.

Historically, collective economic enterprises in general, and philanthropy aimed at the opening of institutions of higher education in particular, have been extremely important for the social development and advancement of African Americans as a group in the United States. We need to build upon this important cultural legacy to plan collectively for African America's social, economic, and political future.[24]

NOTES

1. For information on the various types of "capital" needed for economic enterprises, see Pierre Bourdieu, "The Forms of Capital," in Johns G. Richardson, ed., *Handbook of Theory and Research in the Sociology of Education* (New York, 1986), 241–258. See also James S. Coleman, "Social Capital in the Creation of Human Capital," *American Journal of Sociology* 94 (Supplement): S95–S120; Robert D. Putnam, "Bowling Alone: America's Declining Social Capital," *Current* 356 (October 1993): 4–9; and "The Prosperous Community: Social Capital and Economic Growth," *Current* 356 (October 1993): 4-9; Francis Fukuyama, *Trust: The Social Virtues and the Creation of Prosperity* (New York, 1995); and "Social Capital and the Global Economy," *Foreign Affairs* 74 (Sept.–Oct., 1995): 89–103.

2.   Marxist social scientists were the first to use the terms "social capital" and "cultural capital." For the Marxists "social capital" referred to the resources and wealth produced through "family connections and group membership"; "cultural capital" referred to the wealth that the bourgeoisie and the intelligentsia in capitalistic societies derive from being in a position to legitimize and determine "cultural tastes and artistic styles"; see Bourdieu, "The Forms of Capital," 241–258.

3.   James B. Stewart, "Toward Broader Involvement of Black Economists in Discussions of Race and Public Policy: A Plea for a Reconceptualization of Race and Power in Economic Theory, " *Review of Black Political Economy* 23 (Winter 1995): 13–35.

4.   For discussion, see V.P. Franklin, "Social Capital, Cultural Capital, and Empowerment Zones: A Strategy for Economic and Community Development," in *State of Black Philadelphia: Economic Power—Leveling the Playing Field* (Philadelphia, PA, 1998), 19–23.

5.   See, for example, Don A. Cass, *Negro Free Masonry and Segregation* (Chicago, IL, 1957), 65–90; John Sibley Butler, *Entrepreneurship and Self-Help Among Black Americans: A Reconsideration of Race and Economics* (Albany, NY, 1991), 79–142. For a discussion of the "self-determinist cultural values" that historically underpinned black-controlled organizations and enterprises, see V.P. Franklin, *Black Self-Determination: A Cultural History of African-American Resistance* (Brooklyn, NY, 1992).

6.   Robert C. McMath, *American Populism: A Social History, 1877–1898* (New York: Hill and Wang, 1993), 108–142; Gerald F. Gaither, *Blacks and the Populist Revolt: Ballots and Bigotry in the New South* (Birmingham, AL, 1977); and William F. Holmes, "The Demise of the Colored Farmers' Alliance," *The Journal of Southern History* 41 (1975): 187–200.

7.   The Atlanta University Studies edited by W.E.B. Du Bois at the turn of the century contain much information on cooperative economic activities among African Americans, see *Some Efforts of American Negroes for Their Own Social Betterment, The Negro in Business, Economic Cooperation Among Negro Americans,* and *Efforts for Social Betterment Among Negro Americans* (Atlanta, GA, 1898, 1899, 1907, and 1910). See also John Hope II, "Rochdale Cooperation Among Negroes," *Phylon* 1 (First Quarter, 1940): 39–52.

8.   Richard Robert Wright, Jr., *The Bishops of the African Methodists Episcopal (AME) Church* (Nashville, TN, 1963), 70–73; Carol V.R. George, *Segregated Sabbaths: Richard Allen and the Rise of Independent Black Churches, 1760–1840* (New York, 1973), 49–88.

9.   George, *Segregated Sabbaths,* 76–77; Carter G. Woodson, *The Education of the Negro Prior to 1861* (1914; reprinted New York, 1968), 144–145; V.P. Franklin, *The Education of Black Philadelphia: The Social and Educational History of a Minority Community, 1900–1950* (Philadelphia, PA, 1979), 30–31.

10. Daniel Alexander Payne, *Recollections of Seventy Years,* edited by Rev. C.S. Smith (1888; reprinted New York, 1968), 220–223.

11. Ibid., 224–225; see also Juanita Jackson High, "Black Colleges As Social Intervention: The Development of Higher Education within the African Methodist Episcopal Church," unpublished Ed.D. dissertation, Rutgers University, 1978, 48–53.

12. Payne, *Recollections*. Page numbers for quoted material are placed in parentheses in the text. See also, Frederick A. McGinnis, *A History and Interpretation of Wilberforce University* (Blanchester, OH, 1941), 22–30.

13. Daniel A. Payne, *The History of the African Methodist Episcopal Church* (Nashville, TN, 1891), 430–431.

14. High, "Black Colleges As Social Intervention," 33–37.

15. Ibid., 37–39.

16. Joseph Turner McMillan, "The Development of Higher Education for Blacks During the Late Nineteenth Century: A Study of the African Methodist Episcopal Church; Wilberforce University; the American Missionary Association; Hampton Institute; and Fisk University," Unpublished Ed.D. dissertation, Teachers College, Columbia University, 1986, 85–95.

17. McGinnis, *A History*, 56–60; David A. Gerber, "Segregation, Separatism, and Sectarianism: Ohio Blacks and Wilberforce University's Effort to Obtain Federal Funds, 1891," *Journal of Negro Education* 45 (Winter 1976): 1–20.

18. "The New Wilberforce," *The Crisis* 8 (August 1914): 191–194; High, "Black Colleges As Social Intervention," 60–67.

19. Payne, "Thoughts about the Past, the Present, and the Future of the African Methodist Episcopal Church," *AME Church Review* 1 (July 1884): 1–8.

20. Payne, *History of the AME Church*, 448.

21. High, *Black Colleges As Social Intervention*, 71–94.

22. Ibid., 94–110.

23. Ibid., 116–128.

24. See, V.P. Franklin, "Social Capital, Cultural Capital, and the Challenge of African American Education in the 21st Century" in this volume.

CHAPTER 4

OUR SCHOOL
IN OUR COMMUNITY

The Collective Economic Struggle
for African American Education in Franklin,
Tennessee, 1890–1967

Carter Julian Savage

In Tuskegee, Alabama, in the early 1880s, Booker T. Washington, a novice principal and fundraiser, initiated a capital campaign to construct permanent buildings on Tuskegee Institute's barren campus. The young school was growing and drawing students from across the countryside. The old, rickety, but clean cabins on the school grounds were no longer sufficient to accommodate the school's needs. All told, Washington needed $6,000 to build this new, spacious facility. But, where would he get it? Seeking the local black community's support of this project, he called a meeting of community elders. Washington, who was neatly dressed, stood erect in front of his economically impoverished neighbors and precisely articulated his vision for the school, its students, and the emerging campus.

Although many of them were clad in rags, spoke in broken English, and were illiterate, they cheered this bold, brown-skinned brother who proposed the key to their children's future—an education. As Washington and his trusted colleague, co-teacher, and wife, Olivia Davidson, stood before the crowd, "an antebellum colored man" rose to speak. He had come 12 miles to attend this meeting and had a large hog in the back of his ox-

Cultural Capital and Black Education, pages 49–79
Copyright © 2004 by Information Age Publishing
All rights of reproduction in any form reserved.

cart. Probably pondering his decades in unpaid chattel service as well as the hope this new school could bring to the black community, he announced that he had no money to contribute, but he did have two fine hogs. And he intended to give one of these hogs in support of the school. He concluded that anyone of his neighbors who has love for their race, or any respect for themselves, would bring a hog to the next meeting.[1]

In this anecdote of the early days of Tuskegee Institute, Booker T. Washington claimed that an elderly African American farmer traveled 12 hard miles to donate a hog to support the establishment of Tuskegee Institute in the mid-1880s. Although quite poor, this farmer felt the education of black children in his community was important enough for him to donate a substantial portion of his personal wealth. His act underscored the appreciation that many 19th-century African Americans had for education. The African American farmer's donation of the hog and his subsequent challenge to his fellow citizens to do the same captures African Americans' desire for education, their zeal for socioeconomic mobility, their race pride, and their belief in self-determination. This story provides a glimpse of African American agency and the use of cultural capital for schooling in the South in the 19th century.

This chapter presents the history of four public, segregated, African American schools in Franklin, Tennessee, between 1890 and 1967.[2] It examines how the black community in Franklin utilized cultural capital to establish, maintain, and enhance its schools, in spite of the discriminatory policies imposed by local, all-white school boards. I argue that Franklin's black community exhibited an agency that stemmed from an African American ethos of self-determination and social advancement. Franklin's cultural capital was a product of this community-wide agency. The agency and cultural capital produced by African Americans in Franklin was exhibited in three areas: community-wide resource development, community leadership, and the dedicated service of the teachers and principals.

- *Resource development.* Because of the limited funding of their schools (whether private or public), Franklin's African Americans taxed themselves to provide the resources—monetary or material—that ensured the success of their schools.[3]
- *Community leadership.* Community members, as individuals or as part of a group, created the desire and provided the necessary resources within their community to establish and maintain their schools in spite of the opposition from the larger white community.[4]
- *Extraordinary service.* Although teaching was their profession, principals and teachers provided extraordinary service to their students. Principals maneuvered district policies and provided resources to equip their schools and introduced new curricula and activities to enrich their students. Finally, principals and teachers provided pro-

fessional leadership and technical assistance to the black community's efforts to support the school economically.

Their agency and cultural capital grew from small, close-knit communities surrounding the schools. Specifically, it sprang from an African American community that had (1) a long-standing belief in the power of education as a force for social change; (2) self-contained physical and social structures created under segregation; and (3) an appreciation for the central importance of the school in the community. This environment established long-standing enclaves with diverse levels of employment, education, motivation, and wealth; and provided their schools with a wide array of community resources.

AFRICAN AMERICAN AGENCY AND CULTURAL CAPITAL IN THE SOUTH

Historically, African Americans have struggled to obtain effective education through numerous self-determinist strategies.[5] From the holding of Bible-reading classes on southern plantations to the establishment of segregated public schools, southern black parents and teachers have utilized self-determinist strategies to overcome oppressive Black Codes and Jim Crow ordinances and provide schools in their communities.[6] Whether it was a prominent educator like Booker T. Washington or the little-known principal of Franklin Training School, amazingly similar techniques were used to combat the local forces opposed to African American education. It is these empowering, self-determinist strategies that I define as agency.

Historian James Anderson described these self-determinist actions—this agency—of southern black teachers and communities in their efforts to provide schooling for their children. For Anderson, this agency included both pro-active movements for social change and defiant stances against injustice. Molefi Asante's 20th-century concept of "Afrocentricity" depicts "agency" as proactive movements or perspectives that result from the African "centeredness" within a community. Historian V. P. Franklin's work on the African American cultural value system suggests that this behavior reflected African Americans' cultural value of self-determination and that it stems from an "ethos of service" that called upon those who acquired literacy to transfer this knowledge to others in the black community. Julius Rosenwald Foundation executive Edwin Embree wrote in 1928 about this spirit among African Americans, suggesting that this agency was composed of four elements:

1. African Americans' zeal for education
2. the African American community's propensity to give to their schools
3. the devotion of poorly paid, African American teachers
4. the willingness of African American students to attend "distressingly poor facilities"[7]

The earlier anecdote about the southern black farmer suggests how cultural capital was used by African Americans to develop and maintain schools. V. P. Franklin defines cultural capital as the "'sense of group consciousness' that is utilized as a resource in the development of collective economic enterprises." Specifically, this "capital" is created when African Americans join together and create resources to meet the important social, political, and economic needs in their community. Schooling for African Americans in the South, particularly in the early phases (1867–1935), was often dependent upon cultural capital. Because their schools received no public support or were extremely underfunded, African Americans in the South joined together to create the resources to support public or private schools in their community.[8]

In her history of African American education in Tennessee, Cynthia Fleming noted that African American Tennesseans had acquired school buildings and were covering teachers' expenses by the fall of 1866. African Americans underwrote the entire expenses for 22 schools, partially supported 15 others, and owned 26 buildings. By November 1867, they were completely sustaining 30 schools, and partially funding 40 more. This level of contribution fluctuated throughout Reconstruction, but African Americans in Tennessee were supporting 30 schools in May 1870. The vast majority of these schools were located in urban areas. The rationale behind these locations for schools was economic. In urban areas, African Americans had access to more lucrative jobs. These higher-paying positions allowed a large number of cooperative-minded African Americans to pool their resources to improve the literacy levels in their community, especially among their children.[9]

These schools did not necessarily represent a new era in African American educational history, but were a continuation of the "native schools" founded before the Civil War. Moreover, they represented the link to the schools founded by free blacks in the North and South as early as the turn of the 19th century. These schools also represented a continuation of the ethos of cooperation essential for the freedom and social mobility of African Americans.[10]

There was no monolithic approach to generating the capital necessary to open these new schools, but various strategies were employed. For example, Louis Harlan argued that Tuskegee Institute was founded as a result of Lewis Adams, a black leader in Alabama, securing the black vote for the Democratic party. With no money to start a school, Laurence Jones founded the Piney Woods Country Life School in 1909 with only three students, "under the long leaf yellow pine trees of South Mississippi." Students from this Tuskegee Institute offshoot remember Jones seating the students "on a big long oak log and he was sitting on a little homemade stool right in front of us teaching." During this same period, the members of the African American religious denominations aided the development of secondary schools. Bishop Isaac Lane, representing the Colored (Christian) Methodist Episcopal Church (CME), preached and raised money throughout the South and Southwest to establish Jackson CME High School (now Lane College) in 1882 in Jackson, Tennessee.[11]

To be sure, the work of these school leaders would have faltered without the support of average African American citizens, who understood the meaning of collective sacrifice. They pooled their resources to pay for the construction of school buildings, teachers' salaries, building maintenance, and school supplies. In 1869 John Eaton, the first superintendent of public instruction in the state of Tennessee, described African American monetary contributions for their schooling.

> In the early autumn of 1862, Miss Lucinda Humphrey . . . opened an evening school for the colored employees of the hospital at Memphis. Others followed, increasing from year to year, until in the winter of 1864–65 a method was provided for the colored people to enter activity into the work of supporting their own school, and after which, in about five months they paid for the [building], some four thousand dollars, and the attendance was reported in and around Memphis, as high as 1,949, in April 1865.[12]

Local African Americans provided support for teachers by housing them in their own homes. Finally, whenever possible, they sacrificed some of their annual income by allowing their children to be in school rather than earning a wage. Historian Vanessa Siddle Walker asserts that although the black residents of Caswell County, North Carolina, were provided inadequate facilities, books, supplies, and equipment, they still did not suffer from a "poverty of spirit."

> In this community, many parents were not silent victims of an oppressive system; instead, through a variety of roles, they actively participated in providing resources for their children. They supplied stage curtains, band uniforms, pianos, and much more to support the academic and extracurricular program. They donated the first bus to be used in the transportation of African American children and later bought another bus back from the county for transporting their children to extracurricular activities.

Even more important than their financial support was the Caswell County Training School parents' advocacy role. Among other contributions, parental advocates lobbied the state to establish a black high school, pushed for the construction of the new school building, and spearheaded the campaign for a gymnasium. In addition, they demonstrated their involvement in the school through their attendance at Parent–Teacher Association (PTA) meetings and other school functions.[13]

In the 20th century African Americans also came together to support the development of public schools across the South. Spurred by the promise of matching funds from Julius Rosenwald, local African Americans provided more than their fair share of land, labor, and money to build and maintain these public institutions. Starting in 1913, the Rosenwald Fund began the largest and most dramatic rural school construction project in the country. Although local residents were required to contribute to the construction of the schools, from 1913 to 1928 African Americans contributed more than local whites. For the fiscal year ending in 1928, African Americans contributed 13.5% or $363,000 of the $2.6 million spent to construct Rosenwald schools in the South; whites contributed 4.5% or $118,000. From 1913 to 1928, African Americans contributed 19%, or $3.9 million, whereas whites contributed only 4.5% or $900,000. From the inception of the school building program, the Fund's total contribution was only $3.3 million. In 1928 the Fund's Director Edwin Embree concluded that, "The Rosenwald contributions, it will be noted, are less than the total raised by the Negroes themselves in small amounts, county-by-county and village-by-village. The Negro's zeal for education is attested by these gifts. . . ."[14]

At the first Rosenwald school in Tuskegee, Alabama, African Americans raised $150 to purchase the land for the school site and donated labor equivalent to $132.50. Similarly, S. L. Smith, a white Rosenwald agent in Tennessee, praised the contribution of the African American community to black education in Fayette County, Tennessee—specifically, the work of their black principal and his wife. In 1915, African American citizens raised approximately $2,200 of the $3,500 needed to build Tennessee's first Rosenwald-supported school. Smith noted that 1,200 black fraternal lodge members gave 936 one-dollar bills in a meeting at an old dilapidated school building. Smith recalled, "I was present on a rainy day. . . . An umbrella had to be held over the money as I counted it, because of the leaky roof." An additional $1,200 was contributed at the next meeting. Thomas Stitley noted that other black residents brought "corn, hens, eggs, and potatoes" in lieu of a monetary gift. The Fayette County principal and his wife's continuing fundraising efforts led to building twenty additional Rosenwald-supported schools in Fayette County between 1915 and 1920. For the Shelby County Training School, African Americans raised $500 to purchase extra land for agricultural projects. Finally, in rural Williamson County, African Americans raised $750 of the $1,670 to build Lee Buckner School; raised $200 of the $1,750 to build Locust Ridge School; and raised $750 of the $3,400 to build the school at Thompson Station.[15]

"Rosenwald Days" became annual celebrations to raise funds for African American schools. During the 1920s, Rosenwald Days provided the teachers and administrators in these schools the opportunity to celebrate their year-long drives to raise funds for school operation. For example, in 1931, over 1,900 Rosenwald schools across the South raised more than $81,000 and raised $9,400 on Rosenwald Day alone. In Tennessee's 187 schools, the 1931 "Rosenwald Day" raised $514; the students and teachers raised approximately $8,000 for the year. Similarly, Jeanes teachers supplied by the Jeanes Fund, another philanthropic foundation, organized Home Makers' Clubs for African American women and girls. In 1916, S. L. Smith, the state agent for Negro Education, wrote that the Home Makers' Clubs in Tennessee raised $8,200 for improvements in their schools; Williamson County Home Makers' Clubs raised $163. In 1918, there were 500 clubs in Tennessee that raised $35,000 for both school and home improvement.[16]

Southern African Americans contributed more than their fair share of money, land, and labor to public and private school development. Black Franklinites, like their contemporaries across the South, provided an unprecedented amount of cultural capital for educational institutions. Historian James Anderson suggested that the resources provided by black community members represented a form of "double taxation," where African Americans paid taxes for public schools, but had to supplement them with their own financial donations and other materials. This discussion of black agency and cultural capital should not suggest that there was total agreement and participation among African Americans. Thomas Stitely's research on Rosenwald Schools described some internal community power struggles and denominational rivalries in Tennessee. However, these conflicts did limit school development in their communities. With little national or regional leadership, African Americans at the local level acted as a cohesive group determined to provide schooling for their own children and for future generations.[17]

EARLY AFRICAN AMERICAN EDUCATION OF WILLIAMSON COUNTY, TENNESSEE

Franklin, Tennessee, located approximately 15 miles south of Nashville, is presently a wealthy, rapidly growing, suburban community. However, in 1865, Franklin was a poor, agrarian township that served as the seat of Williamson County, which was the home of a large number of klansmen and witnessed its share of racial confrontations. Like other southern African Americans at the end of the Civil War, Williamson County freedpeople sought schooling as an immediate cure—not only for past injustices, but also as their chief means of personal and community development.[18]

Initially, free public schooling in Williamson County was not well received within the white community. In 1869, School Superintendent J. A. Edmonson reported that "our people's dislike for free schools has given way very much, and many are getting to be actively friendly." The white residents took particular issue with public schooling for African Americans. In this same report, Edmonson noted that 300 masked men rode through the village of Franklin at night to protest against black public schools. They rode to the house of a district director of the Williamson County school system. After a long discussion, the masked men agreed to schools for African Americans as long as there was white control over their operation.[19]

In the late 19th century, one-room, poorly constructed shacks epitomized African American education in rural Williamson County. The Ninth District—which contained the town of Franklin—had only one school for African Americans. Many older African Americans recall their parents being educated in isolated, one-room schools in the towns of DuPlex, Hard Scuffle, Grassland, Mudsink, Bradley's Bend, Thompson Station, Bingham, and Westwood.

In these rural school buildings approximately 30 children sat on long benches facing the teacher and a large, chalky blackboard; they completed their lessons on tablets that they laid in their laps. Books and other materials were in such short supply that teachers could not count on having them. Attendance often depended on the season, the weather, or the economic conditions of the families; thus, most children progressed in an uneven fashion. In most rural "colored" schools, one teacher taught multiple grades, usually 1–8. The level of teaching varied from school to school. During this period (and into the first quarter of the 20th century), African Americans who graduated from the eighth grade were able to secure teaching jobs in other one-room schoolhouses in the same county.

Although it is unclear when (or where) the first African American school, public or private, was opened in Williamson County, there probably was a public school in Franklin as early as 1869. The first newspaper account of a separate school for African Americans in Franklin, the Ninth District Colored School, was recorded in 1881. As early as 1874, there were 26 public African American schools with 29 African American teachers serving approximately 3,600 black children in Williamson County.[20]

The Ninth District Colored School of Franklin was the most stable African American school in Williamson County. On a smaller scale, the town of Franklin, like Nashville, provided greater economic opportunities for African Americans than the more rural communities of the county. African Americans residing in cities and towns had access to more stable jobs. These early African Americans were able to start businesses, buy land, build houses and churches, and support schooling. This more consistent income allowed them to invest their time and money in the development of Ninth District schools and African American children residing in Franklin had more time to devote to schooling than their rural counterparts.[21]

The exact locations of the Ninth District Colored School are currently unknown. Given the opposition to black education, the Ninth District Colored School changed sites frequently. Most likely, this school opened in the late 1860s or early 1870s in space leased from the local black church, Franklin Primitive Baptist Church, in a section of the black community called "Hard Bargain." Franklin Primitive Baptist Church, also known as the "Church on the Hill," was founded in 1867 and was the pulpit of some of the early progressive leaders of the black community. Probably moving from site to site, the black school served as many as 210 children with only two teachers.[22]

Claiborne's Institute

The story of the African American schools on Natchez Street in Franklin begins with Claiborne's Institute, opened sometime in the late 1880s. The history of Claiborne's Institute, which was an L-shaped, clapboard building with at least four classrooms, may never be fully known. Property deeds suggest that the local district school directors, along with a group of African American investors known as the "Langston Association," purchased the property on Natchez Street for a school for African Americans in 1888. However, oral histories from older African Americans in the community, including one Claiborne's Institute student, revealed that the school was named after an African American named Willis Claiborne who provided the land for the school. Claiborne's Institute served Franklin's African American community between the late 1880s and 1907. Providing an academic curriculum with a strong religious base, the students began each morning with chapel, and then were sent to classes in reading, writing, arithmetic, and history. In its heyday, Claiborne's Institute had one principal, three teachers, and approximately 250 students.[23]

Franklin Colored School

From 1867 to 1907 the operation of the schools in the Ninth District was the responsibility of the Williamson County Board of Education with specific oversight from its respective district directors. In April 1907, Franklin's Board of Mayor and Aldermen constituted a city board of education "for the uses and purposes of a public school for white children in said town." With the establishment of the city school district, the two existing primary schools, one white and one black (Claiborne's Institute), were transferred into the jurisdiction of the city of Franklin.[24]

According to oral histories, Claiborne's Institute burned down in the spring of 1907. The new Claiborne's Institute, then referred to as the Franklin Colored School (FCS), was housed in a square-shaped building on Natchez Street with a recessed, rectangular porch. A set of brown, wooden steps led to the entrance of this white, clapboard structure. The front door opened into a long hallway that led straight through to the back door. This six-room school had three classrooms on each side, with one "big, old pot gut heater" per room. The FCS included grades 1–8, with high school subjects offered beginning in 1923. The school drew students from Franklin as well as from "the rim," the immediate surrounding areas. School records indicated that 284 students were enrolled in 1911.[25]

Franklin Training School

The old, clapboard Franklin Colored School was not built to last. By the early 1920s, the members of the African American community had begun to complain about the school's condition. Led by Henry Ewing, an African American contractor, a group of black citizens requested a new building. What they got through the Rosenwald Fund and the Williamson County government was a long, perpendicular attachment to the existing square building. The transition from FCS to Franklin Training School (FTS) signaled a gradual change from a small country school to a comprehensive high school, and the institution's evolution from an important center of education for children to a center of community life. African Americans no longer wanted industrial education and "May Days," but football teams, bands, proms, and formal commencements. These events were not purely for the development of youth, they also supported the social needs of black parents and community members.[26]

Unfortunately, the new FTS was also poorly constructed. Students described huge gaps in the floorboards, extremes in the building temperatures, and close calls with fires. For approximately ten years, the African American community lobbied school district officials for a new building.

Finally, in 1950, a new, red-brick and cinderblock Franklin Training School was built. Still standing today as the Claiborne-Hughes Nursing Home, this building housed both an elementary school and a larger high school. In 1958, another all-black elementary school was constructed, the Charles S. Johnson School (now Johnson Elementary School), and the Franklin Training School became a high school.[27]

Natchez High School

The evolution of FTS into Natchez High School (NHS) was somewhat anticlimatic.[28] George Northern, a science teacher at FTS and NHS, remembered the idea for the name change was brought up at a faculty meeting by Bobbie Jean Ray. Carrie Amos Harrison, NHS's English teacher, suggested the desire for change stemmed from the growing displeasure among African Americans with the title "training school." She indicated that African Americans no longer accepted the idea that "manual training and labor" was schooling. Principal C. B. Spencer took the idea to the Williamson County Board of Education (WCBOE) and the September 19, 1961, board minutes included a simple, but unobtrusive statement: "Motion was made and passed by the Board to change the name of Franklin Training School to Natchez High School."[29]

Although it seemed like an eternity to many of the informants, Natchez High School existed for only six years (1961–1967). For the most part, Natchez High School was simply a continuation of FTS. Between 1961 and 1967, the WCBOE did make substantial improvements to the building. However, these improvements were made within the context of discussions of public school desegregation. These improvements were attempts at appeasement of local African Americans, but public school desegregation was inevitable. On January 10, 1967, the county school board passed its final desegregation plan and NHS was closed as a separate high school in May 1967 and subsequently converted into the vocational annex of the white high school, Franklin High School.[30]

To many students and faculty, the closing of NHS was a traumatic event. Students and community members felt they had lost part of their soul. For teachers and administrators, NHS's closing represented an uncertainty of employment in the larger, predominantly white public school system. As a group, few African Americans remembered the days of Claiborne's Institute and the early years of FTS. But most of them had warm memories of the heyday of FTS and NHS, their school in their community.

EXTRAORDINARY SERVICE: JAMES K. HUGHES
AND THE ERA OF INDUSTRIAL EDUCATION

Over its 42 years of existence, FTS had five principals: J. K. Hughes, Dr. I. H. Hampton, E. E. Pitts, J. R. Watkins, and C. B. Spencer.[31] Each of these principals brought something different to the school. Each in his own way expanded on the work of his predecessors and provided significant challenges to another generation of students, teachers, and school board members. Each principal, through his leadership, rallied the black community and coaxed the white community to support improvements in the school. These principals provided not only the institutional leadership, but technical assistance and expertise to lay leaders within the black community. In sum, these principals were charged with generating cultural capital within the black community while remaining politically connected to the white community. This section describes how James K. Hughes and his colleagues created and maintained school resources, and generated the political will needed in their encounters with Franklin's white community.

In 1921 James Kemp Hughes was elected principal and superintendent of the FCS. Hughes, known as "J. K." to African Americans, was one of the best known figures in Franklin, black or white, during his years of prominence. J. K. Hughes was born sometime in the early 1880s in Bingham—a rural community in Williamson County. He was the son of former slaves, Tom and Matilda Hughes, who sold their farm and moved to the town of Franklin. According to Alice Patton, his daughter, when the family moved to Franklin, he went to school either on Natchez Street or in Hard Bargain. Whether J. K. received an eighth-grade diploma is unclear, but according to Patton, he did do "some extra work" at Tuskegee where he met his future wife, Edna Foy Coleman.[32]

According to a 1936 newspaper article, Hughes spent most of his early teaching career in one-room schoolhouses in the county. "[B]eginning when he was not much more than a boy," Hughes started his career at the Hill's Valley School in the Sixth District, moving later to the Lyon's School. In 1903, a salary payment document provides the first evidence of his teaching in the Ninth District at Claiborne's Institute. When Claiborne's Institute was transferred to the city's Board of Education, Hughes left the Ninth District. For a number of years Hughes was Williamson County "supervisor of the colored rural schools," a title he kept even after he was named principal of FCS and FTS.[33]

On June 28, 1921, the members of the Franklin Board of Education elected J. K. Hughes principal of Franklin Colored School and they also hired his wife, Edna, as the domestic science teacher. At that time, Hughes was the supervisor of the rural black schools. Believing he was the best candidate, the school board allowed Hughes to continue his "educational work in the county."[34]

Physically, James K. Hughes was a large, dark-skinned man who stood about 6 feet tall and weighed about 250 pounds. A large, balding head stood erect atop his broad shoulders; thin, wire-rimmed glasses resting snugly on his nose. He had a heavy, deep voice, in contrast to his reputed soft touch. Alice Hughes Patton confirmed that her father was a "gentle man . . . I would say he was the type of person who saw some good in everybody." Upon Hughes's death in 1936, the Franklin *Review-Appeal* wrote: "James K. Hughes, one of Franklin's most respected colored citizens, died Tuesday morning at 3:15 o'clock. . . . He was liked by both the white and colored population, being courteous and respectful at all times."[35]

Hughes was also a quiet man who loved to read. Will Kelton, a former student, said, "[He] was a man who believed in education." His favorite subject was history. Many of his students remember vividly his lessons in U.S. and Tennessee history. Hughes had a particular interest in the history of the city of Franklin. According to his daughter, students from Battle Ground Academy, a local, private white academy, would come down to the school. These students would sit for hours and ask him different questions about Franklin's history.[36]

Until 1918 there was no difference in the prescribed curricula for white and black students in either the city or county school systems, according to the "Course of Study and Grade Limit" first published by the Franklin Board of Education in 1913. All students had their share of academic and manual training classes. Former students recall studying from spellers, geography texts, readers, and history books. In 1911 Carrie Otey, principal of FCS, did not provide any courses in manual or industrial education. She reported to the superintendent that all 284 students were enrolled in orthography, reading, writing, arithmetic, geography, physiology, U.S. history, Tennessee history, algebra, rhetoric, advanced English, and "civil government."[37]

In 1919 the Board of Education initiated a movement toward the introduction of industrial education through a grant from the John Slater Fund. The board strengthened its commitment to this new approach by hiring a former Tuskegee student, James K. Hughes, in 1921. As part of this new industrial education program, students were offered agricultural, domestic science, and vocational courses, in addition to the traditional academic subjects. Hughes and his wife, Edna, taught many of these courses. Boys in Hughes's shop class learned to make washboards, furniture, and baskets. Janelle Lesley, a student in Edna Hughes's class, recalled, "Mrs. Hughes [taught] us how to cook; we learned how to make candy and cook salmon; and we would eat that after it was all over." "May Days" were the culmination of the school's industrial education programs. Students from FCS as well as other black schools in the county would come together for a county-wide display of their crafts, food, and games.[38]

Hughes remained principal of FTS until 1927. During his tenure, the school became well known and well liked in both the African American and white communities. As mentioned earlier, African Americans thought Hughes was a congenial man, a knowledgeable teacher, and a good discipli-narian. The white community, as noted in newspaper articles, seemed to be charmed by his personality (although I suspect they were sold on the man-ual training programs he set up). The headline of a 1925 story in the *Review-Appeal* announced: "Local Negro School, One of the Best in the State." The reporter declared that,

> James K. Hughes, colored, who is the principal of this splendidly conducted school for [N]egroes, is to be congratulated upon the work he and his asso-ciate teachers are doing. There is an atmosphere of cleanliness and effi-ciency around the establishment which is far beyond that of other schools of this section.

Similarly, in 1926, a *Review-Appeal* article announcing Hughes's reappoint-ment stated: "The school is making rapid strides under the management of Jim Hughes and is now one of the best colored schools of the kind to be found in any Town of the size of Franklin."[39]

In much the same way as his former teacher, Booker T. Washington, Hughes built support for the school by engaging the white community in some of its manual training activities. One such event was an annual lunch he hosted at the school for prominent whites of the community. In many ways, this was an attempt to ensure continued funding for his school.

> Members of the Board of Aldermen of the Town of Franklin, the city recorder, city marshal, members of the Board of Education and representa-tives of the local press, were guests of the local colored school faculty last Wednesday at lunch when the domestic science class of the school served a bountiful meal of deliciously prepared foods for their guests.

After the meal prepared by members of Edna Hughes's domestic science class, some of the guests spoke out in support of the school. These speakers believed that southern whites understood the needs of black southerners, applauded the construction of a "substantially built" new school, and described themselves as lifelong "friends" of African Americans.

> The building is extraordinarily well equipped and substantially built. The stu-dents are taught subjects which will prove really beneficial to them upon graduation. This building and the facilities therein represent substantial evi-dence of just how much the southern people think of the [Negro] and how much they sympathize with him and desire his advancement. In the language

of one of the after-dinner speakers for the occasion, "there is no section in this great country where the [Negro] has greater opportunities for advancement than in the South and there is no people who more thoroughly understand the [Negro] than we of the South."

The highlight of the luncheon was the reading of a letter written by Mrs. Alex Ewing, member of the Board of Education, which "was endorsed by a rising vote" after it was read. She wrote:

> To Jim Hughes, his Teachers, and the pupils of his School—I regret very much my inability to be present at your annual celebration, as has been my privilege for several years past. . . .
>
> I wish to take this means, therefore, of extending to you my best wishes, to commend you for the good work you have done, to congratulate you upon your improved facilities and to encourage you to press forward, onward and upward, making the best possible use of the means at hand for the development of your people.
>
> I hope you will continue in the future, as I think you have in the past, to instill into your children the high principles of honesty, of industry, of thrift, of fair dealing, of clean living and of righteousness which alone marks the true progress of any people.
>
> It is with much pleasure that I can in this much respond to the courtesy which you have shown me by asking me to be present today and speak a word to you and I am glad to be able to send you these well wishes and to call myself your friend.[40]

As a principal, Hughes became a school and community leader, an African American spokesperson, and was considered a friend of the white community. This complex set of relationships was his greatest achievement and the source of his ultimate downfall. Seemingly in much the same way as his former teacher, Booker T. Washington, Hughes built support for the school by engaging the white community in the school's activities. At the same time, his role as the principal/superintendent as well as a church leader solidified him as a leader in the African American community.

However, this praise and glory ended in 1927. For the preceding two years, the minutes for the Franklin Board of Education meetings indicated that Hughes had been elected unanimously as either superintendent and/or principal of the school, and that he had received incremental salary increases each year. However, on Monday, May 9, 1927, the minutes show that "a delegation of colored citizens appeared and filed a petition protesting the re-election of James K. Hughes as principal, [and] Edna Hughes, and Mattie Stewart [as teachers] at the colored school."[41]

After considerable discussion, the Board Chairman appointed a committee to investigate the charges leveled by the delegation and to make recommendations to the Board. The committee reported back by the June 20, 1927, meeting, and only called for the reinstatement of Mattie Stewart as a teacher at FTS. Interestingly, at the next meeting on July 5, Dr. I. H. Hampton and his wife appeared in application "for work in the colored high school." On August 1, the committee recommended I. H. Hampton as principal of FTS. With a five-to-one vote, Hughes was terminated as principal and Hampton was elected.[42]

The minutes do not indicate why members of the African American community objected to Hughes and his colleagues. Alice Patton, his daughter, claims the black parents sought a principal with much more education. There could have been a growing objection in one segment of the African American community to the manual training emphasized at FTS. Perhaps this group was offended by the white community's support of the industrial programs at the school (making Hughes a "sell-out" to his community). Rejecting this Washingtonian approach to education, this group might have sought a principal more like W. E. B. Du Bois, an African American leader and intellectual who challenged the emphasis on industrial education.[43]

To his credit, Hughes had rallied the community, raised new funds, instituted new ideas, and initiated significant changes in the school. Hughes was hired to run Franklin Colored School, but laid the foundation for Natchez High School and had instituted high school work in the 1922–23 school year. From 1922 through 1925, he worked with black community leaders on the construction of a new black school in Williamson County. However, within two years these leaders sought a new direction and a new principal for their school.[44]

COMMUNITY LEADERSHIP

Another of the ways Franklin's black community provided cultural capital for black schools was through community leadership. Community leadership was essential to the establishment and maintenance of the earliest black educational institutions. Not only did these individuals and groups raise the funds to establish schools, community leaders made requests of white school officials, criticized their policies, and challenged the functioning of the public school system with less likelihood of retaliation than black teachers or principals. Moreover, in school districts that provided few educational necessities and no amenities, community support was the only hope for obtaining these materials. Black community leaders were always the backbone of the success of black schools in Williamson County, especially in the period between 1900 and 1930. Yet, as black residents became more economically secure and the school became a more important social component of the community, many local citizens became involved in the schools' operation. Most importantly, it was the community's cultural ethos about the power of education that helped to sustain the school through racial conflicts and discriminatory policies and practices.

This community leadership can be seen in the campaign for the erection of the first Franklin Training School. The African American community led by Henry Ewing argued successfully for a new school building in the early 1920s. Moreover, during the 1930s and 1940s, community leaders continually requested a new school facility. Finally, in 1950, the last Franklin Training/Natchez High School was built and still stands today.[45]

Archival sources suggest that when Claiborne's Institute burned down in 1907, the school board moved to find alternative accommodations for its black students. The "colored Baptist church" was repaired and rented for $60 per year to house the "colored school." But by 1911, the school had been moved to an old, six-room, square-shaped building with one "big, old pot gut heater" in each room.[46]

In April 1914, the city school board minutes indicated that FCS had some structural problems and was too small for the number of children who wanted to attend. These problems had prompted several members of the African American community to appear before the board on several occasions to suggest improvements to the school.[17]

The culmination of these efforts was an appearance by another delegation of African Americans led by contractor Henry Ewing on May 31, 1922.

> A delegation composed of patrons of the colored school appeared before the board to urge the enlargement and improvement of school for colored children. . . . H. J. Ewing, colored, a resident of the town of Franklin, engaged in contracting and building, submitted plans for a building estimated to cost $5,000.[18]

Henry Ewing, who lived two doors from the school, is described as an extraordinary person. Without a doubt, Ewing was a self-made man and typical of ambitious African Americans of that period, he was proficient in many trades, from embalming to architecture. Rev. William Scruggs, also a building contractor, credits his early training to Ewing:

> Henry Ewing was the most brilliant builder that I have ever seen even to this day. He was brilliant. I guess back in those times you would call him an architect or engineer or contractor or all of those things. He was a multitalented person, and he was an undertaker. And he was one of the best embalmers that I have ever seen. The man was self-taught. He didn't go to school for this. . . . He moved the AME Church from down below town, down by the Catholic church, on 2nd Avenue, to where it is now. Built it, finished it up and moved it up there. He was great builder.[19]

In response to Ewing's plans, the Board of Education moved that the matter should be forwarded to Franklin's Board of Mayor and Aldermen for discussion. An attempt was made to get the Rosenwald Fund to provide matching funds for the FCS's expansion, however, the request was turned down because the foundation only supported the construction of *rural* black schools. Ultimately, in August 1922 the Board of Alderman approved $5,000 for the FCS expansion which was completed two years later. While it is unclear from county school board records whether the school officials used Henry Ewing's design for the school addition, it was the persistent lobbying by community leaders that led to the significant improvements in what came to be the Franklin Training School.[50]

"PIE STRUTS," "CAKE WALKS," AND "QUEEN DRIVES:" COMMUNITY RESOURCE DEVELOPMENT TO SUPPORT THEIR SCHOOLS

One of the most explicit ways the black community used cultural capital for education was the area of "resource development." As a rule, local public school officials did not provide adequate resources to the separate black schools. Teachers were not only in need of books, equipment, and supplies, but they were also underpaid in comparison to their white counterparts. Yet it was these underpaid teachers and principals as well as their neighbors who raised the money and resources their school so desperately needed.[51]

The FTS's Parent–Teacher Association (PTA) was an important institution for a number of reasons. First, teachers were valued members of the community. Because this was a close-knit community, parents and teachers had relationships outside of the classroom. They were church and club members together, lived next door, and talked to one another at the grocery store and at social events. "Teachers were respected at that time," Mary Mills recalled:

> Teachers were held in high esteem by the community, and if you got into any trouble at school, you knew you were in trouble at home. Right or wrong, [parents] usually took the teacher's point of view, so you didn't have that much trouble; you had [parents'] support.[52]

Moreover, parents participated actively in the school's events. To be sure, it was considerably easier for city parents to participate than those in rural areas. To be respectful of their circumstances, the school scheduled major events for Friday nights. Thelma Battle, a student at FTS in 1952, remembered her mother attending her sister's school dance.

I remember [my] sister was invited to a seventh or eighth grade party, and the boy met her at school with a flower, and there was my mother and me and my sister . . . this was in the cafeteria . . . the kids danced . . . the mothers would have their places against the wall . . . and they [the mothers] could just sit there and talk. . . . All of the mothers didn't show up, but a lot of them did.

Louise Patton, a student and later a teacher at FTS, commented on the early bond between parents and teachers:

We had so much cooperation from the parents and at that time it seemed that everybody was so happy to be going to school. The parents were happy to send the children; the children were happy to come. And they didn't have a lot of hang-ups about different things. And so the learning was much easier; the teaching was much easier.

Although this relationship was not perfect, parents and teachers were in agreement—all they did was for the betterment of the children.[53]

Parents and teachers were linked together through the PTA. The primary function of the PTA was raising funds. The PTA "was a strong organization. They were the backbone of being able to organize and raise money," said Thelma Battle. Remembering the early days, Louise Patton confirmed:

The PTA, Parent–Teacher Association, and I think we met every month. It was organized, and when things needed to be done for the school like football uniforms or if we need equipment for the . . . kitchen or things that we were not given by the board, then . . . we would have a spaghetti supper, chittlin' suppers, and different ways to raise money to help the school.

In addition to spaghetti suppers and chittlin' dinners, the PTA sponsored pie struts and cake walks. Thelma Battle described a typical pie strut:

The pie struts was where you'd just walk around a table . . . a long cafeteria table . . . with some of the best pies some of the best cooks in the county had made . . . and they play some music, and the idea was just to see these people strut, and you would just strut. . . . They would strut around the table to the music, and whenever they got tired of watching everybody strut, they stop the music . . . when the music stopped they would call off a number . . . then it was time to look under the pie . . . and if your number was under that pie, you won. . . . And that was entertainment . . . they did things that brought the community together and they raised money to put back into the schools.

Later, the process for fundraising became streamlined in such a way that parents' attendance was no longer mandatory. Whereas PTA meetings were still well attended, teachers began to handle more duties, according to Mary Mills. By the 1960s, parent participation could be considered almost "invisible." At Natchez High School, George Northern revealed that although parent attendance was light, the school could count on parent participation through notes sent home, and through announcements. Although they knew parents supported the school, teachers wanted to have parents regularly attending PTA meetings.[54]

Despite the lower attendance rates, Carrie Amos Harrison, a teacher at FTS and NHS, vividly recalled the fundraisers implemented by teachers and parents. With teachers leading the charge, the fundraisers extended the work week for teachers into the weekends. Although this extended work week imposed upon their personal time, teachers recognized that the normal school hours were inconvenient for working parents, particularly those living in rural areas. Thus, if they wanted parents' participation in the PTA and other programs, the hours had to be adjusted to fit the parents' schedules. According to Harrison,

> Now fund-raising, . . . the parents were behind 100%. We had a Queen Drive, and parents really rallied behind this, trying to make it a big thing because the school could use [the money] . . . . So the Queen Drive, Queen of Natchez High School . . . was a big project, and the parents really rallied behind it. On Saturdays, we'd be selling spaghetti and fish. And, the teachers worked with the parents. The parents worked with the teachers. You were advisors of a class, and therefore you went on Saturdays and Sunday, afternoons and nights and all to prepare and work with raising this money. . . . Each class tried to out-raise the other . . . and the parents supported this. . . . If we decided that this was what needed to be done, the respect was there. This is for the benefit of our children so we will do this. . . . And, they came and supported all activities.

The money from fundraisers compensated for the lack of supplies and equipment from the school district. None of the schools had adequate supplies, equipment, or facilities to perform their job effectively. Mary Mills remembered the PTA taking on larger projects, such as buying curtains for the stage.

> When we had to raise money to build the stage, the parents were behind us or we couldn't [have done it]. . . . The school wouldn't have any money to do it, so the parents helped out. They bought some beautiful wine [-colored] curtains with an "F" up there.[55]

Collectively, teachers and parents raised substantial funds to support the short- and long-term needs of the school; however, the significance of this relationship was not simply the dollars raised, but the shared activity of helping the children in the community.

AFRICAN AMERICANS' RURAL BUS SERVICE

Like their counterparts in Caswell County, North Carolina, described by Vanessa Siddle Walker, students living outside of the Franklin city limits found it nearly impossible to get to FTS. These children attended elementary grades in or near their communities of DuPlex, Thompson Station, College Grove, Nolensville, or Grassland. FTS, however, was the only high school for African Americans in the county. Whereas the county provided bus service for white students coming to Franklin High School (which was located only a couple blocks from FTS), no such option was available to the black students.[56]

For example, in 1932 Louise Patton moved back from Detroit to the Arno community in Williamson County, where she intended to continue her high school education. The Arno community, located between Franklin and Murfreesboro, Tennessee, was much too far from FTS to travel each day to school. Patton remarked:

> I had to stay in Franklin when I was coming to high school because at that time we had no buses, and it would have been very inconvenient. In fact, it would have been impossible for [my father] to get up every morning and bring me in to school and having to farm. So I stayed with a cousin during the week, and I'd go home on weekends.

Most rural African Americans during this period were not as lucky as Louise Patton to have relatives to stay with while attending city schools.

> Back at that time when the children finished the 8th grade in the county, they had to either go to Nashville and live with relatives to go to a high school. Or, they could come to Franklin and live with a relative; but, if you had no relatives or anything, sometimes a high school education was not accessible to you.[57]

Elease Reames Parrish, who started FTS in 1944 as a freshmen, remembered that many students were forced to drop out due to the lack of bus transportation. Parrish said:

> We had a freshman class of 40. We started out with 40 I believe it was, which was a large class. And before the end of the year—I've forgotten just how many we lost, but we lost quite a few. . . . See we didn't have buses and they didn't have enough transportation to get in to school, and some just dropped out because they just couldn't get enough rides to get them in daily. . . . They'd get here in the morning and have problems getting back home in the afternoon. . . . Several of the girls found places to stay. Seemingly, more of the girls had places to stay than the boys.[58]

In an April 22, 1938, letter to Dr. Hampton, Rosenwald State Agent, W. E. Turner commented on the bus situation:

> There is no transportation provided at county expense for pupils of this school. Twelve or fifteen of the students now enrolled in your school came from a considerable distance in the county. I feel that these students could be accommodated and many more could be enrolled in the school if you had transportation facilities provided. However, this is an administrative matter for the County Board of Education to consider.[59]

Given that situation, African American community members, led by Tom Patton, founder of Patton Brothers Funeral Homes, banded together to purchase a bus. Louise Patton recalled:

> The issue came up about transportation for the black children . . . and then Tom Patton . . . said that he would give $100 to get a bus started so the black children could come in. I think Dr. [Charles C.] Johnson was another person. . . . I don't remember exactly all of the men [who] helped at that time. . . . But the bus was bought by black citizens.[60]

Mary Mills said the leaders of this group were "Mr. Darden, Mr. Hemingwood, Mr. John Sanford, Dr. Hudson, Thomas Patton—Louise Patton's father-in-law. They went together and bought the very first bus." With this money, the leaders of the group approached the superintendent and "wanted to know why the black kids didn't have a bus. They got a deal and [the superintendent] said if we'd buy one, they'd give us one," said George Northern, a student at FTS and science teacher at NHS.[61]

Not all African American families supported the movement to purchase a bus. Their lack of support did not indicate their opposition to giving rural black children an opportunity to attend high school; instead, they felt that providing bus transportation was the county's responsibility. George Northern was born in 1931 in Grassland, 7 miles north of Franklin. Northern recalled his parents' disagreement over the bus purchase:

> The biggest conflict I've ever known between my mother and father was about that [purchasing the school bus], so they finally ended up giving $25. . . . I remember some people gave almost $100. . . . My father thought it was not their place to buy a school bus, and he was just against it. He thought the school district should buy the bus. And my mother was saying, "You know they're not going to do it, so give the money." So, they eked out $25 between the two of them.

Because of the dearth of public records, it is not clear if the county paid the salaries of the bus driver, whether another community fund existed, or if these drivers volunteered their time. Furthermore, there are few records to demonstrate any increases in enrollment because of the purchase of these two buses. The important aspect of the community's decision to purchase buses was the proactive movement of African Americans to improve the educational opportunities available to their children.

AGENCY AND CULTURAL CAPITAL IN FRANKLIN'S AFRICAN AMERICAN SCHOOL DEVELOPMENT

To be sure, there is virtually nothing good to say about the legalized racism imposed upon Franklin's African American community under segregation. Southern Jim Crow laws limited travel and access to public accommodations. Tennessee state laws restricted black students' access to the resources available in white public schools. The Franklin Special School District and the Williamson County Board of Education instituted separate and unequal salary scales for black and white teachers. The black community was given dilapidated buildings, secondhand books, minimal school funds, and inadequate equipment.

The response of Franklin's African American community to this system was quite interesting, but not atypical of other southern communities. Sara Lawrence-Lightfoot explained it this way:

> The white community became "irrelevant." Segregation pushed African Americans to virtually ignore the whites who sometimes lived only a block or two away. For most of the informants, particularly the senior citizens, there was little unsolicited discussion about the whites or their impact on the African American community. Furthermore, many informants described punishments from their parents if they ventured too far away from their community. It was truly two communities, divided and unconcerned with each other.[62]

Whereas this separation may appear to be negative, it was not always. Another way of viewing this phenomenon is that Franklin's African American community became more introspective and independent. Segregation, as a legal institution, became a social force that created a closed community and economic system. As Booker T. Washington suggested, it forced African Americans to look within their own communities (as opposed to the white community) to find the economic and social resources. Segregation required African Americans to collectively create, within their own community, all the civic, political, social, spiritual, and economic institutions necessary for community life. As a result, Franklin's black community had grocery stores, restaurants, barber shops, churches, funeral homes, a hospital, and social organizations.[63] In the interview Rev. William Scruggs recalled Franklin's black businesses as vibrant:

> During those segregated times, we had black store[s], some kind of black business on every corner in the black community. . . . George Kinnard's grocery, Porky Morton's grocery. . . . We had Kate Patton's restaurant . . . Jack Scruggs' barber shop, [and] Henry Douglas' barber shop. . . .

There were doctors, masons, contractors, plumbers, entrepreneurs, and political spokespersons.

Although this system of legal segregation created numerous problems and conflicts for the community, African Americans in Franklin adjusted to this system, developing their own internal logic within it. Furthermore, during almost 100 years of this system (in one form or another), this separate community took on a life and functioning all its own. On one hand, the system was discriminatory and morally unjust. On the other hand, by the mid-1960s, it had fostered a sense of community and civic pride; it provided a sense of ownership. Scruggs, pondering the duality of legal segregation, stated:

> There is something about oppression and depression that makes kids strive. Some of our best educators, some of our richest blacks came out of schools back in those times; and, I still think there is something about pressure that helps black folks even now.

Furthermore, segregation provided role models and examples of strength outside of the family. In the interview Walter Rucker recalled that,

> [G]rowing up, I relied not only on my mother and father, but I had my grandparents that were there. I had aunts that were there. I had teachers [who] were there. I had store owners [who] were there. . . . So, at any time I needed some examples of success, I only had to turn and look down the street; and, there was somebody there.

DESEGREGATION AND THE LOSS OF CULTURAL CAPITAL

The closing of Natchez High School in 1967 represented more than simply the desegregation of Williamson County Schools. Although there had been three other transitional periods between the establishment of Claiborne's Institute and Natchez High, they represented expansions, name changes, and renovations. The school had never closed; it had simply evolved. The closing of Natchez High evoked a variety of emotions—anger, sadness, hopefulness, and pain. In short, it was not simply the end of an era, it was the loss of tradition, ownership, and the collapse of a school community.

That was more than 30 years ago. What does this story tell us about African American schools and the cultural capital found in the Franklin community? From my personal knowledge of Franklin and the data gathered from the informants, I would suggest that the school, surrounded by small, close-knit communities, facilitated agency and the generation of cultural capital by the residents. The agency and cultural capital produced by parents, teachers, principals, and community resulted in: (1) a long-standing belief in the power of education as a force of social change; (2) a self-contained community and social structure created under segregation; and (3) the centrality of the school in the community. Thus, the community's diverse levels of employment, education, motivation, and wealth provided youth with both role models and examples of the consequences of aberrant behavior. These enclaves, where teachers and parents shared churches, grocery stores, and social groups, promoted stronger bonds between the school and the community. Intergenerational traditions bound alumni to the schools and provided a strong rationale for supporting them. The aura surrounding the school captured the attention of its future students.

The tradition and aura of Natchez High School was created under the conditions of legal segregation in a small, rural, southern community. These components of school life were not only the result of legalized segregation, but also the isolation in the rural south. The most important element was the central place of the school in the community. This centrality resulted in community-wide participation in the schools' programs by adults and strong pride for the students. Community-wide participation resulted in a collective support for an underfunded school. School pride resulted in, at the very least, a greater student interest in remaining in school. It was a rallying point of work and community service for teachers, administrators, parents, and community leaders. Their resource development efforts, though diverse and continuous, were never sufficient to fully meet the school's ongoing needs, but they demonstrated the importance of a collective response to the maintenance and advancement of African American schooling.

In the long run, it may be impossible to recreate all of the positive components of FTS and NHS in contemporary black public schools. Although legal segregation drastically limited their development, these Franklin neighborhoods, specifically Natchez Street, were vital centers of economic development and education for the black community. Thirty years later, these same neighborhoods have been reduced to public housing units, and the residents suffer from high rates of poverty, unemployment, and school failure. With other housing options available, middle-class families left these neighborhoods. In addition, rural communities are not as isolated as they were, and individuals and families are much more mobile. Improvements in transportation, both public and private, have made it possible for parents and teachers to travel farther for work and shopping.[64]

The opening story mentioned an old black farmer who donated a hog to Tuskegee's building fund. Subsequently, he petitioned his fellow community members to contribute in a similar fashion. Whereas Tuskegee and other schools like it educated what W. E. B. Du Bois called the "talented tenth" in these southern communities, this concept assumed the use of cultural capital to advance the entire group, as advocated by Booker T. Washington and Du Bois. Washington popularized and Du Bois ultimately supported the idea that all African Americans, not just the talented tenth, were responsible in some capacity for the social, political, and economic progress of the community.[65]

The story of the African American community in Franklin, Tennessee, demonstrates this point. Over the 70-year period, African Americans rallied around their schools. Collectively, they raised the money, repaired the buildings, developed the curricula, and prepared their children for the future. Cultural capital was important for their children, for their schools, and for their community.

NOTES

1. Booker T. Washington, *Up From Slavery* (1899; reprinted New York, 1986), 140–141.

2. This research relies heavily upon the oral and life histories of 33 former students, teachers, and community activists, as well as the analyses of personal and private records of this community. Having worked in the community for 10 years, many of the informants were familiar faces and were easily accessible. Additional informants were recruited through a "community insiders" and through a "snowball" sampling technique. Informants ranged from age 46 to 103. They were interviewed between one and three times for an average of 2 hours per interview. Participants were interviewed individually as well as in groups. Interviews were tape recorded and transcribed. Informants were asked about their family histories; their family's values on education; the schools they attended; significant teachers, principals, and community members; their careers in education; and their community activism. Personal and public records buttressed their testimonies. Although there were few public records of the black schools, the local school board minutes generally supported individual testimonies. Personal records—diplomas, pictures, and yearbooks—also gave firsthand accounts of the life of the schools, its teachers, and students.

3. James Anderson, *The Education of Blacks in the South, 1860–1935* (Chapel Hill, NC, 1988), 153–156.

4. V. P. Franklin, "They Rose or Fell Together: African American Educators and Community Leadership, 1795–1954," *Journal of Education* 172 (1990): 39–64.

5. For an overview of these efforts, see Anderson, *Education of Blacks*; June O. Patton, "The Black Community of Augusta and the Struggle for Ware High School," in V. P. Franklin and James Anderson, eds., *New Perspectives on Black*

Educational History (Boston, 1978), 45–59; J. R. Coan, *Daniel Alexander Payne: Christian Educator* (Philadelphia, 1935); Edwin Embree, *Julius Rosenwald: A Review of June 28, 1928* (Chicago, 1928), 21–29; Cynthia Fleming, *The Development of Black Education in Tennessee: 1865–1920*, Ph.D. dissertation, Duke University, 1977; V. P. Franklin, *Black Self-Determination: A Cultural History of African American Resistance* (Brooklyn, NY, 1992), 147–167; Issac Lane, *Autobiography of Bishop Issac Lane with a Short History of the C.M.E. Church in America and of Methodism* (Nashville, TN, 1934); Vanessa Siddle Walker, "Caswell County Training School, 1933–1969: Relationships between Community and School," *Harvard Educational Review* 62 (No. 2, 1993): 161–182; Thomas Sowell, "Black Excellence: The Case of Dunbar High School," *Public Interest* 35 (Spring 1974): 3–21. Washington, *Up From Slavery*.

6.   Siddle-Walker, "Caswell County," 166.

7.   Anderson, *Education of Blacks*; Molefi Asante, *Afrocentricity* (Trenton, NJ, 1987). V. P. Franklin, "They Rose or Fell Together," 39–64; Franklin, *Black Self-Determination*, 147–167; Embree, *Julius Rosenwald*, 26.

8.   V. P. Franklin, "Cultural Capital and Black Higher Education: The A.M.E. Colleges and Universities as Collective Economic Enterprises, 1856–1910," in this volume.

9.   Fleming, *Development of Black Education*, 24–25.

10.   Anderson, *Education of Blacks*, 6–7.

11.   Louis Harlan, *Booker T. Washington: The Making of a Black Leader, 1856–1901* (New York, 1972), 113–115. A. Cooper, *Between Struggle and Hope: Four Black Educations in the South, 1894–1915* (Ames, IA, 1989), 56–57. H. C. Savage, *The Life and Times of Bishop Isaac Lane* (Nashville, TN, 1958), 78–123.

12.   State Superintendent of Public Instruction, *First Report of the Superintendent of Public Instruction of the State of Tennessee, ending Thursday, October 7th, 1869* (Nashville, TN, 1869), 91–92.

13.   G. W. Hubbard, *A History of the Colored Schools of Nashville, Tennessee* (Nashville, TN, 1874), 5; Washington, *Up From Slavery*, 111–113; Siddle-Walker, *Their Highest Potential*, 200. Similarly, W. E. B. Du Bois stated that black freedpeople did not have a "poverty of spirit." In fact, Du Bois noted that "the very feeling of inferiority which slavery forced upon them fathered an intense desire to rise out of their condition by the means of education." W. E. B. Du Bois, *Black Reconstruction in America, 1860–1880* (1935; reprinted in New York, 1992), 637–38.

14.   Embree, *Julius Rosenwald*, 29; see also Anderson, *Education of Blacks*, 158–159.

15.   Embree, *Julius Rosenwald*, 24; Samuel L. Smith, *Builders of Goodwill: The Story of State Agents of Negro Education in the South, 1910–1950* (Nashville, TN, 1950), 156; Thomas Beane Stitely, *Bridging the Gap: A History of the Rosenwald Fund in the Development of Rural Negro Schools in Tennessee, 1912–1932* (Ed.D. dissertation, George Peabody College for Teachers, 1975), 22; Anderson, *Education of Blacks*, 166. The information of the Rosenwald schools in Williamson County was found in the Rosenwald Papers at Fisk University. This particular document listed Rosenwald's activities in Tennessee as of 1930.

16.   Anderson, *Education of Blacks*, 174; Samuel L. Smith, "Report of Some Special Work Among Rural Negro Schools in Tennessee, 1915–16," in State Superintendent of Public Instruction, ed., *Biennial Report of the State Superin-*

tendent of Public Instruction for the Scholastic Years Ending June 30, 1915–1916
(Nashville, TN, 1916), 287–289; State Superintendent of Public Instruction,
*Biennial Report of the State Superintendent of Public Instruction for the Scholastic
Years Ending June 30, 1917–18* (Nashville, TN, 1918), 15. Jeanes Supervisors
were supervisors to a county's black schools, funded in part by the Anne
Jeanes Fund. These supervisors not only met monthly with teachers, but
also provided instruction in home economics and assisted in the organiza-
tion of Rosenwald Days.

17.   Anderson, *Education of Blacks*, 156; Stitely, *Bridging the Gap*, 34–36.

18.   Lyn Sullivan Pewitt, *Back Home in Williamson County* (Franklin, TN, 1996),
83–90; Richard Warwick, *Williamson County in Black and White* (Franklin, TN,
2000), 71–106; Anderson, *The Education of Blacks*, 118–129.

19.   State Superintendent of Public Instruction, *First Report Ending Thursday,
October 7th, 1869* (Nashville, TN, 1869), CXLIX–CL.

20.   Ibid.; "Ninth District Colored School," *The Review and Journal* (September 1,
1881); State Superintendent of Public Instruction, *Annual Report of John M.
Fleming, State Superintendent of Public Instruction for Tennessee for the Scholastic
Year Ending August 31, 1874* (Nashville, TN, 1875), 139.

21.   "Ninth District Colored School"; Fleming, *Development of Black Education*, 25.

22.   This information came from a handwritten, unpublished report entitled,
"Report of School Directors of District No. 9, Williamson County," dated
1875. In this report, the Ninth District reports one elementary school led by
two black teachers (one male and one female).

23.   The description of Claiborne's Institute is based on an interview of Ms.
Johnnie Winstead, the last living alumni of the school. Winstead, interviewed by Carol Jones, tape recording, 1993, Franklin, TN; The deed for the
actual school property can be found in the *Williamson County Deed Book*,
1888, 190–191; Records of the Williamson County Archive provide information on an African American teacher and landowner named Willis Claiborne. Willis Claiborne's property deed can be found in the *Williamson
County Deed Book*, 1885, 190–191. However, Claiborne's land is in Hard Bargain. The oral history accounts of Claiborne's Institute are discussed later in
this chapter. The number of students attending Claiborne's Institute is a
rough guess based on known attendance figures reported in 1875 and 1911.

24.   "Minutes of Franklin Special School District" (June 7, 1907), Franklin, TN
(hereafter "FSSD Minutes").

25.   Most local African Americans do not recall the transition from Claiborne's
Institute to Franklin Colored School. The Franklin School Board referred
to the school as the "colored school." The name, Franklin Colored School,
is the term used by the John Slater Fund in their listing of grant recipients.
Will Kelton, interview by author, tape recording, Franklin, TN, March 13,
1997; Janelle Lesley, interview by author, tape recording, Franklin, TN, May
21, 1997; Lucile Patton Blakemore, interview by author, tape recording,
Franklin, TN, May 20, 1997; Willie Mae Pullen, interview by author, tape
recording, Nashville, TN, August 14, 1997; see *Proceedings of the Trustees of the
John F. Slater Fund for the Education of the Freedmen, Proceedings and Reports* (Baltimore, 1919), 18; This data came from a May 12, 1911, school report entitled, "Teacher's Abstract Made to the County Superintendent," filed by
Franklin Colored School principal, Carrie Otey.

26. FSSD Minutes, May 31, 1922, Franklin, TN; The "stubbed-T"–style building was a typical construction layout of a 10-teacher Rosenwald school. Embree, *Julius Rosenwald,* 22–23.

27. Latham Mills, interview by author, tape recording, Franklin, TN, March 15, 1997; "Minutes of the Williamson County Board of Education," March 16, 1949, Franklin, TN; (hereafter "WCBOE Minutes"), FSSD Minutes, May 13, 1957, Franklin, TN.

28. The black community fondly remembers NHS. Alumni of all ages reveled about NHS and in their time spent at the school. It was quite startling to the author that the school was only in existence for 7 years. George Northern, interview by author, tape recording, Nashville, TN, June 9, 1997; Carrie Amos Harrison, interview by author, Nashville, TN, June 18, 1997.

29. With the addition of high school grades to Franklin Training School, the Williamson County Board of Education was given oversight of the high school grades while the Franklin Board of Education (Franklin Special School District) retained oversight of grades 1–8. As of the date of this article, this policy still constitutes the relationship of the two school districts; WCBOE Minutes, September 19, 1961, Franklin, TN.

30. WCBOE Minutes, April 1, 1964, Franklin, TN; WCBOE Minutes, March 18, 1964, Franklin, TN; WCBOE Minutes, October 4, 1963, Franklin, TN; WCBOE Minutes, December 13, 1966, Franklin, TN; WCBOE Minutes, January 10, 1967, Franklin, TN.

31. Mrs. L. A. Hampton was elected Assistant Principal in 1928.

32. FSSD Minutes, June 28, 1921, Franklin, TN; Alice Hughes Patton, interview by author, tape recording, Franklin, TN, April 16, 1997; Ms. Patton was not sure when J. K. Hughes was born. The estimated birth date is based upon Will Kelton's assertion that Hughes was approximately 50 years old in the 1920s. Alice Hughes Patton said that Bingham was near Hillsboro, approximately 15 miles outside of Franklin. "Respected Negro Died on Tuesday: 'Jim Hughes' Was Familiar to Both Races," *The Review Appeal,* October 15, 1936.

33. "Respected Negro Died."

34. FSSD Minutes, June 28, 1921, Franklin, TN; it appears from the FSSD Minutes that Hughes continued to be paid in part by the Williamson County Board of Education.

35. "Respected Negro Died."

36. Interviews with Will Kelton and Alice Hughes Patton.

37. *Statutes and Ordinances Establishing the Public Schools of the Town of Franklin in Williamson County, Tennessee* (August 1, 1913), 14–24; interviews with Janelle Lesley and Will Kelton.

38. *John F. Slater Proceedings and Reports,* 18. The Franklin Special School District also received $150 in 1921 and $100 in 1922 in support of FCS. *Proceedings of the Trustees of the John F. Slater Fund for the Education of the Freedmen, Proceedings and Reports* (Baltimore, 1921), 20; *Proceedings of the Trustees of the John F. Slater Fund for the Education of the Freedmen, Proceedings and Reports* (Baltimore, 1922), 19; FSSD Minutes, January 17, 1919, Franklin, TN; FSSD Minutes, June 28, 1921, Franklin, TN.

39. FSSD Minutes, August 1, 1927, Franklin, TN; "Local Negro School, One of the Best in the State," *The Review Appeal* June 30, 1925, 1; "New Teachers at Colored School," *The Review Appeal* September 25, 1926.

40. "Local Negro School."

41. FSSD Minutes, May 9, 1927, Franklin, TN.

42. FSSD Minutes, June 6, 1927; FSSD Minutes, June 20, 1927, Franklin, TN; FSSD Minutes, July 5, 1927, Franklin, TN; FSSD Minutes, August 1, 1927, Franklin, TN.

43. Harlan, *Black Leader;* W. E. B. Du Bois, *The Souls of Black Folk* (1903; reprinted New York, 1989), 79–95.

44. FSSD Minutes, September 11, 1922; FSSD Minutes, May 31, 1922

45. Walter Rucker, interview by author, tape recording, Franklin, TN, June 22, 1997.

46. On the back of the only remaining picture of Claiborne's Institute, the inscription reads, "burned down in 1907." FSSD Minutes, June 7, 1907, Franklin, TN; FSSD Minutes, July 24, 1907, Franklin, TN; Will Kelton, March 19, 1997; Janelle Lesley, May 21, 1997.

47. FSSD Minutes, April 23, 1914, Franklin, TN.

48. FSSD Minutes, May 31, 1922, Franklin, TN.

49. Rev. W. F. Scruggs, interviewed by author, tape recording, Franklin, TN, June 21, 1997.

50. FSSD Minutes, March 31, 1922, Franklin, TN; Minutes of the Board of Mayor and Alderman, April 4, 1922, Franklin, TN, 601.

51. In an undated set of charts within the FSSD Minutes, comparative teacher salaries are displayed. In 1936–37, the average white teachers were paid approximately $700 per year; black teachers made $395–$400; the white principal made $1,275; the black principals both made $677.50 annually. In 1945–46, the white teachers and principals of Franklin Elementary made approximately $1,300 and $2,400, respectively. The black teachers in the Training School made approximately $990 per year.

52. Mary Mills, interviewed by author, tape recording, Franklin, TN, March 15, 1997.

53. Thelma Battle, interviewed by author, tape recording, Franklin, TN, March 12, 1997; Louise Patton, interview by author, tape recording, Franklin, TN, March 31 & May 7, 1997.

54. Ibid., see also Siddle-Walker, "Caswell County Training School," 180–181.

55. Interviews with Carrie Amos Harrison and Mary Mills.

56. Siddle-Walker, *Their Highest Potential,* 200.

57. Interview with Louise Patton.

58. Elease Reames Parrish, interview by author, tape recording, Franklin, TN, June 7, 1997.

59. This letter was found in the Williamson County Archives in a file on the Franklin Training School.

60. Interview with Louise Patton.

61. Interviews with Mary Mills and George Northern. Elease Reames Parrish recalled a slightly different story. Mrs. Parrish remembered that the WCBOE gave the black community the first bus, and told that if they could support the price of another one, they would give it to the black community at half price. There are no records from the WCBOE from 1944 on to verify

either story. There are few WCBOE records before 1944; Interview with Elease Reames Parrish, June 7, 1997.

62.   Sara Lawrence-Lightfoot, *Balm in Gilead: Journey of a Healer* (New York, 1988), 109–120.

63.   Washington, *Up From Slavery.*

64.   Clarence Hardison, interview by author, tape recording, Franklin, TN, April 8, 1997.

65.   Stitely reported that Rosenwald schools became the social center and the pride of black communities. He contends that these schools help shape black self-identity and resulted in additional resource development. "Negroes began to feel that they had the abilities and responsibility to further themselves for the good of their community and their race." Whereas the schools were the source of community pride, these statements fail to emphasize the history of self-determinist movements, personal sacrifice, group identity, and collective action. These "new buildings" did not initiate these feelings; these buildings were the culmination of an idealism within the black community which emphasized that education was the key ingredient in social uplift. Moreover, these buildings initiated a period of resignation about segregation. If Jim Crow was going to exist, then blacks wanted their own schools, parks, clubs, businesses, and other institutions. Stitely, *Bridging the Gap*, 58–59; Carter Savage, "'Because We Did More with Less': The Agency of African American Teachers in Franklin, Tennessee, 1890–1967," *Peabody Journal of Education*, 76, 2 (2001): 170–203; Craig Allen Kaplowitz, "A Breath of Fresh Air: Segregation, Parks and Progressivism in Nashville, Tennessee, 1900–1920," *Tennessee Historical Quarterly* 62 (Fall 1998): 132–149; Du Bois, *Souls of Black Folk*, 79–95; Washington, *Up From Slavery.*

CHAPTER 5

COMMUNITY, COMMITMENT, AND AFRICAN AMERICAN EDUCATION

The Jackson School of Smith County, Texas, 1925–1954

Peggy B. Gill

This chapter presents a narrative about the Jackson School in Smith County, Texas, utilizing the voices of former teachers and students who experienced its origin and development between 1925 and 1954. It covers the significant events in the story of the school as remembered by African American community members who participated in the day-to-day life of the school. African Americans in Jackson Heights, Texas, faced overwhelming odds in the struggle to provide quality schooling for their community's children. Their stories of self-sacrifice and community effort provide encouragement for today's educators and add to the understanding of the history of African American education. The stories of these people, from a former tenant farmer to a retired administrator, help us understand how a community was able to develop the commitment and resources to provide excellent education in spite of outside political pressures, unequal distribution of funds, and inequitable treatment within the larger community.

Cultural Capital and Black Education, pages 81–96
Copyright © 2004 by Information Age Publishing
All rights of reproduction in any form reserved.

Although this chapter only addresses the period before desegregation, Jackson School continues to be supported by the Jackson Heights community. Local black residents continue to refer to "our school," although the Jackson School currently serves as a primary school for the entire district. Men and women from Jackson Heights drop by the school on a regular basis to have lunch in the cafeteria with the children and share memories of their school. While few written records exist to document the evolution of this school, the personal memories are rich and vivid and provide evidence of the individual and collective efforts to develop social and cultural capital for the community.

Former teachers and students of Jackson School describe a highly successful institution with strong community ties and extensive parent participation. As Peter Coleman reported in studies of school–community relations, "The most important task facing the school in the immediate future is collaboration with parents in building active communities of learners."[1] Michael Fullan indicates that schools and community ideally would function as a unitary whole.[2] That ideal notwithstanding, Coleman found that most schools today exist in constricted worlds where parents and the wider community are outsiders, seldom engaged in reciprocal relationships with the school.

Today's educational and community leaders seek ways to develop and maintain mutually beneficial relationships, but succeed infrequently.[3] Former teachers of Jackson School tell of the essential contribution of resources by the Jackson Heights community that encouraged the development and maintenance of these mutually beneficial relationships. This cultural capital contributed by the community allowed the teachers to fulfill their personal and professional commitments to the children, the school, and the community. It was the material and spiritual support from the African American community that sustained the teachers and allowed them to meet their individual and collective goals.

CULTURE, COMMUNITY, AND EDUCATION

In examining the Jackson School, two recent studies provide understanding of the system of education in place throughout the South during this time period and tell of the interactions of African American culture, community, and education. Vanessa Siddle Walker studied the history of an African American school community in a small town in North Carolina from 1933 to 1969, the period of legal school segregation.[4] While acknowledging the gross inequalities present in the segregated school systems of the South, she chose to study the "successes of the school within the framework of its challenges." Using historical ethnography and drawing on state and local documents and interviews with former students and teachers, Siddle Walker explored parent involvement with and advocacy for the Caswell County Training School, and the ethic of caring demonstrated by the teachers and principals of Caswell County Training School. She focused on the period from 1933 to 1969 in an effort to provide an understanding of the history of African American communities and their schools in order to address some of today's problems.

Carter Savage examined four segregated African American schools in Franklin, Tennessee, between 1890 and 1967. Intrigued by the apparent contradiction between the quality and characteristics of the segregated schools described by parents, students, and teachers and the commonly shared narrative of an inferior segregated system, he examined the African American schools in the segregated system. Successfully using oral history and school records, he found community leadership and the centrality of the school as two significant elements in the perceived high quality of the former segregated system. Savage concluded that small, closed communities allow a greater interest and participation from the community, but suggested it may not be possible to replicate this interest in contemporary school settings.[5]

The story of Jackson School adds to this body of scholarship about African American education in the South prior to desegregation. While Siddle Walker and Savage explored schools supported by small towns, Jackson School is an example of an African American school in rural East Texas that drew upon the cultural capital in the community to build an outstanding educational facility recognized throughout the state.[6] Examination of the history of Jackson School provides the opportunity to see how a group of people successfully created a sense of community around the school through a collective effort to support and maintain that school to expand social capital in the community.[7]

This narrative of collective community commitment was constructed using the voices of those constituents of Jackson School who experienced the struggles of establishing and maintaining a school for black children in a rural area in which African Americans had little political or economic power. The participants in the study were selected from those who identified themselves as present or past members of Jackson School's community. Each participant was selected because of his or her ability to provide a personal perspective on the formation of "community" in relation to Jackson School.[8] A purposeful sampling technique was employed with each participant being asked to identify additional participants. Information was gathered from former administrators, teachers, parents, and students, as well as from those persons currently associated with the school. In addition, historical documents, photographs, school board proceedings, and school and community records provided additional information.

THE HISTORICAL CONTEXT

Because the story of Jackson School is embedded in the larger narrative of African American education in the South, in Texas, and in Smith County, we must first look at the context in which this school began. Until the 1870s, there was no system of public education for African American or white children in Texas. In 1871 Texas organized a statewide public school system of 35 school districts (later reduced to 12). At the time, this was hailed as an amazing opportunity for all children to be educated. From the beginning, schools for African American children were seriously overcrowded and local churches either opened their buildings for use as classrooms or built new buildings with church funds.[9]

The possibilities of equal educational opportunity offered by a free public education for all were gradually worn away for most African American children in Texas over the next thirty years as a system of segregation was put in place and sanctioned by legal authority. With legal sanction for "separate but equal" policies established by the Supreme Court's *Plessy v. Ferguson* decision in 1896, the Texas public school system was reorganized in 1900.[10] Under the 1900 plan of reorganization, previously independent schools for African American students were placed under the control and supervision of all-white school boards. With this reorganization, the system of dual education that would exist in Texas for the next 70 years was established as part of the social fabric of the state.

In 1926, the State Department of Education, as reflected in its bulletin *Negro Education in Texas: Special Activities and Industrial Aid,* supported the establishment of "county training schools" and the erection of model schoolhouses through financial assistance provided by the Rosenwald Fund. County training schools were not accredited high schools but instead focused on the study of agriculture and home economics. As envisioned by state officials, the entire community would benefit from a county training school because the school provided schooling for both children and adults.[11]

SMITH COUNTY AND JACKSON SCHOOL

Formal schooling for African Americans was officially sanctioned in Smith County during the Reconstruction period under the Freedman's Bureau. In 1886, the first public school for African Americans in the county opened in Tyler, the county seat. By 1900, there were seventy-two schools for African Americans in Smith County, including both publicly and privately supported institutions. The state's reorganization of schools in 1900 resulted in all black-controlled districts being brought under the supervision of local all-white school boards, either within independent or common school districts.[12] Whereas before 1900, African Americans in Smith County had controlled their own schools, under this reorganization plan African Americans were relegated to the status of ex-officio board members. In 1921 there were 63 common school districts in Smith County for white children and 53 for African American children. All of these common school districts had an all-white Board of Trustees and were under the direction of the county superintendent, Robert Spurgeon Bolton. Jackson Common School District (CSD) #27 had only a handful of white students attending the Browning School and over 200 African American students attending the Piney Grove School and the Chapel Hill School. Browning School had a 9-month term while both Piney Grove and Chapel Hill operated for only 6-months. Realizing the need for a comprehensive high school for African American children in the county, Bolton approached the local board about establishing a high school for African American children. In 1922 all the white students in CSD #27 were transferred to Holts School in an adjoining district, creating an all–African American school district. The white members of the school board of CSD #27 resigned because "they could not serve under such condition."[13] With these resignations the door was open for the creation of an all-black school board to lead the building of Jackson School, the county training school for Smith County.

Jackson Heights, chosen as the location for the new school, was about halfway between the two existing black schools. Founded in 1925 with the help of the Rosenwald Fund, the new school cost $5,500, of which only $1,100 was contributed by Rosenwald. Residents of Jackson CSD #27 contributed the remaining $4,400.[14] This poor, rural community voted a $1.00 school tax to fund a $3,000 bond issue. One dollar was the maximum school tax allowed under state law. Jackson was the only school in the county, for blacks or whites, to levy the maximum school tax. In addition to the bond issue, the community held picnics, staged plays, and took up church offerings to raise additional money. The need to raise additional funds within the community stands in stark contrast to the reality for white school districts. State aid to schools for white children was generally sufficient to provide adequate facilities, teacher salaries, and necessary supplies and materials.[15]

The original school was a "four-teacher model" built on twenty acres of land using the Rosenwald-prescribed building plans. Later, a three-room shop, a library, and a teacher's house were added. To finance these additional buildings, the community again sought aid from the Rosenwald Fund and raised additional funds through picnics, talent shows, and various other community fundraising events. The school expanded to serve the eastern portion of Smith County where the population was almost exclusively African American.

This area of Smith County was at one time the home of large plantations. The land was rich and fertile with significant virgin timber available. Over the years most of the land was inherited by descendants of the plantation owners who no longer lived in Smith County. By the 1920s the land was generally farmed through a system of sharecropping. Only a few African Americans owned land in the area.[16]

By 1935 Jackson School had 63 students in grades 8–11, with a total school enrollment of 273 (grades 1–11). Three full-time secondary teachers provided all instruction to the high school, and five teachers were employed for grades 1–7. The secondary curriculum included classes in vocational education, home economics, and trade and industry.[17]

In the 1950s, Jackson School consolidated with the all-white Chapel Hill Independent School District (ISD). The school had expanded and consisted of separate buildings for the elementary and high schools, and later buildings were added for vocational training and a separate gymnasium. Although with consolidation, the direction and control of the school passed to Chapel Hill ISD, the Jackson Heights community continued to be closely tied to Jackson School because it served as the only school for African Americans within the consolidated district. In the 1970s the district was desegregated and has since gone through several reconfigurations as new schools have been built to meet the changing needs of the growing district. Jackson School served as a junior high school and an elementary school. Jackson School is currently one of two primary-level campuses in the district with classes from pre-kindergarten through second grade. In addition to the predominantly black Jackson Heights community, the school's attendance zone includes white and Hispanic neighborhoods. Jackson Primary School's student body is representative of the district and is approximately one-third white, one-third Hispanic, and one-third African American. Throughout the demographic changes and reconfigurations, the school has continued to have strong ties to the Jackson Heights black community.

The African American Community and the Jackson School

This brief historical overview of Jackson School does not tell the larger story of Jackson School as experienced by the members of the local black community. The story of the community's commitment to Jackson School is a powerful one. It is a narrative of personal testimonies about the importance of cultural capital in establishing and maintaining quality education for African Americans in this rural area. It is a conversation begun over 75 years ago that continues today. The voices in the conversation are those of people with varying degrees of education, different levels of wealth, and diverse connections to Jackson School and the Jackson Heights neighborhood. While many people contributed stories about Jackson School, this chapter focuses on the experiences and testimonies of Lila McAllister, Sarah Ryder, John and Mary Mosley, Lillian Kissam, and Espanola Davis.[18]

Lila McAllister is a retired teacher and school administrator. Born in 1907, she grew up in the area around Jackson Heights, and although she currently lives about thirty miles away, she still owns her family's farm and has numerous relatives in the community. She attended Cole Hill School, one of the schools that voted to consolidate with Jackson School. Her younger brothers and sisters attended Jackson School and her younger brother taught math at Jackson School for over thirty years.

Sarah Ryder was born and reared in the area of Jackson Heights. She and her husband farmed in the community until his death. As a 90-year-old great-grandmother, she continues to provide support and direction for her children, grandchildren, and great-grandchildren. Her story begins in 1925 as a student at Jackson School. She is currently a member of an area church and participates regularly in activities at the local community center.

John and Mary Mosley are in their late 70s and have lived in Jackson Heights all their lives. They attended Jackson School during their academic careers and they raised twelve children who also attended the school. Now retired from farming, they regularly attend church in the community and attend school activities for their grandchildren. Ten of their twelve children still live in the community. They currently live down the street from Jackson School.

Lillian Kissam and her husband, William Kissam, were education and community activists who worked as a team of vocational teachers, joining the Jackson School faculty in 1941. Educated at Prairie View A & M College, the Kissams were determined to promote community growth and to involve others with them to make things happen. Since William Kissam's death, Lillian Kissam lives alone across the street from the Jackson School. She continues to be involved in her community and frequently attends school events.

Espanola Davis has been a member of the Jackson School community for over fifty years. She and her husband, N. L. Davis, came to Jackson Heights during the 1940s as teachers. He taught agriculture and was trained at Prairie View A & M College. Espanola, trained at Jarvis College and Texas College, taught both elementary and high school. A gifted educator, she used her musical talents and playwriting ability to encourage and support the children of the district. For some years she taught at Douglas School, a nearby community school that later consolidated with Jackson. She also taught at Jackson School and after the desegregation of public schools in the Chapel Hill ISD. Her teaching career in the district spanned thirty-eight years. She continues to be active in the community.

Each of these interviewees provided a unique picture of the community and the school. In examining their stories told about Jackson School, the concepts of place, relationships, and meaning emerge as essential constructs in explaining the commitment of a community's cultural capital to the development of social capital and human capital. John Dewey suggested that meaning is intimately tied to one's experience and that meaning is judged by its benefit to a society.[19] The community of Jackson Heights, with apparently limited financial capital compared to more affluent and less oppressed communities, valued the education of the students in their community (place) enough to build on strong personal ties (relationships) with a shared goal of enhancing and redefining their social and economic reality.

JACKSON SCHOOL: CULTURAL CAPITAL IN A COMMUNITY OF PLACE

A common location has been a traditional focus in the study of community. The Jackson School is both a specific location that engenders a sense of community in terms of place and the symbolic representation of that community of place. Nell Noddings, in her study of community in contemporary schools, points out the importance of people acquiring a sense of belonging to a community. Sharing a common place establishes a common identity and fosters a sense of belonging.[20] Cultural capital is developed when the members of a particular ethnic or cultural group, in this case African Americans, utilize their material and spiritual resources to support economic activities that benefit the entire group, such as schools and other social and cultural institutions.[21] Sarah Ryder, a member of the first ninth-grade class (1926), told of the importance of Jackson School for the African American community. She explained that three men, Laney Mosley, Tommy Redwine, and Lot Allen, were leaders in securing the school for the area. Ryder declared that, "It was important to have the school in your district because your community has an identity. A school was more than just a place to learn. It meant you had teachers living in your community. Teachers were important people. They were your leaders."

The community's pride in the new school was symbolized by the formal ceremonies held at each of the elementary schools that would close and consolidate to form Jackson School. Ryder recalled that the first day that Jackson School opened, students gathered at their former schools and lined up by grades with the oldest children in the front. "We were really proud. Jackson was the first real high school we had. We walked in a line all the way. Students came walking in from all the little schools. We stood outside while the new principal talked, and then we came in and marched to our rooms."

This first day of school was a celebration of the community's commitment to establishing their school. Before Jackson School was built, children attended small schools in space provided by area churches. Mose Chapel, Lane Chapel, and Cole Hill were the names of the area schools. These schools generally had one teacher who provided instruction for grades 1–8. As Lila McAllister pointed out, if a student's family wanted their child to continue beyond the eighth grade, the family arranged for the child to stay with relatives in Tyler and paid tuition for their child to attend either Emmett Scott, the public high school in Tyler, or Texas College, a small parochial college with a secondary curriculum. Very few families in the area could afford this expense so most children did not attend school beyond the eighth grade. The benefit to the community of having a high school cannot be overemphasized. Although it was a sacrifice to send any child to school since most families relied on their children to work on farms, having the high school within the community increased the likelihood of a child's remaining in school to graduation.

While the small elementary schools that consolidated to form Jackson School were poorly funded, they were important to the individual families whose children attended them and to their commmunities. In an example of the initial community commitment to Jackson School, these communities voted to close their individual schools and consolidate with Jackson School when it opened in 1926. Losing the small schools was significant, as Sarah Ryder pointed out, because the school gave a community its identity. Lila McAllister recalled that the parents voted to close Cole Hill School because the new school brought additional benefits to the children.

> When Jackson School opened, the parents at Cole Hill voted to send their children there. They knew they needed to get more education. It meant a long walk for some of the kids, but it was important. The church and the school were the only things in Cole Hill, but they voted to give up the school. You might say they gave up part of who they were so their children could go to a better school.

This sense of place represented by Jackson School was demonstrated through the interdependence of people in the community and reinforced by the images and the language they employed. John and Mary Mosley, students at Jackson School during the 1940s and 1950s, referred to the students' shared responsibility in ensuring the day-to-day functioning of the school. This was their school and it was their responsibility to see that wood was provided for heat and water was provided for the younger children. John Mosley remembered,

We had a big wood stove. A group of the older boys had to cut the wood. They'd go out, get the brush and the kindling, and break the big limbs up. All the boys wanted to get the wood. It was a privilege. You had to have all your work done, and you couldn't be in any trouble. After school, you would get the wood so it would be ready the next day. You'd come early, while it was still dark outside and start the fire.

During the winter when a great deal of wood was needed to heat the school, men in the community would cut wood and bring it to the school. Although most people had little money to share with the school, many people volunteered their services. John Mosley recalled that during the early days of the school, basketball was the only team sport available to the students. Football was too expensive with the need for uniforms and equipment, but basketball only required the purchase of a ball. Men from the community cleared a dirt court beside the school and erected metal hoops at each end of the court. Games were arranged with other schools in the afternoon. A local farmer took off work and piled the basketball team in the back of his wooden-sided truck and drove them to the games. Without this support, the teachers could not have added this extracurricular dimension to the school program.

The benefits to the community of having a county training school extended beyond the educational opportunities given to the children. The Kissams and the Davises, married couples who taught at Jackson School from the 1940s until the 1970s, worked to improve the overall conditions in the community, knowing, as Lillian Kissam observed that, "Neatness was catching and improvement rubbed off." Improvement of their "place" was important. Mrs. Kissam explained her role in improving the entire community:

> The State Department sent us up here. We came as community activists. We came to build this community. The state paid our salary. We were both certified vocational teachers from Prairie View College. Most of the community didn't have anything when we moved here, but we showed the people how to go and ask for what they needed. Everybody in the community used to have a water well. My husband organized the community to develop and build a water system for Jackson Heights.

JACKSON SCHOOL: CULTURAL CAPITAL WITHIN A COMMUNITY OF RELATIONSHIPS

Cultural capital was developed through the personal relationships in the Jackson Heights neighborhood. In this community defined by its relationships, individual circumstances counted, relationships were cooperative, and students were encouraged, accepted, and loved. Images suggested by the words family, obligation, responsibility, pride, respect, and love were often found in the stories about Jackson School. The most common expression was that of love. Lillian Kissam and Espanola Davis used very similar words to define the foundation for relationships within the school. Each told how love was the very foundation of their classroom practice.

A community may be defined by the norms, expectations, and trust created in the relationships among people.[22] Lillian Kissam described a faculty that intuitively recognized the importance of building and maintaining strong, loving relationships. She identified love as a fundamental construct in Jackson School and its community. She remembered, "We taught the love and they taught the love to their children. The love just keeps on going."

The relationships recalled by Kissam and Davis are similar to Mary Rousseau's description of the altruistic love that is the essence of community.[23] Sociologist Amaiti Etzoni suggested that this love or ethic of care created the "web of social bonds" that carried both rights and responsibilities. Within these social bonds parents and teachers accepted this shared responsibility for the success of every child even when economic distress resulted in poor attendance for some children. Although Jackson School offered a nine-month term, many children were only able to attend seven months or less. Families from Jackson Heights left East Texas in August to go "out West" to pick cotton. Families went as far west as Arizona and many children did not enter school until November or December. John Mosley described how the teachers expressed their love and shared responsibility: "The teachers knew I'd be coming in late. They held a packet of work for me. I had to do it, and I had to do it right. They'd help me with it, but I had to catch up." Children were not blamed for their lack of attendance or lack of progress, but were included in the school as full and contributing members. No student was sent to a special program or excluded from classroom activities.

Even the provision of a basic requirement such as lunch was seen as a community responsibility. Sarah Ryder was raised by her grandparents after her mother died when she was eight. Her grandparents insisted she go to school, but did not have enough money to provide her with shoes to wear or basic school supplies. Not having shoes or school supplies was not an unusual occurrence among these students, but in Sarah Ryder's family there was not even enough food to give her a lunch to carry. The "web of social bonds" that was modeled by teachers and community members extended to the young people within the school. She recalled, "At lunchtime the other kids would share with me. We'd sit on that big log and they'd give me some of theirs. I always had something to eat." Within a few years after initial construction, Jackson School added a "lean-to" kitchen to cook hot lunches. Lillian Kissam recalled, "The government subsidies just weren't enough. The community had to give food." Families donated vegetables from their gardens to provide adequate lunches for the children.

Eventually more state funding was provided to help with the school lunch program, but each student was required to pay a small amount for lunch. For many students in the community, even a small amount was more than the family could afford on a daily basis. Teachers joined together to ensure that each child received something to eat each day. Lila McAllister remembered how the teachers saw to it that all children were fed. "They charged a little for the lunches. At that time, even 25 cents was hard to come by. I knew some of the teachers, and they'd always be sure children had something to eat. They'd give any child the four cents for milk. Nobody went hungry."

The community's commitment to the children of Jackson School to encourage the development of social and human capital is exemplified in Lillian Kissam's recollection of a student trip to North Carolina. Mrs. Kissam taught music and led a boys quartet. This quartet won local and state competitions and was eligible to participate in a national competition in North Carolina. Kissam and her husband had a Model T Ford to drive the boys to North Carolina, but needed help with the entry fees, the cost of gasoline, and other expenses associated with the trip. The community began fundraising activities, and raised the money needed to send the quartet to the competition. Kissam remembered, "We had to take those boys to that competition. There were white boys and black boys singing there. We had to let the boys know that everywhere was not [segregated] like here. Everybody pulled together so we could go."

JACKSON SCHOOL: CULTURAL CAPITAL WITHIN A COMMUNITY OF SHARED MEANING

These informants described the evolution of shared values, assumptions, beliefs, and knowledge. These shared meanings and experiences became common possessions and part of the community's cultural capital.[24] In many of these shared experiences the community contributed time and services as part of their commitment to the school. John Mosley told of the importance of these shared community activities in his discussion of "School Closing." "School Closing" was held the last week of every school year. Each evening a group of children would perform a play, recite verses, and celebrate the conclusion of a successful school year. The final night a graduation ceremony was held for the graduating seniors. A few weeks before the event, men in the community would build an outdoor stage and put up tall posts to hold lanterns. As Mosley remembered, "Everybody would have a part in the program. Everybody's family would come. That program is the thing I remember most." This school program was a shared activity that involved most of the community either in writing the plays, building the stage, sewing the dresses or providing the refreshments. Community members shared their talents to provide a successful experience for the schoolchildren.

Community leaders reinforced these shared values by bringing the people together for various activities. From the early days of the canning kitchens, through the style shows, school plays, and athletic events, community members shared in the ongoing development of collective and individual memories. William and Espanola Davis moved to the community in the 1940s. Their work exemplifies the benefits available to the community from the collective commitment to building a quality program. Since Jackson School was the only county training school, it ensured that talented and committed teachers were drawn to the area. These teachers provided the necessary knowledge to strengthen the local students' skills. Espanola Davis noted one important change that came with the new teachers:

> This was a strictly black community and they were poor country people. They didn't even have screens on their windows and doors. After we got there, the high school boys went around and made screens and put on the windows. They made screen doors for the people too. My husband taught them how to weld, and many of those boys ended up making their living as welders.

As a vocational education teacher, W. L. Davis was hired to work with both the students in the school and the adults in the community. Espanola Davis recalled that he set up programs for the boys in Jackson School and for the men in the community. Under the Davis's guidance men from the community built a log cabin on one side of the school campus to use as a canning kitchen. People would bring their vegetables and work together to can them. It was both a practical chore and a social event for the community. Davis also mentioned that her husband taught the young boys to salt and smoke hams and held night classes to instruct the adult farmers in the latest agricultural practices.

The parents, faculty, and students of Jackson School created a complex social tapestry that bound and supported their sense of community. It was this sense of community that helped them to cope with economic hardship, establish traditions and ceremonies, and face challenges. In most ways, this sustaining of community appeared to be a natural and integral part of the daily activities at Jackson School. The story of community commitment in relation to Jackson School is one in which the members functioned as a unitary whole, as described by Michael Fullan.[25] Regardless of the need identified, the members of the community stepped forward to meet that need. Community members contributed money, time, and resources such as food and materials to advance their children and themselves. Although white schools in the county received money for supplies, black schools did not. Pencils, paper, crayons, and chalk had to be purchased by the faculty. Espanola Davis recalled asking students to have their mothers make box lunches to sell to raise money for school supplies. Teachers frequently bought supplies for the children, but with salaries almost half that of white teachers, little extra money was available. Teachers relied on the support of the community to help provide the necessary supplies for the children.

Interconnectedness existed throughout the community with school, work, and church serving as aggregating and stabilizing entities. Beginning at a time of social and economic oppression, individual differences and needs were tolerated with the understanding that personal, family, or financial pressures might take precedence over needed schooling. Leaders of the school and community responded with an ethic of care. Children were viewed as the responsibility and reflection of the community so that each child's behavior and success was important. Education was not limited to academic subjects, but included social and cultural education. Musical and theatrical presentations provided opportunities for the entire community to gather in shared and valued activities. In addition, the educational programs at Jackson School were not limited to children six to eighteen years old, but included adult education classes that encouraged lifelong learning. Community members worked with the school faculty to realize the community's shared vision of the value of education.

CONCLUSION

The narrative of a community's commitment of cultural capital to Jackson School unfolded as former teachers and students reflected upon their experiences at the school and in the community. These recollections provide rich historical, personal, and cultural information. Community commitment was defined by the informants in terms of place, relationships, and shared meaning. Sharing a common location with strong ties among people and a common understanding of the importance of education to the community created a clear vision that reinforced community dedication to establishing and maintaining an outstanding school. While these recollections add to the body of scholarship on African American education, they also provide important information for contemporary educational leaders who face challenges in today's schools. Teachers and community members of Jackson School did not rely on achievement tests or college entrance exam scores to measure the success of the school. Success was determined in terms of individual student participation and achievement, parental participation in and support of the school, student employability, and benefits provided to the community. Like the church, the school was a social agency that served the entire community. Learning opportunities for adults and children benefited the larger community. The teachers encouraged the development of social capital and human capital for the community. Skills needed within the community were identified and courses designed to develop these skills. Today's educational leaders might consider the important relationship between a community and its school(s). While there are areas of high achievement that are essential to all schools, each community brings a unique identity and cultural background that must be considered and incorporated within the school to expand the definitions of success to meet the needs of a diverse society. Members of a community will work to provide cultural capital in the form of money, time, and services to ensure a school's success where community improvement is a shared value and the school is seen as central to that advancement.

NOTES

1. Peter Coleman, *Parent, Student, and Teacher Collaboration: The Power of Three* (Thousand Oaks, CA, 1998), 43.

2. Michael Fullan, *Change Forces: The Sequel* (New York, 1999).

3. Coleman, *Parent, Student and Teacher Collaboration*, 43–45.

4. Vanessa Siddle Walker, *Their Highest Potential: An African American School Community in the Segregated South* (Chapel Hill, NC, 1996).

5. Carter Julian Savage, *From Claiborne's Institute to Natchez High School: The History of African American Education in Williamson County, Tennessee, 1890–1967* (Ed.D. dissertation, Vanderbilt University, 1998).

6. Texas State Historical Association, *The Handbook of Texas* (Austin: *www.tsha.utexas.edu/handbook/online/index*, 1999).

7. For additional stories about African American education in the segregated South, see T. Sowell, "Black Excellence: The Case of Dunbar High School," *Public Interest 35* (1974): 1–21; James Anderson, *The Education of Blacks in the South, 1860–1935* (Chapel Hill, NC, 1988).

8. John Creswell, *Qualitative Inquiry and Research Design: Choosing among Five Traditions* (Thousand Oaks, CA, 1998).

9. Henry Bullock, *A History of Negro Education in the South: From 1619 to the Present* (Cambridge, MA, 1967).

10. *Plessy v. Ferguson, 163 US 1138* (1896).

11. For a discussion of the controversy surrounding the Rosenwald Fund, see E. Anderson and A. Moss, *Dangerous Donations: Northern Philanthropy and Southern Black Education, 1902–1930* (Columbia, MO, 2000).

12. James Smallwood, *Born in Dixie: Smith County from 1875 to Its Centennial Year* (Austin, TX, 1999), 12.

13. Robert Spurgeon Bolton, "Fifty-Four Years in Public Education in Smith County," *Chronicles of Smith County* 19 (1980): 1–18.

14. Texas State Historical Association, *The Handbook of Texas*.

15. Bolton, *Fifty-Four Years in Public Education*, 1–18.

16. Editorial, *Tyler (Texas) Journal*, April 25, 1930.

17. State Department of Education, *Negro Education in Texas: 1934–35* (Austin, TX, 1935).

18. Additional background information is given in my dissertation, "Since We Bought the Land: The Story of Community in Relation to School" (Ed.D. dissertation, Stephen F. Austin State University, 2000).

19. Lila McAllister, interview with the author, Jacksonville, TX, August 13, 15, 27, 2000; Sarah Ryder, interview with the author, Jackson Heights, TX, May 15, 2000; John and Mary Mosley, interview with the author, Jackson Heights, TX, September 13 & 15, 2000; Lillian Kissam, interview with the author, Jackson Heights, TX, August 3 & 21, 2000; Espanola Davis, interview with the author, Jackson Heights, TX, May 25, August 6 & 12, 2000.

20. John Dewey, *Reconstruction in Philosophy* (Boston, 1948).

21. Nell Noddings, *The Challenge to Care in Schools: An Alternative Approach to Education* (New York, 1992).

22. V. P. Franklin, "Social Capital, Cultural Capital, and the Challenge of African American Education in the 21st Century" in this volume.

23. Coleman, *Parent, Student, and Teacher Collaboration*.

24. Mary Rousseau, *Community: The Tie that Binds* (New York, 1991).

25. Amitai Etzoni, *The Spirit of Community: The Reinvention of American Society* (New York, 1993).

CHAPTER 6

"SISTER LABORERS"

African American Women, Cultural Capital, and Educational Philanthropy, 1865–1970

Bettye Collier-Thomas

In 1899 Mamie Donohoo, a black church woman, published an article entitled "Woman as a Philanthropist," in which she described the multidimensional philanthropic work of women. Donohoo stated that "To be a philanthropist one need not necessarily be a millionaire as we use the term, yet the heart must be an unceasing fountain sending forth streams of love, charity, and benevolence. It is her philanthropic heart that prompts her to acts of kindness and deeds of mercy." Utilizing historical and biblical figures, Donohoo described an inclusive context that encompassed women's service to the church and to society, a melange of benevolent acts and gifts, including monetary donations—all of which constituted an extensive base of overlooked community philanthropy. Emphasizing that women who engaged in reform work were philanthropists, Donohoo cited the work of Harriet Beecher Stowe, the author of *Uncle Tom's Cabin*, and Ida Wells Barnett, the noted antilynching crusader. Stowe was described as "a fearless heroine" and one of the greatest philanthropists of the time, a woman whose writing impacted the nation and helped to bring an end to

Cultural Capital and Black Education, pages 97–115
Copyright © 2004 by Information Age Publishing
All rights of reproduction in any form reserved.

the institution of slavery. And Ida Wells Barnett was depicted by Donohoo as the foremost figure in leading a campaign "against mob violence," which "kindled so great a flame in the rational world that the ruthless hands of prejudice and seething floods of superstition cannot quench it."[1]

Portraying women as "sister laborers," Donohoo contended that African American women engaged in Sunday School and church activities and temperance and rescue work, raised funds to build schools, orphanages, and homes for working girls and the aged, formed auxiliaries to male organizations to raise funds for hospitals and a variety of other causes. They filled the coffers of denominational missionary organizations as they embraced their "special mission" to evangelize Africa and redeem the virtue of women of color, both at home in North America and abroad in Africa, South America, and the Caribbean. For examples of church women who participated in this type of philanthropy, Donohoo cited women leaders in her denomination, the African Methodist Episcopal (AME) Zion Church. Katie Hood, the president of the Woman's Home and Foreign Missionary Society, was the first lay member of the church to contribute $50 to the work of that organization. Katie Walters "exhibited her philanthropic nature in assisting the spread of the gospel" by engaging in missionary work. In 1898 Walters raised the largest amount of money in the New Jersey AME Zion Annual Conference.

Hood and Walters built upon the foundation that was laid by the AME Zion's first women's organization, the Female Benevolent Society, commonly known as "The Mother Society," established a few years after the beginning of the 19th century for the purpose of serving the needs of the New York City members of the church. The society ministered to the sick, buried the dead, and assisted in the support of the orphaned children of deceased members. In 1821 the AME Zion United Daughters of the Conference, a national organization, was founded to assist the needs of unsalaried ministers, to raise funds for erecting churches and assisting in paying their expenses; and to support a variety of charitable causes aimed at the poor. Following the end of slavery, Eliza Ann Gardner and several other women in the New England Daughters of Conference raised funds to send and support several ministers in the South as missionaries. Subsequently, they organized branches of the Daughters of Conference throughout the South to aid in paying preachers' salaries and to fund a host of benevolent causes.[2]

Concluding her essay, Donohoo posed several questions:

Who are the agitators of the humane movement? Who is it that advocates the Reform movement for our unfortunate girls? Who makes religious attacks upon dives of sin and vice and with tear stained faces implore the inmates to abandon their mode of living and turn to Him who said "He that is without a fault let him cast the first stone." It is our women—The Relief Corps of Heaven—last at the cross—first at the tomb, and faithful to every charge.[3]

Mamie Donohoo provided an all-encompassing definition of how African American women defined philanthropy and their roles as philanthropists. Donohoo suggested that philanthropy, with its multiple meanings and dimensions, was a central element in the lives of black women, and that their philanthropic activities were in part defined by their social position as women of African descent. In 1899 African Americans were only thirty-four years removed from slavery. As part of an oppressed and despised group, struggling to earn a livelihood and establish schools and social welfare institutions, Donohoo and her "sister laborers" were fighting to reclaim their womanhood—their sense of dignity and self-respect. To do this, in 1896 African American women organized the National Association of Colored Women (NACW), their first national secular organization. The NACW established "Departments of Work," and defined strategies for addressing the innumerable problems of race, class, and gender they confronted.[4]

Why did African American women in secular and religious organizations raise funds and undertake national campaigns aimed at eradicating illiteracy, poverty, lynching, sharecropping, the chain gang, and addressing broad-based educational needs?[5] They organized philanthropic activities to benefit the African American community in general, and black women in particular.

AFRICAN AMERICAN WOMEN AND CULTURAL CAPITAL

Black women's philanthropic efforts can be described and understood by the use of the concept "cultural capital." V. P. Franklin, James Stewart, and other African American scholars use the term cultural capital to refer to the sense of group consciousness and collective identity that serves as an economic resource to support collective economic or philanthropic efforts. Economist James Stewart argues that in explaining economic activities among African Americans, we must begin with the assumption that "the production of collective identity has value to members of a group and is a normal activity undertaken jointly by individuals and groups." These groups of conscious or culturally aware individuals engage in economic activities not merely for self-interest, but to enhance their cultural identity and to advance the social development of the group. Thus the sense of group consciousness becomes a resource, cultural capital, that is used for social and economic development.[6]

Black women's social organizations, and other networks of cultural institutions, voluntary civic associations, and family and kinship groups in African American communities, raised the funds or donated other resources
or services, which served as the cultural capital necessary to build schools
and other community and charitable institutions, and to support a variety
of causes important to African Americans as a group.[7] Linda Gordon, in
her article, "Black and White Visions of Welfare: Women's Activism,
1890–1945," provides a clear example of how black women used their
human capital to create much-needed cultural capital, and how the fundraising activities of black women reformers may be distinguished from
those of white women:

> Black women welfare reformers created schools, old people's homes, medi-
> cal services, [and] community centers. Attempting to provide for their peo-
> ple what the white state would not, they even raised private money for public
> institutions. . . . Thus a large proportion of their political energy went to rais-
> ing money, and under the most difficult circumstances—trying to collect
> from the poor and limited middle class to help the poor. White women
> raised money, of course, but they also lobbied aldermen and congressmen,
> attended White House conferences, and corresponded with Supreme Court
> justices; black women had less access to such powerful men and spent pro-
> portionally more of their time organizing bake sales, rummage sales, and
> church dinners.[8]

The scholarship on black philanthropy is extremely limited. Many scholars have written about the nature and extent of self-help in the black community, but have not defined it as an aspect of black philanthropy.[9] Extant
scholarship consists of a handful of books, curriculum guides, and articles
that either focus on contemporary issues in black philanthropy, or in many
cases simply employ the existing African American history topical framework, that is, slavery, Reconstruction, the Progressive Era, the Depression,
the Civil Rights Movement, and afterward, to examine black philanthropy.[10]
     In order to counter the commonly held assumptions and explode the
myth of black apathy regarding community needs frequently articulated by
white as well as black Americans, the Joint Center for Political and Economic Studies undertook in 1986 the first comprehensive national study of
black philanthropy. In 1989, the statistical findings were published in *The
Charitable Appeals Fact Book: How Black and White Americans Respond to Different Types of Fund-Raising Efforts*, written by Emmett D. Carson, the director
of the Joint Center's project on black philanthropy. The study found that
African Americans from every socioeconomic background engaged in
charitable activities.[11]
     In 1993, the Joint Center published a companion study, or what Center
President Eddie N. Williams called an "extended essay." *A Hand Up: Black*

Philanthropy and Self-Help in America, also authored by Emmett D. Carson, was the first study to trace the history of African American giving patterns and to do so under the rubric of philanthropy. In the foreword to this book, Williams explained that one of the reasons for the low visibility of black philanthropy was that African Americans donate their money and volunteer services primarily to black organizations, frequently to their churches, the NAACP, the United Negro College Fund, and the Black United Fund.[12]

Most scholars of American philanthropy have preferred to emphasize white philanthropic efforts on behalf of African Americans and have tended to ignore African American contributions to black organizations.[13] Thus writers wax eloquently about the contributions of white philanthropists such as Andrew Carnegie, Julius Rosenwald, William H. Baldwin, Jr., Anna T. Jeanes, and others and practically ignore the support of African American religious organizations and individual donors whose contributions provided the bulk of the support for black colleges and universities, and was a significant factor in the sponsorship of public schools, as well as other community institutions and causes.[14]

The history of African American women and philanthropy has not been written. In the emerging scholarship that discusses the importance of black philanthropy in the development of black institutions, and providing charitable services to the community, women are not visible. Similar to the earlier histories of African Americans, most of the published works on black philanthropy discuss the importance of the church, benevolent and fraternal associations, and national race-specific organizations, such as the NAACP, but rarely point out that women's missionary associations and conventions were the chief source of church philanthropy, and that for fundraising and charitable giving purposes, women were frequently organized as auxiliaries to men's benevolent and fraternal associations.

Moreover, missing in these accounts are well-known black women philanthropists, such as Annie Malone and Madame C. J. Walker, as well as the extensive philanthropic work of the gender-specific national secular organizations, such as the National Association of Colored Women, the National Council of Negro Women, the sororities, namely Alpha Kappa Alpha, Delta Sigma Theta, Sigma Gamma Rho, and Zeta Phi Beta; and other female organizations such as the Links. And of course there are many more female organizations at the local and regional levels that have been significant in generating cultural capital in the black community.[15]

To address this historical oversight and to explore the ways in which African American women were involved in educational philanthropy, this chapter examines the philanthropic work of black women during the last 200 years, identifying (where possible) women who were philanthropists and discussing the philanthropic role assumed by black women's organizations as independent gender-specific associations and as auxiliaries to male-dominated organizations. Utilizing Donohoo's definition, what can be said about black women as philanthropists and the educational activities of African American women's organizations in the 19th and 20th centuries? Where do their philanthropic activities fit in the larger context of African American life and history? First and foremost, black women possessed a strong group consciousness, which was informed by race, gender, and class considerations. It is because of that triple consciousness that they bonded together and assumed the responsibility of using their human resources to support collective economic and philanthropic efforts, which produced the funds, or cultural capital, that became the financial backbone for social and economic development in the black community. The bonding process began in slavery, was deeply rooted in their religious beliefs, and found expression in their quest for freedom and justice. It was in the crucible of slavery that they developed a deep race consciousness and clear understanding of what it meant to be black. And, as enslaved African women, it was their vulnerability to rape and forced seduction that seared into their consciousness the meaning of gender, and additionally, the differences between them and white women.

Following emancipation, black women were determined to reclaim their pride, dignity, and self-esteem, and to construct psychological barriers against the larger society's efforts to define them as delinquent, dependent, immoral, and inferior beings undeserving of respect or personal consideration. It is that dual consciousness of race and gender that has continued to fuel the philanthropic efforts of generations of black women. Thus black women raised funds to support orphanages, homes for the aged, and most importantly facilities for young black women, not merely to allow them to survive, but to demonstrate that now that we are free, we can protect and take care of our own. Moreover, since African American orphans, the aged, and young women were frequently excluded from facilities available to whites, African American women took responsibility for campaigns to raise funds to provide social welfare services to African Americans in need. Poor as well as upper and middle class African Americans contributed funds to these enterprises because they believed they would improve the conditions for African Americans as a group.[16]

Though we do not know many of their names and it is only in the last two decades that scholars of black women's history have begun the arduous task of unearthing these women and their stories, we can say that they number in the thousands. In 1995 Osceola McCarty, an elderly washerwoman from Hattiesburg, Mississippi, donated her entire life savings of $150,000 to the University of Southern Mississippi to provide scholarships for poor students. This event was covered extensively by the national and international broadcast and print media, which was fascinated by the fact that a "poor" black woman had managed to accumulate such wealth and was willing to give it away. When asked why she made the contribution, McCarty said, "I'm giving it away so that the children won't have to work so hard."[17]

Few people knew that Osceola McCarty was part of a long tradition of giving in the black community, and especially among poor, working-class African American women, who frequently left their lifetime savings to support primarily religious institutions and schools. For example, in 1845, a black woman named Catharine Freebody who died in Hartford, Connecticut, bequeathed $1,000 to the African Society of Hartford for the support of the ministry, and $600 to five religious societies. In 1872 Mary A. Goodman, a washerwoman and domestic servant, bequeathed her life savings of $5,000 to the Yale University Theological Department's scholarship fund for "colored young men" studying for the ministry. In 1884 a black woman employed as a cook in Augusta, Georgia, willed her life savings of $600 to the Paine Institute, a Colored Methodist Episcopal Church school. In 1898 Mrs. Sarah Gordon, a poor woman in Philadelphia, willed $5,000 to Bethel AME Church, $2,000 to Allen Chapel AME Church, and the rest of her fortune to relatives and charitable institutions. In 1902, Julia Hanson, better known as "Aunt Julia," a former slave who managed to accumulate property of considerable value in the center of Washington, D.C., gave $10,000 to the Church of the Sacred Heart at Mount Pleasant. In 1910 Nannie A. Foulks, a domestic servant, gave her life savings of $1,000 toward the establishment of a reformatory for black youths in North Carolina. In 1911 Anna Maria Fisher, a former slave from Lexington, Kentucky, who lived in New York, died and left an estate estimated at $65,000. Fisher left $10,000 to both Tuskegee and Hampton Institutes, $5,000 to the Presbyterian Church, $1,000 to the Amanda Smith Orphan Home and the YMCA, and many donations to other individuals and causes. In 1916 Mary Strater, a former slave who worked as a domestic servant for seventy-seven years, willed $1,000 to Talladega Institute, $300 to Tougaloo College, $500 to Tuskegee, and $500 to Hampton Institute. In Little Rock, Arkansas, in 1915, Ellen Bransford, a woman who worked as a domestic servant for fifty years, willed $6,000 to the black Lutheran Church in that city. In 1919, an unnamed African American woman contributed $10,000 to the Freedmen's Work of the Presbyterian Church. A graduate of Scotia Seminary in North Carolina, she said that she sent the check so "that more girls might have the chance that I had," noting that it was two-thirds of all that she had accumulated by keeping a boardinghouse. Similar to working-class black women, educated black middle-class women also gave extensively. For example, in 1933 Lucy Moten, distinguished educator, willed $10,000 to Howard University to support educational travel for students furthering their research. In 1963 Dollie J. Alexander, a noted AME church worker in Atlanta, made a gift of $5,000 to Morris Brown College, her alma mater.[18]

BLACK WOMEN PHILANTHROPISTS:
ANNIE MALONE AND MADAME C.J. WALKER

At the beginning of the 20th century the average black man or woman was employed in agriculture or in domestic service. Black women worked primarily as domestic servants, laundresses, and cooks. There was a small and growing black professional class of preachers, teachers, lawyers, doctors, dentists, and entrepreneurs; however, few earned incomes beyond several thousand dollars a year. The phenomenal success of the first black millionaires, Robert Church of Memphis, Tennessee; Annie Turnbo Pope Malone of St. Louis, Missouri and Chicago, Illinois; and Madame C. J. Walker of Indianapolis, Indiana, and New York City, was widely reported in the black press. Robert Church, a real estate investor, was hailed as the nation's first black millionaire. Annie Malone, the first celebrated black pioneer in beauty culture, was the nation's first black millionairess and was the nation's first major black philanthropist. Madame C. J. Walker, a former washerwoman, was one of the first students to enroll in Annie Malone's beauty culture courses at Poro College, founded in 1900 as the first black institution in the United States to train black women, future Poro agents, in the Poro method of beauty culture, and to manufacture toiletries for persons of African descent. By 1904 Madame Walker was employed as an agent for Poro products. Following her departure from Poro in 1905, Walker became one of the most successful black businesswomen in American history, and by 1915 a millionaire. Competing for a piece of the black beauty culture market, which had been cornered by Malone, Walker matched the large donations of Malone to black educational and social welfare institutions, with contributions of her own to similar causes.[19]

Annie Malone is considered America's first major black philanthropist. Because of her extensive philanthropy, which had no specific focus, she was dubbed by certain members of the black press as a "freak giver." Malone supported nearly every known black charity, donating what were considered at the time huge amounts of money to various educational activities and programs. At one time she reportedly was supporting two full-time students in every black land-grant college in the United States. Numerous black orphanages received donations of $5,000 or more annually. During the 1920s Howard University's Medical School Endowment received over $10,000 from Malone. Between 1910 and 1918 Tuskegee Institute received numerous contributions, ranging between $1,000 and $2,000. In 1916, she and her husband Aaron were said to have established "a world record among colored people" by giving $5,000 to the St. Louis, Missouri Colored YWCA. In 1924 the Malones' gift of $25,000 to the building campaign was used by the St. Louis YWCA to secure large matching gifts from wealthy whites. At the opening of Poro College's new facility in

1918, it was reported that the Malones had made more cash donations to charity and Christian associations than any hundred "colored Americans" in the United States. Throughout her life, Malone was intensely concerned about the material and cultural uplift of her race. She not only made direct cash donations to diverse organizations and causes, but she also served as the chair for fundraising campaigns sponsored by black organizations such as the YMCA.[20]

Madame C. J. Walker, a woman who rose up from the most abject poverty, determined that she would never be poor again, singularly focused upon developing and promoting the Walker products. A part of her success lay in her astute understanding of the needs of black women, and the importance of pitching her message directly to them. Walker never missed an opportunity to reinforce to the masses of poor black women that she was one of them. A dark-skinned woman with broad features and coarse hair, she presented herself as the model of how an ordinary-looking, poor woman could achieve financial power. For the many black women who dreamed of being "beautiful," which at the time meant smooth, light skin and straightened hair, the Malone and Walker beauty products were a panacea for all their problems.

While Annie Malone's philanthropic activities were aimed at the social and economic development of African Americans as a group, or "the uplift of the race," Madame C. J. Walker's charitable efforts were targeted toward African American women, and in her speeches she referred to "women's duty to women." With the exception of a large donation to Booker Washington's Tuskegee Institute, she targeted her contributions primarily to black women's educational institutions, which included annual contributions to Mary McLeod Bethune's Daytona Normal and Industrial Institute (later Bethune Cookman College); Lucy Laney's Haines Institute; and Charlotte Hawkins Brown's Palmer Memorial Institute. She endorsed and supported the most powerful organization of black women, the National Association of Colored Women. In addition, she supported groups organized by W. E. B. DuBois, Ida Wells Barnett, A. Phillip Randolph, and Marcus Garvey. In 1919 she donated $1,000 to the Indianapolis Colored YMCA. She contributed money to the National Baptist Convention's foreign missionary program to aid in the establishment of a school and church in Pondoland, South Africa.

Although Walker's largest reported gift, prior to her death in 1919, was a donation of $5,000 to the NAACP's anti-lynching campaign, she gained much more notoriety for her cash donations and charitable acts than Malone. Walker understood that from a purely business standpoint, it was much more important to regularly give small sums to numerous organizations and causes, which she made sure were publicized in the black press and in *Woman's Voice*, a magazine that she underwrote. A shrewd marketer of herself and her beauty culture business, in her speeches she never missed an opportunity to inform the public of her philanthropic activities in educational areas. The combination of her giving and public relations strategies with her articulation of her relationship and fealty to the cause of black women and the race assured her the support of the African American community and the purchase of her products by black women.[21]

BLACK WOMEN'S ORGANIZATIONS
AND EDUCATIONAL PHILANTHROPY

Turning our attention to the collective endeavors of black women's organizations, we find that these activities began in the church. For over two centuries the African American church has been the most cohesive institution in the black community. Its ability to reach major segments of the black population and to raise large sums of money was a recognized asset. In the 19th and 20th centuries, women, constituting the majority of the black church population, were often the most dynamic force in the educational efforts within their churches.[22]

Female religious organizations, mutual-aid associations, and secret societies were the forerunners of the independent black women's club movement, which began in 1896 with the founding of the National Association of Colored Women. From 1800 to 1880 the social service work of black women in voluntary associations was largely concentrated in the church and in benevolent and secret societies. Assuming a key role in fundraising for most of the 19th century, black church women's philanthropic efforts were essential for the funding of church construction and restoration, raising the salaries of ministers, and providing for sick and indigent members. After 1880, the development of denominational missionary societies and women's conventions centralized church women's philanthropic activities and targeted it to national projects defined by the denomination. By 1918 most of the national black Methodist and Baptist denominations had developed powerful networks of women at the local, state, regional, and national levels. Dividing their work between domestic and foreign missions, these organizations raised thousands of dollars annually.[23]

Numerous local and state church-affiliated charitable organizations organized by African American women were connected with the major black religious denominations. In the African Methodist Episcopal, African Methodist Episcopal Zion, Colored Methodist Episcopal (CME), and Methodist Episcopal (ME) churches, the work of the various circles of the King's Daughters, the Epworth League, and the numerous women's home and foreign missionary societies was well known and widely respected. The ME Willing Workers were recognized for their work among the poor and elderly. By 1914, the members of the Mercy and Help Department of the

Epworth League were engaged in social service work among families and young children. In the 20th century Baptist women's domestic and foreign charitable activities were centralized in the women's conventions affiliated with The National Baptist Convention of America, Incorporated (NBC), The National Baptist Convention of America, Unincorporated (NBCA), and The Progressive National Baptist Convention (PNBC). In the Church of God in Christ (COGIC) and in other Pentecostal and Holiness churches, the women's conventions engaged in similar activities, establishing missionary schools and raising funds for charitable social welfare programs in the United States, Africa, and the Caribbean that reflected their cultural background identification.[24]

After 1880 black church women also became more active in the development of secular organizations. They began to focus their efforts on addressing needs beyond their individual denominations and members and to join with other women interested in the creation of cultural capital for the economic, political, and social development of their communities. Between 1880 and 1895 local black organizations focused on numerous goals, ranging from self-improvement, the establishment and support of a variety of homes for children including orphanages, nurseries, and detentions; and facilities for unwed mothers, working girls, and the aged. Settlement houses were set up to meet the needs of rural and urban African Americans; and an extensive network of associations evolved for the purpose of performing rescue and relief work among destitute African Americans. In the educational arena, women in secular and religious organizations raised funds for primary and secondary schools and colleges and universities. The founding of the NACW, an organization comprised of many local and state-based black women's clubs, provided a more unified character to this diverse philanthropic work. It also, for the first time in history, provided black women with a powerful political base. The NACW became a training ground for black women leaders, many of whom developed other national organizations.[25]

Between 1905 and 1920 at least twenty national organizations of African American women were founded. The continuing discrimination in the white women's club movement, the general exclusion from positions of leadership in male-controlled organizations, disaffection in the NACW ranks, as well as the need for professional organizations encouraged black women to develop organizations with more narrowly defined purposes. In the 20th century black women established a network of YWCAs and YMCAs; conducted campaigns for the financial support of protest movements aimed at social and political advancement and for providing social welfare services specifically for African American women; for summer camps, playgrounds, and recreational centers for black children and adults; and in urban areas they operated employment bureaus.[26]

In the 1920s, as more white church women expressed an interest in interracial cooperation, they joined black women to protest lynchings, to improve race relations, and to eliminate segregation and discrimination. During this period women's race relations committees formed under the aegis of the Federal Council of Churches to work on a variety of interracial and interdenominational projects, and black women worked with the state-based Commissions on Interracial Cooperation. After 1950 this work was continued under the National Council of Churches. In the 1920s and 1930s African American church women were a potent force in raising funds to aid the growing number of poor African Americans caught in the throes of the Great Depression. From the early 1940s through the 1950s, 1960s, and 1970s, black church women lent their leadership and support to the emerging Civil Rights Movement.[27]

In recent years as scholars have begun to research and write biographies of black men and women leaders, and recover the history of national organizations such as the NACW and the women's religious associations in the major black denominations, as well as other well-known mixed-gender organizations, evidence of extensive black philanthropic activities has begun to emerge. However, frequently it is not labeled or discussed as philanthropy, but referenced as self-help and uplift efforts. Large donations to institutions and causes, representing thousands of dollars, are often celebrated; however, individual donors who give anywhere from $1.00 to a couple of hundred dollars are overlooked. Little effort has been made to document the collective donations of women's religious organizations connected to the historically black denominations.

There are numerous examples of African American women's organizations generating substantial cultural capital to support black charitable, social welfare, and educational institutions. Let us look at three different types of black women's organizations: the Order of Eastern Star, a fraternal organization; the Woman's Convention Auxiliary to the National Baptist Convention, a religious organization; and the Questers, a contemporary local organization. The Eastern Star was first organized as an auxiliary to the Prince Hall Masons in 1874. Initially chapters were established in Washington, D.C.; Alexandria, Virginia; Baltimore; and Philadelphia. By 1915 the Eastern Star had chapters in cities throughout the United States, Ontario, Canada, and Liberia, Africa; and by 1925 they had organized a Grand chapter and became an independent body comprised of 3,434 chapters and 120,101 members with a national treasury of a half million dollars. Each chapter paid one cent per member in dues to the national office. Figures for the local chapter treasuries remain uncollected.[28]

The purpose of the Order of Eastern Star (OES) was to cooperate with and support the goals of Masonry by "assisting in and in some respects directing the charities and other work in the cause of human progress."

The OES operated burial funds and endowment departments, printing establishments, and juvenile departments in which they provided valuable leadership training to members' children. By 1925 the Eastern Star had accumulated a substantial amount of property, consisting of temples, which served as headquarters for local OES chapters, and a network of widows and orphans homes.[29]

The Woman's Convention (WC) Auxiliary to the National Baptist Convention (NBC), was formed in 1900. Although "Auxiliary" is included in its name, it functioned as an autonomous organization, which set its own agenda and managed its own budget. At its founding the organization listed twenty-six state vice presidents. In 1900 the NBC, with a membership of over three million, represented the largest African American religious organization. As the majority of church members, black Baptist women through the WC and its vast local, state, and regional network had the ability to access thousands of members and exert major influence upon millions of nonmembers. Baptist women represented the mainstay of financial support for the denomination's churches throughout the nation. Their networking power was demonstrated in terms of the number of WC women who held high offices in other black organizations. Throughout most of the 20th century they dominated the leadership of the National Association of Colored Women. Between 1909 and 1925, the WC raised the funds needed to establish and operate the National Training School for Girls in Washington, D.C. Through their domestic missionary work they contributed to the establishment of schools, settlement houses, leadership training institutes, and public health programs.[30]

The WC's extensive educational and charitable efforts in Africa demonstrated the strong cultural connections that underpinned their fundraising activities. In Africa they built nursing schools and hospitals and sent food, clothing, household needs, appliances, and medical and surgical supplies to Baptist missions. Missionary boxes sent by local and state women's conventions were usually valued at anywhere from $300 to $800. Between 1900 and 1920 the WC underwrote the educational expenses of a number of African students in the United States. The WC also sponsored individual missionaries, paying their annual salaries. In 1932 WC President S. Willie Layten requested that 5,000 of the 18,000 missionary circles in churches allied with the NBC donate 25 cents per month for foreign missions. This would provide $1,250 per month for Africa. In 1953, at a cost of $83,500, the WC purchased a building to be used as a Missionary Retreat Home for retired missionaries.[31]

Each year the WC state conventions raised large sums of money, which were sent to the national office. For example, for the fiscal year July 1, 1928, to June 30, 1929, the WC raised $80,396.74 for foreign missionary work.[32] In 1942 when the NBC Foreign Mission Board launched a drive for

$100,000, the Woman's Convention agreed to cooperate and share in this effort by enlisting 5,000 new monthly contributors whom they called "Minute Women." At the 1944 annual meeting of WC held in Dallas, Texas, the WC reported that it had raised over $35,000. Similar to the Order of Eastern Star, district and state conventions also raised money for their local educational institutions. For example, in 1927 the Woman's Baptist District Convention of the Mt. Olivet district, meeting in Cranford, Mississippi, reported that $900 was donated to the West Point Ministerial Institute and College.[33]

The Questers, an organization founded in Washington, D.C., in 1962, was a small membership organization that relied on donations, fundraising, and volunteerism to finance and carry out programs that reflected their collective cultural identity. Each year the organization sponsored a luncheon fashion show, which raised a substantial amount of money. Between 1964 and 1984 the Questers dispersed over $81,000 for a variety of educational and health-related projects, including the Howard University Center for Sickle Cell Disease, the Department of Pediatrics at Howard University Hospital, Pilgrim Baptist Mission Hospital in Africa, the NAACP, and the National Council of Negro Women. In addition they gave scholarships totaling $25,000. In 1985, Mabs Kemp, a columnist for the Washington *Afro-American*, declared that, "Such a track record is phenomenal considering the fact that the Questers are only 26 members strong. But because their efforts in the community stand out like a beaming star, supporters back them to the hilt."[34]

This survey of black women's philanthropic activities in the areas of education, health, and social welfare covering over 100 years documents their significant role in the generation of cultural capital in the African American community. Again, the reason African American women engaged in these activities was to benefit African Americans as a group and African American women in particular. Charitable philanthropic efforts, along with self-help organizations and activities, have been the foundation for the provision of schooling and social welfare services within African and African American communities.

A full examination of black women's philanthropic organizations, as well as those of African American religious institutions, mutual benefit societies, fraternal organizations, economic cooperatives, and community development corporations, will provide a better understanding of the role of cultural capital in the social, economic, and educational development of African Americans and provide a much-needed comprehensive history of African American philanthropy in the United States and abroad.

NOTES

1. Mamie Donohoo, "Woman as a Philanthropist," *AME Zion Quarterly Review*, October 1899–January 1900, 45–48; for a discussion and comparison of the reform activities of black and white women, see Linda Gordon, "Black and White Visions of Welfare: Women's Welfare Activism, 1890–1945," *Journal of American History* 78 (September 1991): 559–590. The author wishes to thank the Lilly Endowment, Inc. and the Ford Foundation for their generous support for the research for this chapter.

2. Donohoo, "Woman as Philanthropist," 45–48; Bishop William Jacob Walls, *The African Methodist Episcopal Zion Church: Reality of the Black Church* (Charlotte, NC, 1974), 134–137.

3. Donohoo, "Woman as Philanthropist," 48.

4. Stephanie J. Shaw, "'Black Club Women' and the Creation of the National Association of Colored Women," in *"We Specialize in the Wholly Impossible": A Reader in Black Women's History*, eds. Darlene Clark Hine, Wilma King, and Linda Reed (Brooklyn, NY: Carlson Publishing, 1995); for histories of the National Association of Colored Women, see Elizabeth Lindsay Davis, *Lifting As They Climb* (Chicago: National Association of Colored Women, 1933); Charles Harris Wesley, *The History of the National Association of Colored Women's Clubs: A Legacy of Service* (Washington, DC, 1984); for examples of the types of philanthropic activities supported by NACW women, see Kathleen C. Berkeley, "Colored Ladies Also Contributed: Black Women's Activities from Benevolence to Social Welfare, 1866–1896," in *Black Women in United States History*, ed. Darlene Clark Hine, Elsa Barkley Brown, Tiffany Patterson, and Lillian S. Williams (Brooklyn, NY, 1990), 61–83; and Cynthia Neverdon-Morton, "Advancement of the Race through African American Women's Organizations in the South, 1895–1925," in *African American Women and the Vote, 1837–1965*, ed. Ann D. Gordon with Bettye Collier-Thomas, et al. (Amherst, MA, 1997), 120–133.

5. For an example of how African American women organized at the local and state level, particularly in the NACW state federations, see V. P. Franklin and Bettye Collier-Thomas, "For the Good of the Race in General and Black Women in Particular: The Civil Rights Activities of Black Women's Organizations, 1915–1954," in *Sisters in the Struggle: African American Women in the Civil Rights-Black Power Movement*, ed. Bettye Collier-Thomas and V. P. Franklin (New York, 2001), 21–41.

6. V. P. Franklin, "Cultural Capital and Black Higher Education: The AME Colleges and Universities as Collective Economic Enterprises, 1856–1910," in this volume, and "Social Capital, Cultural Capital and Empowerment Zones: A Strategy for Economic and Community Development," in *The State of Black Philadelphia—Economic Power: Leveling the Playing Field* (Philadelphia, 1998), 19–23; James B. Stewart, "Toward Broader Involvement of Black Economists in Discussions of Race and Public Policy: A Plea for a Reconceptualization of Race and Power in Economic Theory," *Review of Black Political Economy* 23 (Winter 1995): 13–35; see also James Earl Davis, "Cultural Capital and the Role of Historically Black Colleges and Universities in Educational Reproduction," in *African American Culture and Heritage in Higher Education Research and Practice*, ed. Kassie Freeman (Westport, CT, 1998), 142–152.

7. For information on the various types of "capital" needed for economic enterprises, see Pierre Bourdieu, "The Forms of Capital," in John G. Richardson, ed., *Handbook of Theory and Research in the Sociology of Education* (New York, NY, 1986), 241. See also James S. Coleman, "Social Capital in the Creation of Human Capital,"*American Journal of Sociology* 94 (Supplement): S95–S120; Robert D. Putnam, "Bowling Alone: America's Declining Social Capital," *Current* 373 (June 1995): 3–9, and "The Prosperous Community: Social Capital and Economic Growth, "*Current* 356 (October 1993): 4–9; Francis Fukuyama, *Trust: The Social Virtues and the Creation of Prosperity* (New York, 1995), and "Social Capital and the Global Economy," *Foreign Affairs* 74 (September–October, 1995): 89–103.

8. Gordon, "Black and White Visions of Welfare," 560–561; On the question of black women "raising private money for public institutions," Gordon cites the Atlanta University study of 1901 conducted by W. E. B. DuBois, which found that in Virginia, North Carolina, and Georgia the private contribution to the black public schools was greater than that from tax moneys. Also, the tax money spent on African American schools was proportionately and quantitatively far less than that spent on white schools. See W. E. B. DuBois, ed., *Efforts for Social Betterment among Negro Americans* (Atlanta, GA, 1909), 29.

9. Many general African American history books as well as institutional studies of the black community include examples of black philanthropic activities. See John Hope Franklin, *From Slavery to Freedom: A History of Negro Americans* (5th ed., New York, NY, 1980); Benjamin Quarles, *Black Abolitionist* (New York, NY, 1969); James D. Anderson, *The Education of Blacks in the South, 1860–1935* (Chapel Hill, NC, 1988); Robert A. Hill, ed., *Marcus Garvey and the Universal Negro Improvement Association Papers* (Berkeley, CA,1983); Aldon D. Morris, *The Origins of the Civil Rights Movement* (New York, 1984); V. P. Franklin, *Black Self-Determination: A History of African American Resistance* (Brooklyn, NY, 1992).

10. For a brief historical overview of black philanthropy, see Emmett D. Carson, *A Hand Up: Black Philanthropy and Self-Help in America* (Washington, DC, 1993); for discussions of contemporary black philanthropy, see Emmett D. Carson, *The Charitable Appeals Fact Book: How Black and White Americans Respond to Different Types of Fund-Raising Efforts* (Washington, DC, 1986); Alicia D. Byrd, ed., *Philanthropy and the Black Church* (Washington, DC, 1990); James A. Joseph, "Black Philanthropy: The Potential and Limits of Private Generosity in a Civil Society." First Annual Lecture delivered to the Association of Black Foundation Executives, June 3,1991, Washington, DC. Emmett D. Carson, "Black Volunteers as Givers and Fundraisers," Working Paper (New York: Center for the Study of Philanthropy, Graduate School, CUNY, 1991). For curriculum guides that utilize the African American history topical framework, see Colin Palmer, *Topics in Black American Philanthropy Since 1785 Curriculum Guide # 3* (New York, NY: Center for the Study of Philanthropy, Graduate School and University Center, CUNY, Spring 1998); Colin Palmer, *A Graduate Curriculum Guide to Topics in Black American Philanthropy Since 1785* (New York, 1999).

11. "Helping Our Own," by Emmett D. Carson, *Essence* (May 1988), 160.

12. Carson, *A Hand Up*, "Foreword," n.p.

13. Henry Snyder Enck, "The Burden Borne: Northern White Philanthropy and Southern Black Industrial Education, 1900–1915," Ph.D. dissertation,

University of Cincinnati, 1970; Edwin R. Embree and Julia Waxman, *Investments in People: The Story of the Julius Rosenwald Fund* (New York, NY, 1949); Raymond B. Fosdick, Henry F. Pringle, and Katherine Douglas Pringle, *Adventure in Giving: The Story of the General Education Board, a Foundation Established by John D. Rockefeller* (New York, NY, 1962); Louis R. Harlan, *Booker T. Washington: The Making of a Black Leader, 1856–1901* (New York, NY, 1972); Louis R. Harlan, *Booker T. Washington: The Wizard of Tuskegee, 1901–1915* (New York, NY, 1983); Ellen Condliffe Lagemann, *The Politics of Knowledge: The Carnegie Corporation, Philanthropy, and Public Policy* (Middletown, CT, 1989); Ullin Whitney Leavell, *Philanthropy in Negro Education* (Westport, CT, 1970); Judith Sealander, *Private Wealth, Public Life: Foundation Philanthropy and the Reshaping of American Social Policy from the Progressive Era to the New Deal* (Baltimore, 1997); Jeffrey Sosland, *A School in Every County: The Partnership of Jewish Philanthropist Julius Rosenwald and American Black Communities* (Washington, DC, 1995); John H. Stanfield, *Philanthropy and Jim Crow in American Social Science* (Westport, CT, 1985); Louise Ware, *George Foster Peabody, Banker, Philanthropist, Publicist* (Athens, GA, 1951); M. R. Werner, *Julius Rosenwald: The Life of a Practical Humanitarian* (New York, 1939); Steven C. Wheatley, *The Politics of Philanthropy: Abraham Flexner and Medical Education* (Madison, WI, 1988); Philip Whitwell, *An Unofficial Statesman: Robert C. Ogden* (New York, 1924).

14. For figures and discussion regarding black contributions to public and private secondary and higher education for African Americans, see Monroe Work, *The Negro Yearbook: An Annual Encyclopedia of the Negro* (Tuskegee, AL) See editions for the years 1912, 1913, 1914–1915, 1916–1917, 1918–1919, and 1921–1922.

15. For studies on African American women's voluntary associations and philanthropic activities, see Linda Perkins, "Black Women and Racial `Uplift' Prior to Emancipation," in Hine et al., *Black Women in United States History,* 1077–1094; Shirley Yee, *Black Women Abolitionists: A Study in Activism, 1828–1860* (Knoxville, TN, 1992); Elizabeth Lindsay Davis, *Lifting As They Climb* (Washington, DC, 1933); Bettye Collier-Thomas, *Daughters of Thunder: Black Women Preachers and Their Sermons, 1850–1979* (San Francisco, CA, 1998); Bettye Collier-Thomas, "The Role of Black Women in the Development and Maintenance of Black Organizations," in *Black Organizations: Issues on Survival Techniques,* ed. Lennox S. Yearwood (College Park, MD, 1980), 135–144; Bettye Collier-Thomas, *Black Women Organized for Social Change, 1899–1920* (Washington, DC, 1984); Stephanie Shaw, "Black Club Women and the Creation of the National Association of Colored Women"; Evelyn Brooks Higginbotham, *Righteous Discontent: The Women's Movement in the Black Baptist Church, 1880–1920* (Cambridge, MA, 1993); Paula Giddings, *When and Where I Enter: The Impact of Black Women on Race and Sex in America* (New York, 1984); Cynthia Neverdon-Morton, *Afro-American Women of the South and the Advancement of the Race, 1895–1925* (Knoxville, TN, 1989); Dorothy Salem, *To Better Our World: Black Women in Organized Reform, 1890–1920* (Brooklyn, NY, 1990); Gordon, "Black and White Visions of Welfare, 559–590. For a study of the philanthropic work of Jane Edna Hunter and Nannie Helen Burroughs, specifically the development of the Phyllis Wheatley Association in Cleveland, Ohio, and the DC based National Training School for Girls, see Darlene Clark Hine, "`We Specialize in the Wholly Impossible': The Philanthropic Work of Black Women," in *Hine Sight: Black*

Women and the Re-construction of American History (Bloomington, IN, 1994), 109–128.

16. Bettye Collier-Thomas, "The `Relief Corps of Heaven': Black Women As Philanthropists," in *Philanthropy in Communities of Color: Traditions and Challenges*, ed. Pier C. Rogers (Indianapolis, IN, 2001), 29–39.

17. "Osceola McCarty, a Washerwoman Who Gave All She Had to Help Others, Dies at 91," *The New York Times*, September 28, 1999.

18. *The Liberator*, May 9, 1845; "Bequest to the Yale Divinity School," *New Haven Daily Palladium*, February 1, 1872; "General News in Brief," Philadelphia *The State Journal*, January 19, 1884; "A Good Example," *The Christian Recorder*, June 23, 1898; "Race Gleanings," Indianapolis *The Freeman*, October 18, 1902; "Gives Savings of a Lifetime," *New York Age*, August 11, 1910; "Anna Maria Fisher Makes Many Bequests," *New York Age*, November 21, 1911; "Notes on Racial Progress," *National Baptist Union Review*, February 13, 1915; "A Gift of Love," *Southern Workman*, July 1916, p. 416; "A Widow's Mite," *Baltimore Afro-American*, July 18, 1919; *Pittsburgh Courier*, December 16, 1933; "Mrs. Dollie J. Alexander, Atlanta Church Worker, Provides Example of Stewardship, "*Christian Recorder*, July 23, 1963.

19. Lester C. Lamon, "Church, Robert Reed, Sr. (1839–1912)," in *Dictionary of American Negro Biography*, ed. Rayford W. Logan and Michael R. Winston (New York, NY, 1982), 109–110; Bettye Collier-Thomas, "Annie Turnbo Malone, (1869–1957)," in *Notable Black American Women*, ed. Jessie Carney Smith (Detroit, MI, 1993), 724–727; Joan Curl Elliott, "Madame C. J. Walker (1867–1919)," in *Notable Black American Women*, ed. Jessie Carney Smith (Detroit, MI, 1993), 1184–1188.

20. Collier-Thomas, "Annie Turnbo Malone," 726.

21. A'Lelia Bundles, "Sharing the Wealth: Madame Walker's Philanthropy," in *Radcliffe Quarterly* (December 1991): 8–10; "America's Foremost Colored Woman," *Indianapolis Freeman*, December 28, 1912; "Madame C. J. Walker Manufacturing Co., and a Short History of Its Founder," *Christian Recorder*, August 14, 1924. For a discussion of *Woman's Voice*, a magazine created and published by Madame C. J. Walker, and the purposes it served, see Noliwe M. Rooks, *Hair Raising: Beauty, Culture, and African American Women* (New Brunswick, NJ, 1996), 97–100.

22. Collier-Thomas, "Black Women in the Church: A Research Priority," *Christian Recorder*, 1992.

23. Collier-Thomas, *Daughters of Thunder*, 35.

24. Collier-Thomas, "Women in the Church."

25. Collier-Thomas, *Black Women Organized*, 37–45; Gerda Lerner, "Early Community Work of Black Club Women," *Journal of Negro History* 59 (April 1974): 158–167; Bettye Collier-Thomas, *N.C.N.W., 1935–1980* (Washington, DC, 1980), 1, 30.

26. Ibid.

27. Jacquelyn Dowd Hall, *Revolt Against Chivalry: Jessie Daniel Ames and the Women's Campaign Against Lynching* (New York, NY, 1993); Bettye Collier-Thomas, "Across the Divide: The Interracial and Interdenominational Efforts of Black and White Women: An Historical Reconnaissance" in *Black Women's History at the Intersection of Knowledge and Power: ABWH's Twentieth*

Anniversary Anthology, ed. Rosalyn Terborg-Penn and Janice Sumler Edmond (Acton, MA, 2000), 25–34.

28. Sue M. Brown, *The History of the Order of Eastern Star Among Colored People* (Des Moines, IA, 1925), 16, 37.

29. Ibid., 17, 58, 51.

30. For discussion, see Traki Taylor, "'Womanhood Glorified': Nannie Helen Burroughs and the National Training School for Women and Girls, Inc., 1909–1960," *Journal of African American History* 87 (Fall 2002): 390–402.

31. "Women of NBC Hear Address by Mrs. Layten," *Chicago Defender,* September 18, 1943; "Thanks to our Women for Mission Boxes," *Mission Herald,* Sept.–Oct. 1934, 4; "President Layten's Page," *Mission Herald,* May–June 1937, 37; "Our Women Renew Their Efforts in Pushing the Cause of Foreign Missions," *Mission Herald,* October 1932, 6; "National Baptist Convention Incorporated Woman's Auxiliary Pays in Full for Missionary Retreat in Washington, D.C. at a cost of $83,500," *Mission Herald,* Jan.–Feb. 1964, 5.

32. "Contributions for Year July 1, 1928 to June 30, 1929, "*Mission Herald,* September 1929, 12.

33. "The Woman's Convention, Auxiliary to the National Baptist Convention, U.S.A., Inc., Raises $35,035.35 in Annual Session," *Mission Herald,* September–October 1944, 21; S. Willie Layten, "President Layten's Page," *The Mission Herald,* July–August 1942, 17; S. G. Gerdine, "Baptist Women Work for Education," *National Notes,* October 1927, 10. *National Notes* is the official publication for the NACW.

34. "The Questers: A Track Record of Caring Via Fashion Show," *Washington Afro-American,* October 26, 1985.

CHAPTER 7

"MAINTAINING A HOME FOR GIRLS"

The Iowa Federation of Colored Women's Clubs at the University of Iowa, 1919–1950

Richard M. Breaux

This chapter examines the Iowa Federation of Colored Women's Clubs' (IFCWC) campaign to operate a house for African American women at the University of Iowa from 1919 to 1950.[1] It seeks to add to a growing body of literature that focuses on African American philanthropy and collective black economic enterprises. An examination of the experiences of African American women at the University of Iowa and the campaign for the IFCWC Home campaign offers an interesting case study that builds on recent research on African American women's philanthropy.[2] The IFCWC's economic enterprise developed because between 1913 and 1946 the University of Iowa barred African American students from campus dormitories and some student activities. The experiences of African American women at the University of Iowa are unique for two reasons: (1) the house they occupied was one of a few "women's dormitories" in the nation owned and operated by a formally organized group of African American women and (2) the campaign to maintain the IFCWC Home provided mostly middle-class Afri-

Cultural Capital and Black Education, pages 117–141
Copyright © 2004 by Information Age Publishing

can American women students with the organizational, intellectual, and leadership skills necessary to become the next generation of black women activists. In general, the experiences of African American college women at predominantly white coeducational institutions in the early 20th century are unique because white women often had the guidance and support of white women administrators and/or faculty.[3] African American women, on the other hand, had to look outside the university for such mentors and role models. This raises several questions: How did the alliance with the IFCWC help to keep students connected to the African American community and how did the community respond? How did limited employment prospects that resulted from race and gender prejudice help to bring about a sharply focused movement to make a college education available to a number of Iowa's young African American women? I contend that the IFCWC prepared African American women at the University of Iowa to assume positions of leadership in organizations such as the IFCWC, National Association of Colored Women (NACW), the Order of the Eastern Star (OES), and the National Association for the Advancement of Colored People (NAACP), and a host of other local and regional civil rights organizations.[4] Upon graduation, these women also assumed responsibilities in their local communities in their effort to "uplift the race."

This essay places African American women's lives at the center of inquiry in a preexisting historiographical paradigm, which often excludes them through a preoccupation with African American men and white women. A few scholars, such as Linda Perkins, Elizabeth Ihle, Jeanne Noble, and Ellen Lawson, have completed studies on African American women's higher education. Other scholars, such as Amy Thompson McCandless, offer thorough and insightful comparisons of southern white and southern black women's education in the 20th century. Outside the works by this small group of historians, the experiences of college-educated African American women have been marginalized. Particularly missing from current studies is any examination of African American women in the Midwest.[5] Although African American women's historiography has recently focused on Ohio, Indiana, and Illinois, these works provide limited information on African American women's history in midwestern states west of the Mississippi River such as Minnesota, Nebraska, and Iowa.[6] To be sure, this study is not only specific to Iowa, but to African American women who attended the University of Iowa. I contend that racism did not paralyze these women's struggle for equality. They transformed their experiences with racism into a call for social activism, racial uplift, and service to their communities.[7]

As Kevin Gaines, Stephanie Shaw, and other scholars point out, although African Americans agreed on the ideal of uplift, they did not always agree on what types of behavior were appropriate. As a black middle class emerged at the end of the 19th century, conceptions of appropriate behavior became even more contentious. Kevin Gaines argues that there is a historical tension between the two commonly understood meanings of racial uplift: (1) a broad original meaning that emerged after the Civil War and included social advancement and education as liberation for all African Americans; and (2) an ideology shaped by an emerging middle class that stressed "self help, race solidarity, temperance, thrift, chastity, social patriarchal authority, and the accumulation of wealth."[8] The latter of these two, Gaines argues, became manifest as middle-class blacks sought to lead the social, political, and religious activities of the working-class. Black migration literature describes this tension as a battle between the old settlers and the new migrants, but for the IFCWC and African American women at the University of Iowa, uplift ideology and generational difference caused the most tension. Club leaders Sue Brown and Gertrude Rush best summarized the IFCWC's stance when they stated, "The greatest need of the Negro Woman is to set up a standard for her own; that she may regain the confidence of the opposite sex, many of whom are beginning to feel women are losing their finer charms."[9] Gertrude Rush added, "The type of character held up to our girls as a model should be strong prideful morality, strong in point of conduct prompted by a sense of self-respect and honor. Future mothers can't be flappers and retain the respect of their girls."[10] Among students, "appropriate behavior" in the 1920s meant facing up to academic and social challenges on campus, addressing racism and discrimination, and maintaining high scholastic standards, with some social activities on the side. African American women students knew that despite their individuality, their academic and social performances would affect perceptions of the Federation Home. Historians, such as Lynn Gordon and David Levine, describe college women and men in the 1920s, 1930s, and 1940s as individualistic and part of a culture of aspiration, in an era marked by "political conservatism, the absence of an active feminist movement, the Great Depression, World War II, and an insistence" on a return to women's "normalcy." However, African American women at the University of Iowa ascribed to what Stephanie Shaw calls "socially responsible individualism."[11] African American college women shifted their attention and activism from national issues before 1920 to local and regional issues after the passage of the Nineteenth Amendment.[12] These women achieved inside the classroom as individuals, but their success or failure was seen to reflect on their various African American communities throughout Iowa and the rest of the country.

Although the idea of "socially responsible individualism" explains the connection African American students had to various larger African American communities, the concept of "cultural capital" as redefined by V. P. Franklin, James Stewart, and Bettye Collier-Thomas best explains the relationship between mostly working-class and middle-class African Americans and the Federation Home. Franklin and Stewart define "cultural capital" as a sense of "group consciousness" evident when African Americans financially support collective economic or philanthropic enterprises "to advance the group rather than individual capitalists."[13] Such collectives, they argue, are normal, but have significant value to members of the contributing community.[14] As we shall see, African Americans throughout Iowa obviously felt this sense of group consciousness and demonstrated it by the number of people and organizations that gave to the campaign to purchase the Federation Home.

The relationship between the IFCWC and the National Association of Colored Women resembled that shared by other state black women's organizations and the NACW, but the uniqueness of the relationship between the IFCWC and African American women at the university makes this a special case. As the 19th century came to a close, African American women began to set their sights on community activism, service, and local politics. The NACW, established in 1896, brought together many local women's clubs into state organizations. The presence of the NACW also led to the emergence of African American women's clubs around the country. For example, the Iowa Federation of Colored Women's Clubs was founded in 1903. Like other African American women's clubs, the IFCWC engaged in what Anne Meis Knupfer calls "other mothering."[15] Club members filled the role of surrogate mother for the students in the Federation Home. But this home was neither a shelter for the elderly nor a home for delinquent children. In some cases, the students who lived in the Federation Home were the daughters, nieces, cousins, or other blood relatives of IFCWC members; and, in other cases, the students were the relatives of OES, NACW, and state clubwomen from other states. Neither the NACW motto, "Lifting As We Climb," nor the IFCWC motto, "Sowing Seeds of Kindness," properly describes the relationship between the University women and the IFCWC. As we shall see, in several cases club members helped students to cross into the organizations to which clubwomen belonged or urged students to seek employment and political positions that racism often prevented clubwomen themselves from holding. While some women used their church and OES organizational skills to assume positions of power in the IFCWC, other clubwomen married University of Iowa alumni and used their earlier political activism to launch them into prominent IFCWC positions. One such woman, Sue Brown, maintained a central role in the IFCWC for over thirty years. Brown was the wife of S. Joe Brown, a prominent Des Moines lawyer and Phi Beta Kappa member, who became the first African American to graduate from the University of Iowa's College of Liberal Arts and Graduate College. Although Sue Brown only attended the extension courses at the university, because of her extraordinary efforts to secure and maintain the Federation Home, the IFCWC named the house "Sue Brown Hall" in 1934.

The relationship between the IFCWC and the women at the University of Iowa was both similar to and different than those of their white sisters in Iowa and throughout the country. In terms of similarities, Lynn Gordon points out that white college women "created important alliances with clubwomen, reformers, suffragists, and alumnae."[16] African American women at the University of Iowa and all over the United States built similar alliances. White and black sororities also encouraged their members to build leadership skills and take an active role in reform and civil rights campaigns across the nation.[17] But at the University of Iowa in particular, white women enjoyed access to residential space, such as dormitories, and traditionally male-dominated disciplines, such as law, dentistry, and medicine, that African American women did not. For example, Mary Hickey Wilkinson (white) received a law degree from the university in 1873, but Beulah Wheeler, the first African American graduate of the university's law school, did not receive her law degree until forty-one years later.[18] In dentistry, Jesse Ritchey graduated in 1887, and twenty-eight women graduated in dentistry between 1887 and 1906, but no African American woman graduated in dentistry until after 1950.[19] Eight white women made up part of the first class of medical students in 1870; possibly one African American woman enrolled as a medical student before 1950.[20]

Throughout the 20th century, African American women college students outnumbered African American men during every decade except the 1920s. However, African American women's enrollment only exceeded African American men's in the first two years of college. By the third and fourth years, the 2-year teaching credential lured many African American women away from college.[21] This was also the case at the University of Iowa where evidence suggests that African American men outnumbered African American women in every decade before 1950.[22] Despite their relatively small numbers, the lives of African American women at the University of Iowa demand further investigation because these women's experiences provide a glimpse into African American women's educational and political activities in the years between two great political movements—the fight for women's suffrage and the modern Civil Rights Movement.

FINDING HOUSING AND DEVELOPING SISTERHOOD

African American women and men experienced great difficulties with finding housing because Iowa City's African American community remained small and the university continued to bar black students from dormitories. Although the number of white women enrollees created housing problems, most white women had the option of living in the dormitories. Dormitories housed 480 of the 1,260 women enrolled at the university in 1919. An unwritten university policy prohibited African American men and women from residing in on-campus housing.[23] To pay for the cost of their educations, African American women "found homes with various faculty members, where they served as domestics, earning their board and room and sometimes a little spending change."[24] The small African American community in Iowa City only slightly alleviated the student housing shortage. As if being a student wasn't stressful enough, race-based housing restrictions made the experiences of African American women almost unbearable. Fed up with having their shelter rest on the whim of a white landlord's racial views, several women from the university traveled to Marshalltown and Cedar Rapids to attend annual meetings of the Iowa Federation of Colored Women's Clubs. At the request of the students, Sue Brown, the retiring club president, appointed Helen Downey as the chair of the house search committee; and the club proposed to launch a campaign to purchase a home in Iowa City for African American women students.[25]

Initially, the clubwomen proposed two housing options to University of Iowa officials: (1) the university could purchase a home for African American women to be used as a dorm or (2) university administrators could endorse a fundraising campaign for the IFCWC to purchase a home.[26] Although the IFCWC could possibly have involved the NAACP, the association engaged in only a limited number of battles where they challenged institutions on the "separate but equal" doctrine. Such challenges did not become a major NAACP activity until the 1930s. First, the IFCWC wrote university officials in 1920 to document the importance of adequate housing for African American women. In response, Dean of Women Nellie S. Burner wrote:

> So long as colored women attend the university, there can be no question of the need of a suitable house which they may find proper living conditions. The movement of the Iowa Federation of Colored Women's Clubs to provide such a house is a direct response to this need. There can be no doubt that housing conditions are of vital importance in the life of a student.[27]

The IFCWC offered to pay to furnish and maintain a university-owned house. "To be sure," Helen Downey wrote in a letter to President Walter A. Jessup, "if this could be done, it would be a wonderful help to us, and with the money we have we could furnish, put in coal and keep the place in good condition."[28] But university officials rejected the first option and forced the IFCWC to hold a fundraising campaign, which included a drive, tag sales, and other ventures. Because President Jessup was on vacation, the dean of women and other university administrators dodged the issue by citing the state legislature's limited resources.[29] In another letter to Helen Downey, Dean Burner wrote:

> When the communication came from the Des Moines Chamber of Commerce, I took up the matter with Dean Kay and we agreed that nothing could be done because the legislature has made no appropriation for additional dormitories for girls. These are badly needed for more than twice as many girls as we can accommodate have applied for dormitory rooms for the coming year. We regret that our facilities are so limited. We appreciate your effort to secure a home for your girls and trust that it will be successful.[30]

Needless to say, the drive was on.

The alliance between the IFCWC and the African American women at the university became official; and the struggle to establish the Federation Home gave students first-hand experiences with working with local and state officials from the Iowa City council to the governor. Many African American women students worked for and lived with local whites because of limited housing options. According to one source, these students "ran to school in the morning without a chance to glance in the glass, hurrying back at noon to help with the midday meal, then another run to school. When the evening work was done, they were [too] tired to study."[31] Clubwomen expressed interest in students' study habits, working conditions, and the extent to which students represented African American womanhood. Appearance played a significant role in constructing womanhood and in how white university and government officials perceived African American students. African American students did not view their domestic work as an end or preparation for future work. The menial tasks these women were forced to perform were a means to an end. These women "worked the system to accomplish their own goals" by working as domestics, completing their studies, and lobbying government officials to get support for the housing campaign.[32] Clubwomen enlisted the services of the Des Moines Secretary of Commerce and the Governor of Iowa. This represented a rare occasion when African American women had access to and some political influence with powerful white men in government.[33] Students such as Helen Dameron Beshears often met with President Walter Jessup in an effort to garner his support for the proposed housing drive. Jessup showed nothing but indifference toward the IFCWC, the housing drive, and the students' requests. Although the Des Moines Secretary of Commerce Ralph H. Faxon and Governor Frank Jackson gave the campaign the green light, Jessup and other university administrators blamed the failure to act on the state legislature's limited resources.[34] Caught between student demands and the university's indifference, the proposed campaign moved forward.

Cultural capital was provided by African American women's organizations, African American alumni of the university, and the husbands of IFCWC members. Other philanthropic funds and resources came from white state government officials. Alumni contributors included S. Joe Brown ('98), Laurence C. Jones ('07), Archie A. Alexander ('12), J. Wesley Thompson ('17), and Dr. Rufus P. Beshears ('08). In addition, at least three other African American alumni contributed to the campaign. The Princess Zora chapter of the OES, the Oziel Chapter of the OES, and the Des Moines branch of the NAACP also contributed money to the Home fund. Local women's clubs, such as the Mary Church Terrell Club, the Phyllis Wheatley Club, and the Mary B. Talbert Club, gave to the campaign and made annual donations. Clubwomen also contributed old wares for "tag sales." Hundreds of working-class and middle-class African Americans with no club or university affiliation sent money as well. As for white government officials, Iowa Attorney General H. M. Havner and former Governor Frank D. Jackson donated $50 and $25, respectively.[35] The philanthropy and charitable contributions of some whites does not diminish the sense of group solidarity among African American clubwomen, such as Sue Brown, who raised over $800 and the students, such as Emily Gross, who raised over $100. The IFCWC also established a special Home Committee, which usually included an alumna or the wife of an alumnus. Among the leading women on this committee over the years were Sue Brown, Mrs. Audrey Alexander (the wife of Archie Alexander, 1912), Helen Dameron Beshears, and Mrs. Adeline Clark (wife of the first African American graduate of the University of Iowa). Clubwomen also established an annual scholarship to assist women students with the cost of their education. With an increased number of nine African American women registered for the fall of 1919, the *Bystander* read "A Group of University Girls Looking for a Home."[36] Students living off campus were required to live in university-approved housing. Despite their initial indifference to the drive, both president Jessup and Dean Burner wrote letters of support and endorsement of the IFCWC efforts.[37]

With university approval for the fundraising campaign, the IFCWC put a $1,000 down payment on a home. By September 1919, the club selected a "twelve room modern two story residence, at 942 Iowa Ave[nue]."[38] Also in the home was a box to collect donations, rent, and items that could be sold at annual tag sales, including "paper money, silver, pennies, and used textbooks."[39] The house was purchased for $5,300 and the club's trustees appointed Mr. and Mrs. James Dameron to act as manager and matron of the home. Their daughter, Helen Dameron-Beshears, graduated from the University of Iowa in 1920. As a student, Dameron-Beshears developed a strong interest in education and child welfare. Following her graduation, Dameron-Beshears served as academic director of Piney Woods School in

Mississippi, directed the "Negro Girls Reserve" in Cedar Rapids, and earned an appointment as a probation officer in Polk County, Iowa.[40] As a student, Dameron-Beshears kept constant pressure on Jessup. But neither Dameron-Beshears nor the IFCWC could prevent the financial problems that the home would experience in future years.

Because the IFCWC failed to reach their goal of $10,000, Governor Nathan Kendall stepped in to ease the financial burden. The IFCWC made the first payment of $1,000 in September 1919. They agreed to make subsequent payments on January 1 of 1921, 1922, 1923, and 1924 with a 6 percent annual interest. Although the IFCWC made its 1921 payment in full, $825 in interest and principal went unpaid for 1922, and the $1,000 payment for January 1923 became past due.[41] Additional problems with taxes put the home in jeopardy of being sold, but Governor Kendall, who was a former state senator from Albia (near Buxton), stepped in and "discharged the indebtedness entirely, by canceling the interest and donating about one-sixth of the principal." In a letter to Walter Jessup, Governor Kendall wrote, "You will remember my connection with the dormitory for colored girls at Iowa City. The mortgage held by an eastern woman was about to be foreclosed when I purchased it, intending to extend the maturity indefinitely."[42]

Although a lack of financial resources plagued the IFCWC's early efforts, resistance from a white neighborhood association in Iowa City further complicated efforts to secure the house. According to the minutes of the IFCWC, in 1920 club members made an offer on the house and an additional lot in Iowa City, but as they closed "the deal, they found there was a tax assessment pending on an extra lot. This they thought would not come up. But angry because we bought, neighbors began to ask a reassessment of this lot and were successful in getting it through court, and it was reassessed [at] $179, which [was] to be paid in four payments."[43] Stephen Meyer, in his study of racial conflict and residential segregation, contends that campaigns to maintain all-white neighborhoods in the 1920s revealed the depth of racism and the animosity of northern whites toward African Americans. Northern whites often overlooked class and believed that African Americans in the neighborhood, regardless of their socioeconomic status, immediately lowered property values. Meyer reminds readers that "[w]hites accepted African Americans' advancement towards equal citizenship rights as long as they didn't move next door."[44] Sources do not reveal whether the group that forced the property reassessment was the same one that attempted to keep Kappa Alpha Psi from renting a home in Iowa City. According to William E. Taylor, a member of Kappa Alpha Psi enrolled in the law school at the time, as early as 1920 African American students at the University of Iowa appealed to James Weldon Johnson and the NAACP to help end racial discrimination in Iowa City and within the university. William E. Taylor wrote that "the conditions in this city are at present almost unlivable for a colored student. The attitude of hostility is felt most keenly in the matter of housing. No one will rent to colored fraternities and no one will sell in a livable locality." Taylor reported that a local land-lord broke the contract with the fraternity when members of the local Ku Klux Klan chapter organized to outbid the black students. Taylor con-cluded, "I have been in this city long enough to note the crystallization of sentiment against us. There is an organization of the Ku Klux Klan here, and I have not the least doubt but that they are financing the scheme to effect our ruin." Johnson suggested that the students contact local NAACP chapters, but refused to offer any assistance from the national office.[45] In fact, many of the IFCWC members and their husbands belonged to the Iowa NAACP; and S. Joe Brown, then president of the Des Moines NAACP, helped the IFCWC to close the deal on the house. Why the NAACP did not use this opportunity to press for the desegregation of dormitories remains unclear. Resistance from the white neighbors on Iowa Avenue demon-strates that some in the community followed the lead of the university, rental agents, zoning agencies, and the National Association of Real Estate Boards on the issue of residential segregation.[46]

Barred from white women's social organizations on campus, African American women established the "Mary Church Terrell Club" in 1913, to "inculcate high ideals in the girls," and to work "along literary lines with an emphasis placed upon the achievements among Negroes."[47] One year later, students renamed the organization the "Girls of the State University of Iowa."[48] Several months before the house was purchased in 1920, the Afri-can American women students established the "colored University Girls club" to improve their situation on campus.[49] This club resembled the IFCWC, but was strictly maintained by African American women at the uni-versity and it led to the formation of the university's first African American sorority. Through the assistance of the women's club, eight women estab-lished the Delta chapter of Delta Sigma Theta Sorority in 1919. Alumnae Adah Hyde and Vaeletta London counted themselves among the chartered members of the sorority. Emily Gross, Mamie Diggs, Ola Calhoun, Helen Dameron Beshears, Harriette Alexander, and Helen Lucas made up the remainder.[50] For the first 2 years of its existence, the "Federation Home," as it was called, also served as the Delta house. The IFCWC, however, asked students to remove the sorority letters from the house because member-ship in the sorority was not a requirement to live there.[51]

Delta Sigma Theta became an important avenue for African American women to develop leadership and communication skills. A portion of this leadership training included fundraising. Local Delta chapters, such as the one at the University of Iowa, provided financial support to organizations such as the National Council of Negro Women. In general, African Ameri-can Greek-letter organizations "symbolized the right of black students to pursue a liberal arts education at a time when such studies were deemed to be either beyond the intellectual reach of or impractical for, the growing numbers of black students, especially black women, seeking higher education."[52] The Delta chapter, however, hampered by low membership numbers and the restrictions of the IFCWC concerning house residency and sorority affiliation, became inactive. By 1933 many of the African American men enrolled in the university thought that the redevelopment of the sorority chapter in Iowa City might increase the enrollment of African American women.[53]

Although the home represented a major expression of cultural capital, local African American families offered their homes to students, which was another form of cultural capital. Over the years, students came to depend on both. The rent paid by African American women covered most of the expenses of the home. The number of women who lived at the Federation Home varied from year to year. In the 1919–20 academic year the number of residents at the Federation Home was 11. Seven women lived in the house during the 1921–22 school year. By 1929, African American women at the university numbered 25. Seventeen of these women lived in the Federation Home.[54] In subsequent years, African American students also found rooms in the homes of local black residents Helen and Allen Lemme, Estelle "Ma" Ferguson, and Bettye and Junious Tate.[55] During the Fall semester in the 1932–33 school year, six women lived at the Federation Home, seven women lived in private homes run by local African American families, three women roomed and boarded with white families, and one student lived with and worked for a white family.[56]

As the effects of the Great Depression set in, the number of African American women at the University began to decline. In the fall of 1933, only three African American women lived in the Federation Home, and some students, such as Frances A. Nance who enrolled at the university during the depression years, were forced to withdraw for financial reasons. Nance, the oldest of five children born to her parents in Esterville, Iowa, attended grammar school and high school in Cedar Rapids. At age 17, she graduated from high school and entered the University of Iowa in 1931. Nance lived at the Federation Home with seven other African American women. During her first semester, Nance's mother fell sick with tuberculosis. Nance, the only one of her mother's children old enough to supplement the family income, found work as a seamstress and domestic, but also became an active member of the IFCWC. Nance later attended Kirkwood Community College and worked as a library technician in the Cedar Rapids Public Schools and the Cedar Rapids Public Library until her retirement.[57] Low enrollments among African American women in the 1930s crippled the IFCWC's ability to finance the home.

The IFCWC could not afford to operate the home without a significant number of student occupants. When the federation fell on difficult financial times in the mid-1920s, the members launched a campaign to pay the mortgage and property taxes on the Home.[58] In the 1935–36 school year, as an incentive to attract women, the IFCWC instituted a scholarship program to provide $5 in assistance to the first ten African American women students to register as house residents.[59] This method of finding residents, however, proved ineffective. In response, the club took out advertisements in various African American magazines and newspapers in an effort to keep the house in operation. When this strategy also failed, federation members called upon African American male students to help with the struggle to maintain the home. Demonstrating that their sense of "collective consciousness" transcended personal gain, members of Kappa Alpha Psi gave up their house and moved into the Federation Home to help the IFCWC's efforts. During the 1937–38 academic year, five members of Kappa Alpha Psi took over the home.[60] As the decade came to a close, however, the number of African American women at the University slowly recovered and the house continued to function as a dormitory for African American women until 1950. In 1946, five women lived at the home, and Nick Aaron Ford ('45) and his wife served as the house supervisors.[61] In this same year, the university finally ended its policy barring African American women from the dormitories.

Ironically, the university had no *official* rules on African American students' exclusion from the dormitories. The dean of men and women merely claimed that white students would object to black hall-mates.[62] As for local black families, the Lemmes were a mainstay for African American students. One student, Juanita Kidd, who later became a supreme court judge in Pennsylvania, remembered "walking up and down the streets looking for a place to live" until "[s]he noticed a black baby in diapers on the front porch. So she went up to the door and asked if she could stay."[63] Kidd took a room at the home of Helen Lemme. The Lemme family had lived in Iowa City from the early 1900s. Elizabeth and Junious Tate lived on Prentiss Street and by 1940 they owned and operated the "Tate Arms" at 914 South Dubuque, which also welcomed black students.[64]

In addition to the rooms African American families provided, other forms of cultural capital that added to black student life included hair care service, restaurants, social activities, and informal welcoming committees. The Negro Forum, originally founded as a religious group, mobilized in 1925 to address the issue of hair salons owners' refusal to service African American students. Although local business people did not budge on the issue, African American women established alternative services. Some of the women in the Federation Home in the mid-1940s benefited from the services of Barbara Jean Brown-James.[65] Students such as Betty Jean Furgerson and Martha Scales went home, others went to Cedar Rapids, did their own hair, or went to Helen Lemme's house at 603 South Capitol Street.[66] Although African American students could eat at the Memorial Union on campus, black residents in the community also provided meals for students. These services sheltered students from racist soft-drink-counter attendants who refused to serve students, or who only served light-skinned blacks.[67] African American students had similar difficulties finding local restaurants that would serve them, and finally Vivian Trent, an African American graduate of the university in 1934, opened a restaurant in 1937 called Vivian's Chicken Shack. As a student, Trent had lived in the Federation Home. One student reminisced about the atmosphere at Vivian's and other local restaurants:

> We couldn't eat in the restaurants in the city. When I came here in 1937, a Black gentleman whose name I don't recall ran a restaurant for Black students on Burlington, somewhere between Dubuque and Clinton. That's where Black students used to gather at noon everyday for a meal at lunch.... couldn't eat in the Union either. ... They had persons standing at the doors of restaurants in Iowa City, and while I was never refused admission, the person at the door would simply tell the Negro students that they simply didn't serve Negroes.[68]

Not all students could afford to eat at Vivian's often. Elizabeth Catlett, who became a world-renowned sculptor, "waited table for meals at Vivian's." Catlett also recalled that she played bridge with Trent and two other women. Catlett, a graduate of Howard University, received a scholarship to work on her masters in fine arts. For a short time she lived with noted writer Margaret Walker, who later became a professor of literature at Jackson State University.[69] Catlett also lived with Mrs. Estella Scott "near the Alpha House," where she paid $10.00 per month for rent, and in the Federation Home for a year.[70] By the time Catlett arrived in Iowa City, African American alumni and students developed a referral service and student welcoming system. For example, some students wrote Bettye Tate to reserve a room. Other students, like Elizabeth Catlett, were met by a small group of African American students at the train station. These same students drove Catlett around town until she secured a room.[71] Individuals and groups, community people and students all contributed cultural capital to provide a sense of community in an otherwise uncertain time and environment.

TRAILBLAZERS IN CLASS AND OUT

The various African American women who lived in the Federation Home in the early years blazed many trails as University of Iowa students. For example, in 1924, Beulah Wheeler became the first African American woman to graduate from the College of Law. Wheeler, a Marshalltown resident who lived at the Federation Home as a student, helped pay for her education by selling handmade art. She was one of many African American women who attended meetings of the IFCWC to express her appreciation to the Women's Club for their continued support.[72] During her senior year, Wheeler played on the class basketball and volleyball teams where she was one of "the chief score makers for the seniors."[73] She also received a "chevron" for her outstanding record as a volleyball player.[74] Wheeler's exploits, however, were not limited to the ball courts. In 1921, Wheeler won the Women's Extemporaneous Speech Contest with a speech entitled "Uniform Marriage and Divorce Law."[75]

Marie A. Brown and Gwendolyn Wilson were among the first African American women to enroll in the College of Pharmacy. It appears that only Lorena Suggs, a graduate of the College of Pharmacy in 1921, preceded Brown and Wilson.[76] Brown completed the mandatory three-year requirement for a pharmacy degree in 1930. Two years later, the College of Pharmacy increased its graduation requirements to four years of academic courses.[77] Wilson, however, did not graduate from the University. After one year, Wilson transferred to Des Moines College's [later Drake University] pharmacy school where she earned a degree in 1929. Unable to find work in her field due to discrimination, Wilson taught school in Holly Springs, Mississippi, for fifteen years. Despite this diversion, however, Wilson became one of the first licensed African American woman pharmacists in Iowa. She worked as a pharmacist clerk and chemist for the state of Iowa and served four years in Vietnam before she retired in 1974.[78]

Women such as Lorraine Crawford and M. Corine Mathis continued to blaze the trails paved by Harriette Alexander and Beulah Wheeler in women's athletics. At the University of Iowa, African American women participated in sports that were virtually closed to African American men. Lorraine Crawford, a native of Des Moines, played on the women's volleyball team in 1923. After two years at the University of Iowa, Crawford transferred to Drake University where she received her bachelor's degree in 1927. In the same year, her teammate and housemate Corine Mathis of Boley, Oklahoma, played on the women's baseball, track, volleyball, and basketball teams.[79] Mathis had been one of the lead scorers on the sophomore volleyball team. She also competed in track and field events, including the basketball throw, baseball throw, and 8-pound shotput. One year, Mathis placed first in the basketball throw, and she also won in the 8-pound shotput. In the same year, she and three other women broke the university-wide women's record in the mile relay.[80] While no African American woman at the University of Iowa seems to have participated on an athletic team before Harriette Alexander played field ball (field hockey) in 1919, African American women played on athletic teams at other predominantly white schools as early as 1917 when Phyllis W. Waters lettered as a member of the University of Michigan basketball team.[81] Despite advancements in some sports, African American women continued to be prohibited from joining the swimming team.[82]

African American women constructed their own realities and their own ideals of womanhood. Participation in college athletics surely created a dilemma for African American women. Many middle-class African American women sought to redefine ideals of womanhood, which historically excluded them or often cast them in stereotypical roles, such as the "masculinized domineering matriarch, the inept and comical domestic servant, the exotic sex object, and the tragic mulatto."[83] African American women had to fight racial and gender-based social constructs defining their behavior. They used athletics as an arena to undermine popular ideas about the feebleness of women and to combat beliefs about the inherent inferiority of African Americans through open competition with white women. Most importantly, reports of African American women students' achievements in sports and academics added weight to the argument to maintain the home, and helped African Americans across the state to understand that their financial contributions benefited the group.

LEGACIES AND CONNECTIONS TO THE PAST

By the 1940s, opportunities for African American students were slowly changing. African American students developed new ways to address the old problems of finding a place to eat, finding hair care services, and acquiring money for college. The greatest change, especially in regard to earning money, was the enrollment of several "legacies," the children of Iowa alumni. The parents of several students who enrolled in the 1940s had received professional degrees in law, medicine, dentistry, and pharmacy from the university decades earlier. Virginia Harper and Lois Harper-Eichacker of Fort Madison, Iowa, followed in the footsteps of their father Dr. Harry Harper, and their aunt Naomi Harper-Jordan. Naomi Harper, who lived in the Federation Home as a student, became a teacher after her graduation in 1922.[84] Virginia Harper completed three years at the University of Iowa before she transferred to Howard University, and later graduated from the College of Medical Technology in Minneapolis, Minnesota. As a student, she did not have to hold a job and the extra time created an opportunity for her to join the Alpha Kappa Alpha sorority and to participate in other student activities. Although her finances were "taken care of," the racial attitudes of many of her classmates created many obstacles for her. Despite her experiences, Virginia Harper was determined to make conditions better for herself and other African Americans in Iowa. Like some of the women before her, Harper's experiences with racism, during college and after, led her to the presidency of the Fort Madison chapter of the NAACP and membership in the Fort Madison Human Rights Commission.[85] Lois Harper-Eichacker, like her sister Virginia, worked during her post-college years as a coordinator for the Southeast Iowa Community Action Center.[86]

Other legacies, such as Martha Scales-Zachary and Betty Jean Furgerson, were Virginia Harper and Lois Harper-Eichacker's contemporaries. When Betty Jean Furgerson and Martha Scales-Zachary enrolled at Iowa, they were following in the footsteps of their parents and other family members. Both Furgerson and Scales-Zachary's fathers earned medical degrees from Iowa in the 1920s. Betty Jean Furgerson's mother was a student at the time that Scales-Zachary's parents managed the Women's Club house on campus. In addition, Scales-Zachary's aunt attended the university, and her uncle received a medical degree in 1934. Furgerson and Scales-Zachary were two of the nine charter members of the Alpha Kappa Alpha sorority.[87] Betty Jean Furgerson's mother taught elementary school in Waterloo, Iowa, from 1952 to 1971. No African American woman or man had taught in a Waterloo public school before. Ironically, Vaeletta London ('17) had been denied a similar job in the same city three decades before Furgerson's appointment. As a member of the Waterloo NAACP, London helped to push school board officials to desegregate Waterloo's teaching force.

Second-generation students had very different experiences from their parents. Martha Scales-Zachary did not have to work off campus because her father paid for her education. A graduate of St. Joseph's Academy in Des Moines, she attended the University of Iowa from 1947 to 1951. While a student, Scales-Zachary regularly attended university football games with her parents and other African American students. By this time, most African American students had few problems being served in local restaurants.[88] Neither Scales-Zachary nor Furgerson reported having trouble with professors or their fellow students. After graduation, Furgerson became a social worker, educator, and director of the Waterloo Human Rights Commission from 1974 until 1992. Both women were among the second group of African American women to move into Currier Hall, the dormitory from which their relatives had been barred.

Five African American women—Esther Walls, Virginia Harper, Nancy Henry, Gwen Davis, and Leanne Howard—"officially" desegregated Currier Hall in 1946. According to Virginia Harper, however, the first African American women to live in the dorms went unacknowledged because they were "light-skinned." Harper recalled that "African American women were reported if the proctor found them socializing with a white student."[89] Other students, such as Betty Jean Furgerson, remembered "it did not seem as if the proctors wanted us [African American women] in the dorm." Martha Scales-Zachary also remembers that notices were sent to white parents asking if they would allow their daughters to live in the same dorm with African American women. The university operated several houses, where students lived before moving into the dorms. Betty Jean Furgerson had to switch homes because one student's parents objected to desegregated living quarters. As a result, Scales-Zachary and Furgerson then became roommates in a home operated by the university.[90] These arrangements lasted the first semester. The following semester the women from these homes moved into Currier. For the first semester, no out-of-state women were permitted to live in the dormitories. Iowa residency was a prerequisite for African American women students who lived in Currier; this requirement, however, did not apply to African American men.

The sincerity of the University of Iowa administrators in deciding to desegregate the dormitories in 1946 is questionable. Some predominantly white northern schools barred African Americans from dormitories and others segregated African Americans inside campus residence halls. For example, Dickinson College and Bryn Mawr College in Pennsylvania barred African Americans from dormitoriesand all on-campus housing. The University of Chicago allowed African American men into dormitories, but barred African American women from campus housing. These women had to find accommodations some "ten to fifty blocks from the campus."[91] Surely, University of Iowa administrators were pressed to fill the dormitories as a result of the financial strains created by World War II. Administrators also might have feared law suits as the NAACP challenged college segregation in the 1930s and 1940s.[92] Several African American graduate students came to the university from southern states where their graduate education was partially financed by the state governments in an effort to maintain racial segregation in southern white colleges and universities. Students such as Juanita Kidd, a native of Oklahoma, took special interest in college desegregation cases. While a student, Kidd cut classes to hear Charles Houston argue in the *Gaines v. Missouri* case.

> That is the only time in my life, grade school, high school, college, or graduate school or professional school that I ever cut class. But even though I was a teenager, I had heard of Charles H. Houston, and I had a life long ambition to be a lawyer myself; and when I heard that Charles H. Houston was coming

to Jefferson City, Missouri, I cut class and went to the Supreme Court of Missouri that day and I was thrilled.[93]

THE CLOSING OF THE FEDERATION HOME

The postwar era, which saw a greater push for school desegregation by many African Americans and some whites, precipitated the end of the Federation Home. As in so many other cases, desegregation came at a cost. Beginning with the desegregation of Currier Hall, the university began to draw African American women away from the Federation Home and into the dorms. Not all African American women lived in the dorms after 1946. University regulations limited dorm residency to African American women with residency status in Iowa. African American women from the South and other parts of the United States continued to live in the Federation Home. Some women, such as Barbara Jean Brown-James, a third-generation Iowan, and Arlene Roberts Morris lived in the house because the rent was inexpensive compared to other places in town.[94] But by 1949, this situation had changed, and university regulations permitted all African American women to live in dorms, regardless of their state of residency, and with this came the end of Federation Home. The degree to which African Americans mourned the loss of the home remains unclear. IFCWC minutes offer no elaborate explanation of the home's closing. The *Iowa Bystander* and the *Daily Iowan* published no stories announcing the home's end. Moreover, even after the closing of the home, African American women continued to be segregated by rooms within the dorms well into the 1950s. In this instance racial discrimination did not end as much as it changed forms.[95]

Although covert and overt forms of racism and sexism represented obstacles for many of these women, their personal pride, professional goals, and desire to "uplift the race" helped them to translate their experience into lifelong lessons of survival; and much of this would have been virtually impossible without the Federation Home. The home not only belonged to the women's club and the students, but to all of Iowa's African American residents. In fact, residents of the Federation Home may have best captured the relationship between students at the university, the IFCWC, and African Americans across the state when they wrote:

> To the Members and Co-Workers of the Iowa Federation of Colored Women's Clubs: Please accept our hearty appreciation for the faithful work which you have done, and are doing now, toward trying to maintain a Home for us. We want you to know that we realize the many sacrifices which you are making, and we hope that some day our words will become deeds.[96]

Students clearly understood that as socially responsible individuals they would have to use their education to serve their communities; and the communities' sense of group consciousness was evident through their heartfelt donations to campaigns for the Federation Home.

NOTES

1. Earlier versions of this chapter were presented at the annual conference of the Midwest History of Education Society in October 1999, Chicago, and the annual conference of the American Educational Research Association in April 2001, Seattle, Washington. The author would like to thank Karen Mason, Iowa Women's Archives; Matt Schaefer, Iowa City; and Fran Murphy, University of Iowa Archives. Also special thanks to Leslie A. Schwalm, Thalia Mulvihill, Crystal Lewis-Colman, Lyn Lombard, and Adah Ward Randolph for commenting on earlier versions of this chapter.

2. Bettye Collier-Thomas, "'The Relief Corps of Heaven': Black Women As Philanthropists," in Pier C. Rogers, ed., *Philanthropy in Communities of Color: Traditions and Challenges* (Indianapolis, IN, 2001), 25–39.

3. This was especially the case at the University of Chicago, the University of Iowa, the University of Michigan, the University of Wisconsin, and Cornell University. See individual studies on Michigan and Cornell and Lynn D. Gordon, *Gender and Higher Education in the Progressive Era* (New Haven, CT, 1990), 87–102; Barbara Miller Solomon, *In the Company of Educated Women: A History of Women and Higher Education in America* (New Haven, CT, 1985). For a thorough critique of Solomon's text and suggestions for further research in women's higher education history, see Linda Eisenmann, "Reconsidering a Classic: Assessing the History of Women's Higher Education a Dozen Years after Barbara Solomon," *Harvard Educational Review* 67 (Winter 1997): 689–717. This was also true for most women's colleges; see Helen Lefkowitz Horowitz, *Alma Mater: Design and Experience in the Women's Colleges from Their Nineteenth Century Beginnings to the 1930s* (New York, 1984).

4. For more on the NACW, see Deborah Gray White, *Too Heavy a Load: Black Women in Defense of Themselves, 1894–1994* (New York, 1999), 18. For more on the Order of the Eastern Star, see Sue M. Brown, *History of the Order of the Eastern Star Among Colored People*, ed. Sheila Smith McKoy (1925; reprinted New York, 1997).

5. For more on African American women's higher education in the 19th century, see Linda M. Perkins, "The Education of Black Women in the Nineteenth Century," in *Women and Higher Education in American History*, ed. John Mack Fargeher and Florence Howe (New York, 1988), 64–86; "The African American Female Elite: The Early History of African American Women in the Seven Sister Colleges, 1880–1960," *Harvard Educational Review* 674 (Winter 1997): 718–756; David Diepenbrock, "Black Women and Oberlin College in the Age of Jim Crow," *UCLA Historical Journal* 13 (1993): 27–59; Ellen Lawson and Marlene Merrell, "Antebellum Black Coeds at Oberlin College," *Black Women in United States History*, ed. Darlene Clark Hine (Brooklyn, NY, 1990); Ellen Lawson, *The Three Sarahs: Documents in Antebellum College Women* (New York, 1984). Jeanne Noble offers insight into African

American women's history and higher education in "The Higher Education of Black Women in the Twentieth Century," in Fargeher and Howe, eds., *Women and Higher Education in American History* 87–106. The most comprehensive studies on African American women's higher education are Jeanne Noble, *Negro College Woman's College Education* (New York, 1956) and Elizabeth Ihle, ed., *Black Women in Higher Education: An Anthology of Essays, Studies, and Documents* (New York, 1992). In terms of comparing and contrasting black and white women's higher education, and an analysis of the general "twoness" of women's education in the South, see Amy Thompson McCandless, *The Past in the Present: Women's Higher Education in the Twentieth-Century American South* (Tuscaloosa, AL, 1999).

6. Elizabeth Lindsay Davis, *The Story of the Illinois Federation of Colored Women's Clubs* (New York, 1997); Anne Meis Knupfer, *Toward a Tenderer Humanity and a Nobler Womanhood: African American Women's Clubs in Turn-of-the-Century Chicago* (New York, 1996); Wanda A. Hendricks, *Gender, Race, and Politics in the Midwest: Black Club Women in Illinois* (Bloomington, IN, 1998); Deborah Gray White, *Too Heavy a Load: Black Women in Defense of Themselves, 1894–1994* (New York, 1999); a series of studies on African American women in Indiana, Illinois, and Michigan have been produced by Darlene Clark Hine. Also see Gerder Lerner, "Early Community Work of Black Club Women," *Journal of Negro History* 59 (April 1974): 158–167. One of a few histories to cover Iowa, Kansas, Minnesota, and Missouri is Elizabeth Lindsay Davis, *Lifting As They Climb* (Washington, DC, 1933). One study specific to Kansas is Nupur Chaudhuri, "'We All Seem Like Brothers and Sisters': The African American Community in Manhattan, Kansas, 1865–1940," in Darlene Clark Hine, Wilma King, and Linda Reed, eds., *"We Specialize in the Wholly Impossible": A Reader in Black Women's History* (Brooklyn, NY, 1995), 543–560.

7. Linda Perkins, "The African American Female Elite"; Hendricks, *Gender, Race, and Politics in the Midwest.*

8. Kevin Gaines, *Uplifting the Race: Black Leadership, Politics, and Culture in the Twentieth Century* (Chapel Hill, NC, 1996), 1–5.

9. White, *Too Heavy a Load*, 130.

10. Ibid., 129.

11. David O. Levine, *The American College and the Culture of Aspiration, 1915–1940* (Ithaca, NY, 1985); Lynn D. Gordon, *Gender and Higher Education*, 196–197; Stephanie J. Shaw, *What a Woman Ought to Be and Do: Black Professional Women Workers During the Jim Crow Era* (Chicago, 1996), 2, 10.

12. Rosalyn Terborg Penn, *African American Women in the Struggle for the Vote, 1850–1920* (Bloomington, IN, 1998), 5–6. For an example of this local/regional nationalist feminist activism among African American and Alpha Kappa Alpha, see Susan L. Smith, *Sick and Tired of Being Sick and Tired: Black Women's Activism in America, 1890–1950* (Philadelphia, PA, 1995), 149–169; McCandless, *The Past in the Present*, 144, 193.

13. James Stewart, "Toward Broader Involvement of Black Economists in Discussions of Race and Public Policy: A Plea for a Reconceptualization of Race and Power in Economic Theory," *Review in Black Political Economy* 23 (Winter 1995): 13–55; V. P. Franklin, "Cultural Capital and Black Higher Education: The A.M.E. Church and Universities as Collective Economic Enterprises, 1865–1910," in this volume, and "Social Capital, Cultural Capital, and

Empowerment Zones: A Strategy for Economic and Community Development," in *State of Black Philadelphia: Economic Power—Leveling the Playing Field* (Philadelphia, 1998), 21.

14. Stewart, "Toward Broader Involvement"; Franklin, "Cultural Capital and Black Higher Education"; Collier-Thomas, "Relief Corps of Heaven."

15. Knupfer, *Toward a Tenderer Humanity and a Nobler Womanhood,* 7, 13.

16. Gordon, *Gender and Higher Education,* 40.

17. McCandless, *The Past in the Present,* 141–145, 193–194.

18. Philip Hubbard, *New Dawns: 150 Years of Human Rights at the University of Iowa* (Iowa City, IA, 1996), 12.

19. Adrienne Drapkin, et al., *A Century of Caring: The Health Sciences at the University of Iowa, 1850–1950* (pamphlet) (Iowa City, IA, 1998), 56–57. No mention of racial discrimination or the experiences of students of color appears in this text.

20. Drapkin, Harper, Fifth, and Monson, "A Century of Caring," 11.

21. Noble, "Black Women in the Twentieth Century," 89.

22. Herbert C. Jenkins, "The Negro Student at the State University of Iowa: A Sociological Study" (M.A. thesis, State University of Iowa, 1933), 5; Edwin Bayliss, "The Negro Student at the State University of Iowa: His Preparation, Interests, and Achievement," M.A. thesis, State University of Iowa, 1936, 2.

23. Jenkins, "The Negro Student at the State University of Iowa: A Sociological Study," 29.

24. IFCWC Home Brochure, 2, Iowa Federation of Colored Women's Clubs Home File, Iowa Women's Archives, University of Iowa, Iowa City, IA.

25. Ibid., 2.

26. Helen Downey to J. [*sic*] A. Jessup, August 16, 1919, Box 1919–1920, folder 31, Jessup Papers, University of Iowa Archives, Iowa City, IA.

27. "$10,000, Student's Home Drive," in Box 1, 1920 Minutes folder #21, Iowa Federation of Colored Women's Clubs Papers, SHSI Archives, Des Moines, IA.

28. Helen Downey to J. [*sic*] A. Jessup, August 16, 1919, Box 1919–1920, folder 31, Jessup Papers.

29. Secretary to the President to Helen Downing [*sic*], August 18, 1919, Box 1919–1920, folder 31, Jessup Papers.

30. Nellie S. Aurner to Helen Downey, August 19, 1919, Box 1919–1920, folder 31, Jessup Papers.

31. "Tag Day, Tag Day," *Iowa Bystander,* July 11, 1919.

32. Glenda Gilmore, *Gender & Jim Crow: Women and the Politics of White Supremacy in North Carolina, 1896–1920* (Chapel Hill, NC, 1996), 141.

33. Linda Gordon, "Black And White Visions of Welfare: Women's Welfare Activism, 1890–1945," *Journal of American History* 78, (September 1991): 560–561; Collier-Thomas, "'The Relief Corps of Heaven,'" 27.

34. Nellie S. Aurner to Helen Downey, August 19, 1919, Box 1919–1920, folder 31, Jessup Papers.

35. "Home at Iowa City Purchased," *Iowa Bystander,* September 12, 1919.

36. *Bystander,* August 22, 1919. Incidentally, this house was purchased during the Red Summer of 1919, when race riots broke out in several northern cit-

ies. Stephanie J. Shaw offers a brief and limited analysis of the problems African American women students had with housing. See Shaw, *What a Woman Ought to Be and Do*, 47–51.

37. "$10,000, Student's Home Drive," in Box 1, 1920 Minutes folder 21, Iowa Federation of Colored Women's Clubs Papers, SHSI Archives, Des Moines, IA.

38. IFCWC Home Brochure, 2, Iowa Federation of Colored Women's Clubs Home File, Iowa Women's Archives, University of Iowa, Iowa City, IA.

39. "Collected from the Home Box" in Box 1, 1919 Minutes folder 20, Iowa Federation of Colored Women's Clubs Papers.

40. "Helen Beshears Is Appointed Polk County Juvenile Officer," *Iowa Bystander*, October 6, 1933. William H. Beshears, Jr., telephone interview with the author, March 23, 1999.

41. "Financial History of the Iowa Federation Home," in Box 1, 1923 Minutes folder, Iowa Federation of Colored Women's Clubs Papers, SHSI Archives, Des Moines, IA.

42. Nathan Kendall to Walter Jessup, December 10, 1924, 1924–25 folder, Box 64, Jessup Papers.

43. "Scholarship Committee," in Box 1, 1920 Minutes folder 21, Iowa Federation of Colored Women's Clubs Papers.

44. Stephen Grant Meyer, *As Long As They Don't Move Next Door: Segregation and Racial Conflict in American Neighborhoods* (Lanham, MD, 2000), vii. Although much of Meyer's study refers to the urban north and parts of the urban south, his claims hold up in many cases in the rural-industrial north. Furthermore, only the African American student population in Iowa City increased during the 1920s, the city's black population and the number of blacks in the state decreased in the 1920s. The Great Migration was less a factor in the growing student population than the rise of what David O. Levine refers to as the "culture of aspiration."

45. William Edwin Taylor to James Weldon Johnson, November 2, 1921, series C, part 12, reel 10, frame 0598, NAACP Papers, University Microfilm series, University of Iowa Law Library; James Weldon Johnson to William Edwin Taylor, November 10, 1921, series C, part 12, reel 10, frame 0600, NAACP Papers on microfilm; James Weldon Johnson to L. M. Brown, November 12, 1921, series C, part 12, reel 10, frame 0604, NAACP Papers on microfilm, James Weldon Johnson to Mrs. Thetha E. Graham, November 12, 1921, series C, part 12, reel 10, frame 0606, NAACP Papers on microfilm.

46. Meyer, *As Long As They Don't Move Next Door*, 6–7.

47. "Colored Students at the State University of Iowa," *Iowa Bystander*, December 19, 1913.

48. *Bystander*, November 6, 1914.

49. *Bystander*, September 12, 1919.

50. "Family Genealogy," The Lemme Family Papers, folder 1, Iowa Women's Archives, Iowa City, IA; Paula Giddings, *In Search of Sisterhood: Delta Sigma Theta and the Challenge of the Black Sorority Movement* (New York, 1988), 74–76.

51. "Minutes of the Twenty-First Annual Convention of the Iowa Federation of Colored Women's Clubs" in Box 1, 1922 Minutes folder, Iowa Federation of Colored Women's Clubs Papers.

52. Paula Giddings, *In Search of Sisterhood,* 16; Paula Giddings, "Delta Sigma Theta Sorority, Incorporated," in Darlene Clark Hine et al., *Black Women in America: An Historical Encyclopedia* (Bloomington, IN, 1994), 319.

53. Jenkins, "The Negro Student at the State University of Iowa," 27.

54. IFCWC Home Brochure, 2, Iowa Federation of Colored Women's Clubs Home File, Iowa Women's Archives.

55. Helen Lemme was a former Fisk University student and graduate of the University of Iowa in 1928. Lemme (whose formal name is Frances H. Renfrow-Lemme) lived in the Federation Home in 1927–1928. After graduation from college, she worked in Iowa City. Lemme Family Papers, Iowa Women's Archives.

56. Jenkins, "The Negro Student at the State University of Iowa," 19.

57. Maenard Wright, telephone interview with the author, March 14, 1999. Wright is the daughter of Frances A. Nance.

58. Sue Brown to Walter Jessup, April 14, 1924, Box 1923–1924, folder 29, Jessup Papers.

59. "Proceedings of the Iowa Federation of Colored Women's Clubs, Thirty-Third and Thirty-Fourth Annual Sessions," 13, Box 1, 1934–1934 Minutes folder, Iowa Federation of Colored Women's Clubs Papers.

60. Paul D. Haughton, telephone interview with the author, March 18, 1999. Haughton was one of the members of Kappa Alpha Psi who lived at 942 Iowa; "Proceedings of the Thirty-Fifth and Thirty-Sixth Annual Sessions of the Iowa Federation of Colored Women's Clubs," 2 and 10, Box 1, 1936–37 Minutes folder, Iowa Federation of Colored Women's Clubs Papers.

61. Madelyne Walls, telephone interview with the author, December 3, 1998.

62. Jenkins, "The Negro Student at the State University of Iowa," 29.

63. Juanita Kidd Stout quoted in Valoree Armstrong, "Judge Recalls UI's Bar of Blacks," *Iowa City Press Citizen,* November 7, 1990; Juanita Kidd Stout vertical folder, University of Iowa Archives.

64. "Contract for Sale of Real Estate, May 24, 1940," Elizabeth "Bettye" Tate Papers, Iowa Women's Archives.

65. Madelyne Walls, telephone interview with the author.

66. Sister Mary Constance Murray, "The Negro Student at the University of Iowa" (Student term paper, State University of Iowa, 1945), 7, University of Iowa Archives, Iowa City, IA.

67. Jenkins, "The Negro Student at the State University of Iowa," 33.

68. Student quoted in Madgetta Dungy, "African American Graduate School Experiences at the University of Iowa, 1937–1959: An Oral History," Ed.D. diss., University of Iowa, 1997, 118. Dungy's study proved to be invaluable as a lead toward general themes for this study.

69. Elizabeth Catlett, letter to the author, January 16, 1999; Samella Lewis, *The Arts of Elizabeth Catlett* (Claremont, CA, 1984), 13.

70. Elizabeth Catlett, letter to the author.

71. Ibid.; Linda Schreiber, "Housemother Sets Rules: Tate Arm's Opens to U of I Students," *Community Advertiser,* August 16, 1995.

72. "[?] Girls Home at Iowa City," *Iowa Bystander,* May 10, 1924, Clipping in Box 1, 1920 Minutes folder; De Mae Lee Fine, "Proceedings of the Twenty-Sec-

ond Annual Session of the Iowa Federation of Colored Women's Clubs," 13, Box 1, 1923 Minutes folder, Iowa Federation of Colored Women's Clubs Papers.

73.   "Seniors Defeat Frosh In Volley Ball Game: Roose, Spencer and Wheeler Star in First Contest of Tournament," November 27, 1923, Newspaper Clipping, Women's PE Department Memory Book, Box 4, Iowa Women's Archives.

74.   "Backwoods People Frolic and Dance," January 30, [192?] and "W.A.A. Holds First Banquet at Youde's Yesterday," May 21, [192?]; Newspaper Clippings, Women's PE Department Memory Book, Box 4, Iowa Women's Archives.

75.   "Beulah Wheeler Wins Contest by Default," *Daily Iowan,* January 12, 1921; "Women to Speak Tonight at 7:30," *Daily Iowan,* January 18, 1921; "Non-Literary Woman Given First Place in Extempore," *Daily Iowan,* January 20, 1921; and "Women's Extemporaneous Contest," *Hawkeye* (1922), 325.

76.   "Our Neighbors: Iowa City Items," *Iowa Bystander,* July 7, 1921.

77.   Drapkin, Harper, Fith, and Monson, "A Century of Caring," 71.

78.   *Des Moines College Yearbook, 1929;* Rekha Basu, "She Left More Than Her Share," *Des Moines Register,* February 13, 1998, Clipping; William Petroski, "Four Women Named to Iowa Hall of Fame," Clipping in Gwendolyn Wilson-Fowler Papers, Iowa Women's Archives.

79.   University of Iowa *Hawkeye* (1924), 305 and 307.

80.   The same year Wheeler won a chevron, Crawford also won a chevron and Mathis earned a "numeral." Women had to receive one honor to win a numeral, two honors to win a chevron, and captains received stars. "Backwoods People Frolic and Dance," January 30, [192?] and "W.A.A. Holds First Banquet at Youde's Yesterday," May 21, [192?]; Newspaper Clippings, Women's PE Department Memory Book, Box 4, Iowa Women's Archives.

81.   "Miss Phyllis Waters," *Iowa Bystander,* June 20, 1917.

82.   Jenkins, "The Negro Student at the State University of Iowa," 30–33.

83.   Gwendolyn Captain and Patricia Vertinsky, "More Myth than History: American Culture and Representations of Black Female Athletic Ability," *Journal of Sports History* 25 (Fall 1998): 542.

84.   Lois Harper-Eichacker, telephone interview with the author, February 9, 1999.

85.   Western Union Telegram to Virginia Harper dated April 26, 1948, Box 1, folder 1, Virginia Harper Papers, Iowa Women's Archives.

86.   Lois Harper-Eichacker Papers, Iowa Women's Archives, Iowa City, IA; Lois Harper-Eichacker, telephone interview with the author, March 17, 1999.

87.   Marjorie H. Parker, *Alpha Kappa Alpha: In the Eye of the Beholder* (Washington, DC, 1979), 183, 185. According to Parker two chapters were established at the University of Iowa: Gamma Pi in 1949 and Epsilon Theta in 1968. However, some women were initiated at the university before the charter, as shown in a Western Union Telegram to Virginia Harper dated April 26, 1948, Virginia Harper Papers, Box 1, folder 1, Iowa Women's Archives.

88.   Martha Scales-Zachary, telephone interview with the author, March 15, 1999.

89. Virginia Harper quoted in S. Kreimer, "Hall of Fame Inductee Reflects on Difficult Past," *Daily Iowan* September 14, 1992, clipping in Virginia Harper Papers, Iowa Women's Archives, Iowa City, IA. Mary Constance Murray confirms this by writing "during the past year for the first time a Negro girl lived at Currier Hall" in "Negro Students at the University of Iowa," 6. In 1946–47, eighteen men also desegregated various dorms on campus also. Leola Bergmann, "Negro Students in the Town Area, 1946–1947," SHSI Archives, Iowa City, IA.

90. Betty Jean Furgerson, telephone interview with the author, March 11, 1999; Martha Scales-Zachary, telephone interview.

91. "The Year in Negro Education, 1930," *Crisis*, August 1930, 262–263; African Americans at the University of Illinois had similar experiences to those at Iowa, particularly in relation to being prohibited from living in dormitories, see Deirdre L. Cobb-Roberts, "Segregated Students at the University of Illinois, 1945–1955," *Journal of the Midwest History of Education Society*, 24 (1997): 46–51, and Joy Ann Williamson, "An Oral History of Black Students at the University of Illinois, 1965–1975," *Journal of the Midwest History of Education Society*, 24 (1997): 94–101.

92. The operations and strategy of the NAACP in the school desegregation process is covered thoroughly in Mark V. Tushnet, *NAACP's Legal Defense Strategy Against Segregated Education, 1925–1950* (Chapel Hill, NC, 1987). For more on *Brown* and the cases that preceded it, see Richard Kluger's *Simple Justice: The History of Brown v. Board of Education and Struggles for Equality* (New York, 1977).

93. Juanita Kidd Stout quoted in *The Road to Brown* (video recording)—a presentation of the University of Virginia; prod. and dir. Mykola Kulish; written by William Elwood, et al., 58 min. San Francisco, CA: California Newsreel, c1990.

94. Peter Boylan, "This Old House an Isle of Pride, Acceptance," *Daily Iowan*, April 18, 2001.

95. The IFCWC printed portions of the minutes in the campus newspaper in 1934. See "Minutes of the Thirty-Third and Thirty-Fourth Annual Convention of the Iowa Federation of Colored Women's Clubs," 6, in Box 1, 1934–35 Minutes folder, Iowa Federation of Colored Women's Clubs Papers, SHSI Archives, Des Moines, IA. Also see "Federation to End Session This Evening," *Daily Iowan*, May 28, 1934, and "Mrs. Lillian Edmunds Heads Iowa Colored Women's Club," *Daily Iowan*, May 30, 1934. Similar coverage did not surface with regard to the Home's closing.

96. Students to the IFCWC, May 27, 1923, "Proceedings of the Twenty-Second Annual Session of the Iowa Federation of Colored Women's Clubs," 20, Box 1, 1923 Minutes folder, Iowa Federation of Colored Women's Clubs Papers. This was signed by Lorraine Crawford, Alberta Greene, Georgia Grigsby, Beulah Wheeler, Corine Mathis, and Lily Williams.

CHAPTER 8

PARADISE LOST?

Teachers' Perspectives on the Use of Cultural Capital in the Segregated Schools of New Orleans, Louisiana

Monica A. White

W. E. B. Du Bois, in one of his most controversial essays, "Does the Negro Need Separate Schools?", published in 1935, concluded that what the Negro needed was neither segregated schools nor mixed schools; rather, "What he needs is Education."[1] This education, to which Du Bois referred, is what black students received in segregated schools, as opposed to the schooling that was received in mixed settings.

> [A] separate Negro school, where children are treated like human beings, trained by teachers of their own race, who know what it means to be black in the year of salvation 1935, is infinitely better than making our boys and girls doormats to be spit and trampled upon and lied to by ignorant social climbers, whose sole claim to superiority is the ability to kick "niggers" when they are down. . . . What he must remember is that there is no magic, either in mixed schools or in segregated schools. A mixed school with poor and unsympathetic teachers with hostile public opinion, and no teaching of truth concerning black folk, is bad. A segregated school with ignorant placeholders, inadequate equipment, poor salaries, and wretched housing, is equally bad.[2]

Cultural Capital and Black Education, pages 143–158
Copyright © 2004 by Information Age Publishing
All rights of reproduction in any form reserved.

Anna Julia Cooper, a progressive African American educator at Washington Colored High School in the late 19th and early 20th centuries, believed that because of desegregation, African American children would no longer be taught racial pride.[3] Ruby Forsythe, one of the "Elder" teachers interviewed by educational anthropologist Michelle Foster in her study of black educators, saw another threat to achievement coming from mixed or integrated schooling. "Instead of seeing black children winning prizes for their achievements, you see them all in special education classes. . . . Instead of being taught to lead, they are being taught to follow."[4] With regard to teacher behaviors after school desegregation, Everett Dawson, another "Elder" in Foster's study, recalled that "The [white] teachers made it clear that blacks were not welcome . . . a lot of young black brothers get into the classes of white instructors who went into the class saying . . . 'these black kids can't make it.'"[5]

Psychologist James Jones noted that many black teachers thought of their students as "apt and intelligent," related well to them, and employed a type of pedagogy that was beneficial to their cognitive and social development.[6] African American educators in New Orleans who worked in separate black schools during the late 1950s and early 1960s report that they and their colleagues felt the same way toward their students. These educators sought to create academic excellence in their teaching of African American children in New Orleans. In a segregated society they engaged in activity fostering social justice and providing important services, as did many other African American professionals of that time. These educators and other professionals made use of the "cultural capital" that was made available to them by parents, community leaders, and the community at large who shared the cultural value that education was the path to freedom.

Educational historian Vanessa Siddle Walker described "valued segregated education" in her book *Their Highest Potential: An African American School Community in the Segregated South* (1996). She found that traditional educational research on segregated schooling in the South tended to focus primarily on the inferior facilities available in separate all-black schools. Her research on the Caswell County schools, however, demonstrated that while failure may seem inherent in academic settings that were underfunded and poorly equipped, those who attended the "black school," as well as the other members of the community, found great value in the local educational institutions. The focus for them was not on what these schools did not have; rather, its students and community members focused on what they did provide—excellent professional services from teachers who lived and worked in the community, an education focused on individual and collective group advancement, and community pride. Walker's findings suggested that the discourse on segregated black schools needs to be expanded to include the increasing evidence of the positive aspects of all-black schooling.[7] Educator Faustine Jones reported in her study of black student achievement in the all-black Dunbar High School in Little Rock, Arkansas, that in spite of the deficiencies of the segregated southern educational system, this black school provided an education that allowed its graduates to go on to establish "successful, satisfying careers. . . ."[8] Faustine Jones further noted that the teachers imbued their students with the motivation to have an "appreciation for knowledge in general, not just subject matter. . . ."[9] The teachers served as "black intellectual role models" and made sure that their charges received more than just information about subject matter, but received a "sense of racial and academic pride."[10]

Maike Philipsen, anthropologist and author of *Values-Spoken and Values-Lived: Race and Cultural Consequences of a School Closing*, echoed the views of educational researcher Jacqueline J. Irvine on the importance of role modeling provided by African American educators prior to the U.S. Supreme Court's *Brown v. Board of Education* decision in May 1954. Irvine argued, "Immediately after emancipation, black educators assumed the unique task of enhancing the opportunities of newly freed slaves . . . to prepare black children for freedom, respectability, independence, and self-reliance." This same theme resonated throughout the South in all-black schools in the first half of the 20th century.[11] Irvine found that despite the horror and violence of the oppressive system of Jim Crow segregation, "a functional, semi-autonomous black community [emerged] with its own peculiar set of rules, norms, sanctions, and rewards. . . ."[12] Black children who were able to attend school were made aware of the necessity for "learning what was taught in school, and the cost of failing to achieve there."[13] This was carried out in an atmosphere of "support, encouragement, and rigid standards" that helped to foster a sense of self-worth among these children.[14] But the educators also warned their students that "a Negro had to be twice as good to get half as far."[15] Thus, despite inadequate materials and supplies, there were external supports for the children in the community and in their homes. Faustine Jones found that the black public school during segregation was enmeshed in a network of supportive family relations, positive church participation, and cohesive community interest.

Social critic bell hooks went even further and argued, in *Teaching to Transgress: Education as the Practice of Freedom*, that "devotion to learning was a counter-hegemonic act, a fundamental way to resist every strategy of white racist colonization."[16] When she was growing up in Hopkinsville, Kentucky, the teachers at her all-black school were "committed to nurturing intellect so that [students] could become scholars, thinkers, and cultural workers—black folks who used [their] 'minds.'"[17] Despite the limitations of the all-black schools, hooks confirmed that the segregated black "classroom . . . remains a location of possibility."[18] Hooks attributed her success to her teachers' attitudes: "My teachers were on a mission."[19] These educators had a keen awareness that in order to fulfill their mission they needed the assistance of others in the community. Thus, these educators made sure that they knew the families and home environments of their students, the churches they attended, and their economic circumstances. Philipsen offered the views of the black director for research on school closings in "Centerville," a pseudonym for a small town in North Carolina. "Teachers of the past are described as having had a mission or as having assumed 'moral responsibility for the education of children.'"[20]

In a study of African Caribbean-Canadian female teachers, educational researcher Annette Henry reached similar conclusions about the practices of African American educators. Although Henry's informants were not part of a *de jure* segregated school system, their philosophy was the same; that "all kids can learn; . . . education is a means of elevating themselves."[21] Henry's informants clearly relied on the cultural capital generated by African Americans' long-held belief in education as a means of self-improvement and collective liberation from continued economic and political exploitation.

The U.S. Supreme Court's *Brown* decision declared legal segregation in public education unconstitutional. This monumental decision called for the desegregation of public education initially just in the southern and border states, then later throughout the country. In southern school districts desegregation not only resulted in the loss of jobs by hundreds of black teachers and principals, but the loss of the supportive educational environments that these educators had created in the all-black schools. According to bell hooks, "school changed utterly with racial integration," that is, the positive things that happened in all-black schools that contributed to success for black children were no longer there.

According to Maike Philipsen, "the Black community as a whole is perceived as having lost education as a vehicle for social mobility . . . they have lost the most powerful tool in the struggle for equality."[22] Historian Karen Johnson, in her study of educators Nannie Burroughs and Anna Julia Cooper, reported that when Cooper was asked her opinion of the *Brown* decision, she responded, "I'm against it. . . . Under the segregated systems, black children were taught to take pride in themselves . . . desegregation meant the loss of race-conscious education."[23]

The "loss" that Anna Julia Cooper spoke about resulted in black students no longer being "challenged academically, and the [black] teacher . . . not [being] challenged professionally."[24] White teachers sometimes feared the black children they were supposed to teach, and so failed to discipline them. Feeling unchallenged, black students did not take their schooling as seriously as they would have under strict, but caring black teachers. Urban educational researcher June Gordon, in *The Color of Teaching*, reported that black teachers believed these white teachers "underestimated [black students'] abilities, didn't know how to work with them, or were just too lazy and didn't care. . . ."[25] Black educators said they felt they could "understand '[their] own kind' better and that there were certain kinds of knowledge that were more easily transmitted by Black teachers to Black children."[26]

Educator Lisa Delpit, in *Other's People Children: Cultural Conflict in the Classroom*, suggested that the issue was "not the kind of instruction, but the attitude underlying it . . . when teachers do not understand the potential of the students they teach, they will underteach them no matter what the methodology."[27] Similarly, psychiatrist James P. Comer argued "those schools that are attuned to the black community's history and needs represent one of the best opportunities to prepare more black youth for successful performances in school and in life."[28] Historians V. P. Franklin, Christopher Span, Adah Ward Randolph, and others have documented the significance of cultural capital for the funding of black schools in the United States from the Reconstruction era to the 1950s. Cultural capital in the form of the material and spiritual resources provided by members of the African American community allowed black teachers and principals to create positive educational environments for their students. Cultural capital was important for the creation of "valued segregated schooling." But how did cultural capital operate in the day-to-day experiences of African American educators in all-black schools? What aspects of this educational experience were "lost" with the coming of public school desegregation?

RECOLLECTIONS AND PERCEPTIONS
OF ALL-BLACK SCHOOLING

This study focuses on New Orleans, Louisiana, during the late 1950s and throughout the 1960s, when the transition from *de jure* segregation to *de facto* segregation took place in the city's public schools. New Orleans public school teachers and students were subjected to a violent and disruptive desegregation process that commenced in one of the city's poorest sections, the Ninth Ward. The informants in this study were young teachers or students in the New Orleans public schools during the implementation of the desegregation process. Eight participants were initially selected to take part in the study; six responded positively. To maintain their anonymity, each is given a pseudonym. The former teacher participants are Yolanda, Russell, Elaine, and Vicki. The two other participants, Carol and Debra, were students during that period.[29]

An interview protocol was prepared prior to the actual informant interviews. This protocol was based on the issues and topics raised during their interviews with African American educators in the studies conducted by

Michelle Foster, Vanessa Siddle Walker, bell hooks, and June Gordon (see Table 8.1).[30] The questions were used to encourage the informants to recreate details from their pasts and provide a "thick description" of the period (people, educational attitudes, and outcomes) for African American students and teachers in New Orleans. Phil F. Carspecken, in *Critical Ethnography in Educational Research: A Theoretical and Practical Guide*, recommended the use of thick description to "capture a lot of detail . . . for selected periods of time . . ." from interviewees.[31] In addition to reconstructing the past, the questions were utilized to secure each individual's own stories and to infuse their voices throughout the dialogue and discussion. The questions, which appear in Table 8.1, were used as probes in seeking connections between past teacher practices found to be successful in the all-black schools and those activities recommended by the current school reforms.

Table 8.1.   The Interview Protocol

- Tell me about your career in education.

- What was your teacher-training program like? How is it similar/dissimilar to current teacher education programs? Who/what do you credit as the source of what you were able to perform in the classroom?

- Tell me about your students. Their parents? Their participation and involvement? Their achievements? Memorable situations, your relationship with each, etc.

- Describe your role as a teacher. What has been your goal as an educator? How successful were you in that role?

- What were some of the difficult things you had to deal with?

- How do you describe the culture and climate of the schools that you have worked in during the 1960s? What is your assessment of the culture and climate now? Explain.

- How was education regarded during your teaching profession? How were teachers regarded during your teaching profession? Compare that to today's situation. What do you think happened? Explain.

- What do you remember about the desegregation process? What were the effects in your classroom practices, students, parents, community, etc.?

- What practices of teachers are no longer in place that were successful during your tenure? Why are these not common practices any longer?

As with Walker's study of Caswell County Training School, this study builds upon the foundation of previous scholars who have quantified the "success" of all-black schools by using external factors, such as rates of attendance and graduation. In this study, however, more value is attached to identifying the self-defined variables of success that arose from earlier interviews with African American educators.[32] Some of those self-defined variables include student and parent participation, teacher expectations, the importance of school activities, and community support. This study describes the community's positive assessment of these all-black schools and their teachers, and reveals some of the environmental factors that were important in allowing black teachers to produce educational success for their students.[33]

It should be pointed out that the reasons given for educational success in the 1960s resonate with the current theories about the way African American children should be educated. The *Brown* decision sought to end the inequities in all-black schools in comparison to their white counterparts. Instead, the effect was to label the black schools as "inherently inferior" and the burden of desegregation was placed on black children. Thus, if schools were going to be integrated, then African Americans would have to leave their schools and attend or teach in formerly all-white schools. After all, why would the whites, or anyone for that matter, choose to go to a school labeled inferior? This reality, according to some of the informants, had an extremely negative effect on black public schools in New Orleans. Furthermore, they reported that this situation decreased the status of the African American teacher as a leader in the community.

The informants in this study also commented on the New Orleans public schools at the height of the civil rights struggle and those same schools in the 1990s. The poor physical conditions in the all-black public schools served as one of the reasons for pursuing an end to legal segregation. Inadequate supplies, deteriorating physical plants, hand-me-down books, and other materials from all-white schools served as a major indictment of black public education in New Orleans. However, these same conditions existed in the 1990s in the "desegregated" public schools in New Orleans, where African Americans make up over 90 percent of the student population. However, the situation in the 1990s is actually worse than the situation in the 1960s because the all-black public schools in the earlier period had large numbers of respected, committed black educators who utilized cultural capital from the black community to produce educational success for their students.

EDUCATIONAL THEMES

The participants' responses supported several themes related to teacher practices that have been discussed in the works of James P. Comer, Lisa Delpit, Michelle Foster, Janice Hale-Benson, Asa Hilliard, and bell hooks. Eight predominant themes emerged and were recurrent throughout the interviews and discussions (see Table 8.2). The respondents reflected upon the educational practices of the past and compared them to their observations of the current situation.

Table 8.2.

Emergent Themes	1960s De Jure Segregated Schools	1990s De Facto Segregated Schools
Teachers' sense of mission	**Collective.** Teachers felt individually and collectively responsible for student success.	**Fragmented.** The sense of personal responsibility is not a part of every teacher's personal praxis.
Standard of professionalism	Teachers were well respected in the community, and role models to students as well as community.	Teachers are not highly regarded in community because of low pay and influx of external factors out of their control.
Parents	**Insider.** Home visits were encouraged. Parents were welcomed in schools and seen as a help to teachers.	**Outsider.** Home visits are discouraged. School environment not welcoming to parents, but parents are verbally encouraged to visit.
Standards and Accountability	**Self-governed.** Course content based on identified needs of students. Accountable to families and communities.	**Externally controlled.** Course content is heavily regulated by the use of standardized testing in state accountability system.
Teaching practices	**Differentiated** instruction employed.	**Whole-group** instruction primarily. Individual needs of students often met in special programs rather than home classroom.
Curriculum	Teachers gave students what they needed to survive in a world that was primarily against them.	Teachers primarily gave students what was in prescribed curriculum and some of what they needed to survive in a world that was primarily against them.
Leadership	**Ownership.** School-site administrators made decisions that were unique to school sites and implemented ongoing professional development.	**Detachment.** School-site administrators have little autonomy in making individual decisions and professional development programs are relegated to add-on programs and "sit and get" sessions.
Knowledge	**Transformational.** Teachers used knowledge as a mechanism of liberation.	**Informational.** Teachers view knowledge as subject matter information only—"covering standards."

Teachers' sense of mission. Each of the informants recalled that black teachers prior to desegregation had a unity of purpose, and collectively they faced a common enemy—racial oppression. Black teachers at that time felt a moral obligation to prepare each student for success in facing the challenges of discrimination in a racially segregated world.

Standard of professionalism. Within all-black neighborhoods the teachers were considered "pillars" in the community. They were respected as professionals and conducted their daily routines in nothing less than a professional manner.

Parents. Segregated schools were closely tied to the community, and parents were encouraged to be partners with the teachers in the education of children. Conversely, in many public schools currently, an adversarial relationship has developed between parents and teachers.

Standards and accountability. The standards-based curriculum and testing movement of the 1990s has significantly decreased the amount of autonomy that teachers have in deciding what to teach their students. In the 1950s and 1960s teachers made professional decisions about what was taught in classrooms. However, they were held accountable to the parents, and held themselves responsible as well for the success of their students.

Teaching practices. Black teachers in segregated schools reported that there was little use made of a "special education" designation for children. Students with special needs were provided services on an individual basis while maintaining high standards for all children to achieve. Currently, students are often placed in special programs, but their special needs may not be addressed due to insufficient resources. The common practice among many current teachers, according to the informants who are still in the classroom, is to teach toward the middle, that is, the average student. Therefore, the high-achieving and low-performing students do not receive the attention they need.

Curriculum. Unlike the current externally mandated course requirements, determined by state guidelines and geared toward standardized tests, the curriculum in the past was informed by teachers' knowledge of the world facing the students they taught, and their desire to equip them appropriately for success in it.

Leadership. American society today is more litigious than in the past. School site administrators do not have as much control in staffing decisions, course requirements, and educational content as in the past. With teacher unionization, principals' ability to require professional development classes and other types of preparation for teachers outside of the workday decreased.

Knowledge. Prior to *Brown* and in the years immediately following, formal education was viewed as the key to improving the family's lifestyle. African American children were schooled in hopes of not only improving themselves, but their families as well. Currently, that desire for collective advancement is no longer as pervasive. Individual educational achievement is viewed as benefiting primarily the individual. Moreover, societal changes requiring more and more credentials have made it difficult for parents and educators to convince young African Americans that increased formal schooling is the best way to improve their status in life.

The respondents reported that the success of the teachers, despite the poor educational conditions in the 1960s, was due to a strong sense of commitment, a shared collective vision, a desire for freedom from oppressive conditions, and high professional standards. Other prominent themes that emerged from the interviews included concerns about the educational environment, administrator characteristics, and parental and community involvement.

EMERGENT THEMES

Collective Sense of Mission

Some African American teachers would work before and after school hours for the betterment of their students. Yolanda emphatically stated, "It was the commitment. Teachers then knew that [for] the kids they worked with, education was their ticket out. So they [the teachers] took it personally."[34] A collective mission fueled this sense of commitment. Black social critic bell hooks believed her teachers were on a mission. The responses from the participants support this notion of the teachers' missionary zeal. For example, Carol, one of the former student participants, recalled that, "Our teachers used to encourage us and tell us the things we needed to know. . . . Our teachers gave us a lot. They talked to us and told us what we needed to succeed. See those children in the integrated schools didn't get that."[35] Additionally, when asked about the teachers' training, Yolanda noted that those teachers who attended Normal School understood that "they had one way to get out of poverty and that was education." Yolanda recalled that her high school English teacher is remembered well for encouraging her students to challenge what they thought they believed. For example, Yolanda remembered that, "we had debates in class. One topic [I was asked to debate was] 'It is futile to go to college.' I knew that she knew I was going to go to college so I asked her why she would have me to take that position. She insisted that I take that position in order to dig deeper and challenge my thoughts about what I thought about going to school." The comments from this informant made it clear that this teacher did not allow students to make hasty decisions, regardless of how noble they appeared, and the students were challenged to examine why they held their beliefs.

When asked how that is different from what currently occurs in many classrooms, Elaine identified it as a "lack of compassion and understanding." Yolanda concurred, "the demographics are the same, but the results are different because of the *level of commitment of teachers*." Moreover, all students were taught. There were no special education classes. "As teachers, whatever the deficiencies were, we handled them." Russell similarly notes that, "The older teachers had a serious commitment to help students, to encourage young people to get professional degrees. A lot of our students went on to become successful people. . . . We came early and stayed late. We met kids early and stayed after school. . . . We dealt with all of the kids too."[36]

But, things changed, and according to the responses of the participants, desegregation was the line of demarcation. Yolanda described it as a "disturbing trend." She recalls:

> There was a disturbing trend in education with desegregation. The talks in the lounge used to be "'lil' Maya is not getting such and such in my class. She is fidgety. . . ." Then someone else would say, "Oh, this is what you have to do for lil' Maya. Because I tried this with her and it worked." But after integration, it was more like, "'lil' Maya is cutting up. She doesn't want to do the work, something must be wrong with her." See the white teachers would put black children down and the young black teachers would take on the traits of the oppressors. . . . Black teachers took on different views of black children. It was us, all of us, teachers and students. After integration, it was us [the teachers] and them [the students]. And that changed everything because the expectations weren't the same . . . [Integration] lowered the expectations for black children.

Russell noted that to help the situation, the district paid $3,000 to northern teachers to come to the South to work. He says that the northern recruits were good people, but he recalls having to "tell [them] . . . that teaching is not social work." He also felt that they came wanting to show African American children "how sorry they were" about their conditions. The difference between the African American teachers and these recruits was that although they felt sorry for them as well, the black teachers knew the way to change things for them and their families was through "education." Russell defines what he meant by "education" for these students: "having a definition of themselves as bright, intellectual young people who can become something."[37]

Vicki's philosophy of teaching is similar. She noted that when she integrated the faculty of a previously all-white elementary school, her first thought was "You have to know who you are because if you know who you are, then you are able to work with people, children in particular." This philosophy guided her practice. She declared, "I never wanted to lose sight of who I was . . . my background was too important." Currently, this mission is diminishing among African American teachers because, as Russell noted about the younger generation of teachers, "You don't have that as a goal. You feel the society is [already] integrated. And you have arrived. We were trying to overcome the constraints of segregation. . . . We had hope that our legacy was the children's success."

Yolanda, Russell, and Vicki's comments illustrate the use of "sociocultural theory" in the classrooms. Their examples provide the rationale for this theory, which "emphasizes that human intelligence originates in our society or culture, and individual cognitive gain occurs first through interpersonal (interaction with social environment), then intrapersonal (internalization) [relationships]."[38] That is, these teachers went into classrooms with an in-depth knowledge of who they were, but also who the children were—their homes, their likes and dislikes, and their interests. Although their backgrounds were not necessarily the same as their students, in many instances they were astute enough to use their knowledge about the students to assist them in giving the children what they needed.

The Spirit of Professionalism

The teachers interviewed by June Gordon in *The Color of Teaching* reported that "the status and image of teachers were based on the African American experience in the South from the Post-Reconstruction 1880s to the 1950s, . . . when teaching was viewed as the most productive way to bring about the 'uplift of the race.'"[39] The participants in this study recognized a shift in perceptions about the teaching profession as a result of public school desegregation. They mentioned several examples of peer coaching and mentoring and the use of model lessons. Russell describes one of the strategies to assist new or struggling teachers:

> We had what we called the "circuit chairmen." That's when you have one outstanding teacher and about five new teachers grouped together. In these circuits, this is where you got your problems resolved as a new teacher and were mentored on campus. . . . The circuit chairman observed our classes. When we [new teachers] were off, we would visit the master teachers and see how it's supposed to be done.

Yolanda offered a similar observation about the training of new teachers.

> I would propose after 4 years in a Bachelor's program in education that an individual work as an "intern," where the teacher works part of the day with a master teacher. While the teacher is working with a rotation [of master teachers] on various levels, the next year [he or she would] decide on a specialty. The master teacher will pull back more. The teacher may even have a class where she [or he] is responsible for records [and other things].

She notes that this is not an original proposal, for it is similar to what her principal did for new teachers in the 1950s.

Others noted that their experiences with mentors represented hard work and a challenge. Elaine recalls her training to become a principal under an African American male administrator who was well respected in the school district and in the community. She noted, " He was my mentor. He worked me extraordinarily hard."

The respondents discussed school administrators who commanded great respect and served as models of professionalism in the all-black schools. When asked how and why they earned this admiration, Yolanda related the following: "Parents saw [this black principal] at the end of the day standing in the middle of [the avenue] helping the teachers escort students across the avenue to their homes. . . . She had standards and that did a lot for the people in the neighborhood. You knew how committed and serious she was." It was further noted that educators were true "leaders in the community. . . . They were pillars of the church and community. They were elevated to positions of esteem."

Parent and Community Involvement

Since "cultural capital" is defined as the resources that various members of the African American community supplied to support black schooling or other enterprises, the time, energy, and commitment of black teachers was an important resource in the success of many segregated black schools. In my interviews with informants, they also discussed specific instances and areas where parental and community involvement became an important resource—cultural capital—for underwriting the success of these schools.

Elaine noted that when she was selected to integrate the faculty of a previously all-white school, the type and level of parental involvement differed. The all-white schools were usually stocked with the necessary supplies and materials; therefore, activities no longer took place that brought African American parents to school and involved them in things good for their children. Some of those activities included sponsoring "penny parties" to raise money for materials, having "room mothers" to assist in getting more parents involved in school activities, and involving pastors from neighboring churches who often gave their support.

Similarly, Vicki noted that families often supplemented education with activities at home. Her own experiences with being raised close to her grandmother and having "lessons" in science in their garden or at the dinner table prepared her for understanding the importance of family and community in southern black life. While many of these families had limited formal education, they were able to provide their children with "hands-on" learning experiences upon which classroom teachers were able to build.

In addition to providing support for the classroom practices of these African American teachers, the family and community served as resources in their training to become teachers. Many of the participants credited their churches and families for providing them with the knowledge and skills needed to teach African American youth in such a tumultuous time as the 1960s when the New Orleans public schools were being desegregated. Elaine proudly recalls her many speaking parts in church services under the watchful eyes and ears of the "mothers of the church" and the admonitions from her father to always seek the best. Because of both, she concludes, she knew that she could become successful and would commit to teaching others in her community, an economically impoverished area in New Orleans, to do the same.

Debra, growing up in the Ninth Ward, a poor neighborhood, described the conditions in the local all-black school. Having a large family and being one of the youngest meant that teachers and administrators already knew her before she arrived. She recalls her family was poor, but that did not prevent her parents from participating in activities organized by the African American teachers. Sometimes that participation involved sending things to school for fairs, contests, or other fundraising activities, escorting the children walking to school to ensure their safe arrival. Most of the students in her school were poor, Debra recalls, but parents were always supporting them in activities either with their presence or by making sure their children were present.

CONCLUSION

This study utilized oral interviews with African American educators and former students in the New Orleans public schools in the 1950s and 1960s to identify the types of resources that existed in all-black schools that helped to produce educational success for African American students. Following the path of several earlier researchers on the topic of "valued segregated education," this study also found that in spite of the horrific conditions of Jim Crow or legal segregation, the African American community and family pulled together to supplement the meager educational resources and materials provided by the state.

The themes repeated in these interviews were a high standard of professionalism and collective sense of mission among teachers, parental and community involvement, and culturally relevant curricula and teaching practices. The principals and other administrators provided exemplary leadership and often worked closely with other community leaders. While these persons and conditions cannot be reproduced, the lessons learned from these encounters have relevance to the current challenges to African American educators in today's *de facto* segregated schools.

Cultural capital, in the form of the teachers' collective sense of mission, spirit of professionalism, mentoring and role modeling, and standing in the community, was considered important for educational success in the all-black schools. Perhaps African American educators can mobilize this resource once again in their efforts to produce increased academic achievement for African American children currently attending urban public schools.

NOTES

1. W. E. B. Du Bois, "Does the Negro Need Separate Schools?" in *The Oxford W. E. B. Du Bois Reader,* ed. Eric J. Sundquist (New York, 1996), 431.

2. Ibid.

3. Karen Johnson, *Uplifting the Women and the Race: The Educational Philosophies and Social Activism of Anna Julia Cooper and Nannie Helen Buroughs* (New York, 2000).

4. Michelle Foster, *Black Teachers on Teaching* (New York, 1997), xxxiv.

5. Ibid.

6. James Jones, "Psychological Knowledge and the New American Dilemma of Race," *Journal of Science Issues* 54 (No. 4, 1998): 641–642.

7. Vanessa Siddle Walker, *Their Highest Potential: An African American School Community in the Segregated South* (Chapel Hill, NC, 1996).

8. Faustine Jones, *A Traditional Model of Educational Excellence* (Washington, DC, 1981), 6.

9. Ibid., 48.

10. Ibid., 49.

11. Philipsen, *Values-Spoken and Values-Lived: Race and the Cultural Consequences of a School Closing* (Cresskill, NJ, 1999), 59.

12. Ibid.

13. Jones, "Psychological Knowledge," 71.

14. Walker, *Their Highest Potential,* 3.

15. Jones, "Psychological Knowledge," 71.

16. bell hooks, *Teaching to Transgress: Education as the Practice of Freedom* (New York, 1994), 4.

17. Ibid, 2.

18. Ibid., 207.

19. Ibid., 2.

20. Philipsen, *Values-Spoken, Values-Lived,* 60.

21. Annette Henry, *Taking Back Control: African Canadian Women Teachers' Lives and Practice* (Albany, NY, 1998).

22.   Philipsen, *Values-Spoken, Values-Lived*, 69.

23.   Johnson, *Uplifting the Women and the Race*, 89.

24.   June Gordon, *The Color of Teaching* (London, 2000).

25.   Ibid., 69.

26.   Ibid.

27.   Lisa Delpit, *Other People's Children: Cultural Conflict in the Classroom* (New York, 1995), 175.

28.   Johnson, *Uplifting the Women and the Race*, 73.

29.   It should be noted here that the author's personal experiences, knowledge of school district history, and observations as a teacher in the New Orleans Public School were utilized during the analysis of interview data to provide a measure of comparison.

30.   Foster, *Black Teachers on Teaching;* Gordon, *The Color of Teaching;* hooks, *Teaching to Transgress;* Walker, *Their Highest Potential.*

31.   Phil F. Carspecken, *Critical Ethnography in Educational Research* (New York, 1996), 46.

32.   Walker, *Their Highest Potential*, 4.

33.   Ibid., 5.

34.   Interview with the author, New Orleans, LA, March 17, 2001.

35.   Ibid.

36.   Interview with the author, New Orleans, LA, March 25, 2001.

37.   Interview with the author, New Orleans, LA, April 1, 2001.

38.   Jy Wana Daphne Lin Hsiao, "Vygotsky's Sociocultural Theory," *CSCL Theories;* Available: www.edb.utexas.edu/csclstudent/Dhsiao/theories.html#vygot.

39.   Gordon, *The Color of Teaching*, 20.

CHAPTER 9

SOCIAL CAPITAL, CULTURAL CAPITAL, AND THE CHALLENGE OF AFRICAN AMERICAN EDUCATION IN THE 21ST CENTURY

V.P. Franklin

There is a little known statistic that needs to be more widely publicized. While the U.S. news media have been broadcasting the fact that people of African descent have been surpassed by Spanish-speaking citizens as the largest ethnic minority, a more important reality at the dawn of the 21st century is that U.S. African Americans are the wealthiest, most highly educated, and most influential African people in the world. Unfortunately, in many ways this is a dubious distinction because despite their wealth, influence, and education, U.S. African Americans are also victimized by the negative effects of globalization and the expansion of multinational corporate capitalism. The widespread health problems and obesity among U.S. African Americans, the low levels of academic achievement for urban black youth, and the extremely high rates of incarceration for black men and women are symptoms of U.S. African Americans' victimization by the profit-driven decisions made by right-wing politicians and their corporate capitalist sponsors. While most of the people in Asia, South America, the

Cultural Capital and Black Education, pages 159–171
Copyright © 2004 by Information Age Publishing
159

Caribbean, and Africa are the victims of globalization and the exploitative advances of multinational corporate capitalism, U.S. African Americans, resident within the boundaries of the only remaining "superpower," should be in a much better position to do something to change and improve these conditions. Indeed, U.S. African Americans need to mobilize their intellectual and material resources—cultural capital—to counter the negative effects of multinational corporate capitalism on the minds and bodies of African American children.

CONFRONTING THE AIDS, OBESITY AND PRISON EPIDEMICS

There are many serious problems facing African American children and youth as we enter the new century. Many recent reports have focused on the low levels of academic achievement among lower and middle income black students; however, there are other, even more life-threatening issues and problems that need to be addressed. Currently, the rate of HIV infection among African American youth under age 30 is significantly higher than for European, Hispanic, or Asian Americans of the same age. It is likely that the widespread denial in the African American community during the first decade of the epidemic, and the failure to assist and protect our children who are suffering from AIDS, helps to explain the continued rise in the number of HIV infections among African American youth. Many physicians, public health officials, and other medical personnel have asked: Why do we have such high levels of HIV infection among African Americans under the age of 30? Why are AIDS education programs and "safe sex" messages not working for African American youth?[1]

There are very likely many complex reasons for this deadly state of affairs, but we must not rule out the likelihood that the denials and condemnations of those persons in the African American community with AIDS, and who are HIV positive, by black spokespersons and religious leaders during the first 15 years of the epidemic did not help the situation, nor do the negative portrayals and stereotypes about black youth in general, and black males in particular. African American organizations and other agencies need to develop more effective AIDS education programs for African American children and young adults with an emphasis on the need for our children to protect themselves in order to fulfill their destinies as contributing adults and leaders among African people throughout the world.[2]

Unfortunately, for black boys in contemporary American society, if you are not a star athlete or a rap singer, your career options are extremely limited since the only other path upward involves attending and graduating from high school, college, or professional school, and many black boys do not like school. If success in school does not appear to be a possibility, then a cynical fatalism is bound to replace any hope for the future. Given the absence of alternatives presented by the larger society, it is no wonder that more African American males between age 18 and 30 are caught up in the penitentiary system than are enrolled in institutions of higher education. Thus, in addition to the AIDS epidemic, African American children must confront the "prison epidemic" and the increasing likelihood that they will fall victim to the exploitative advances of the "prison-industrial complex" in the United States.[3]

There has recently arisen a new and serious threat to the health and well-being of African American children in the 21st century. For all American children and adults, but particularly for poor African Americans, obesity has developed to life-threatening proportions. Larger and larger numbers of children have been raised on a diet of "fast foods"—pizza, hamburgers, french fries and other fried foods, shakes, and sodas—and as a result, obesity has reached epidemic proportions among adult Americans, and one out of every four American children under age 12 is considered obese. This situation has led to the unprecedented development of numerous cases of non-insulin-dependent diabetes mellitus or Type II diabetes, hypertension, and heart disease among American children. Among poor African American children, the rates of obesity and Type II diabetes have reached epidemic proportions.[4]

WHY ARE WE HERE?

Given these conditions, one might ask: Why have adult members of the African American community failed to meet our responsibilities to protect our children and prepare them for the future? There are numerous possible answers to this question, but the one that I wish to address here is African Americans' increased integration into the larger society in the post–civil rights period. In other words, greater integration into the larger society may have created more problems for African American families and youth than it solved. As a result of the civil rights campaigns of the 1950s and 1960s, and the passage of the Civil Rights Act of 1964 and the Voting Rights Act of 1965, the constitutional barriers to African American and other minority groups' participation in the society as first-class (rather than second- or third-class) citizens were lifted. One of the major results of these struggles for integration has been the movement of significant percentages of African American families and individuals into the American middle class.[5]

Integration has allowed us to accomplish many things, and we certainly do not intend to give up any of the rights and privileges we have struggled to obtain. But we must also admit that integration has been problematic in many areas. The demise of excellent black schools and other cultural institutions has been one result, but even more importantly, with integration many African Americans came to believe that the government would assume responsibility for protecting the health, physical, and intellectual well-being of African American children, and for preparing them for their role as contributing adults in American society. Unfortunately, given the political and economic realities of American society, Democratic and Republican politicians (black and white) have not only abdicated that responsibility, but have acted in a manner that facilitates the exploitation of African American and other children by national and international corporate capitalists. Far from being an end in itself, integration should be considered a means through which the African American population in the United States struggles to achieve its collective vision. Historically, that collective vision has been defined by how we answer the question, Why are we here?

Since the legal enslavement of African Americans was outlawed in 1865, generations of African American leaders, professionals, and average citizens have debated and provided possible answers to this important question. For those socially and culturally aware African Americans who reached adulthood before and during the civil rights era, there were generally two answers given to this question.[6] Many African Americans decided that the reason why black people are here is "to save white America from itself." This integrationist vision is captured in the slogan taken as the theme for the conference that led to the creation of the Southern Christian Leadership Conference (SCLC) in February 1957 in New Orleans. For Martin Luther King, Jr., and the thousands of African Americans who participated in the nonviolent direct action protests that took place throughout the United States in the 1950s and 1960s, black people are here "To Redeem the Soul of America."[7]

While this was a worthy objective in 1957, it is hardly appropriate for the new millennium. Today for those "white" Americans who believe they have a soul, it could hardly be redeemed by a group of people who, by every indication coming from the popular media, is morally, spiritually, and intellectually deficient. Indeed, many have argued that it is Black America's soul that needs redeeming![8]

The second most popular answer given by earlier generations to the question "Why are we here?" was "to save ourselves" and thus serve as an example and model for other oppressed peoples throughout the world. This was the black nationalist response. From Marcus Garvey and the Universal Negro Improvement Association in the 1920s through Elijah Muhammad's Nation of Islam, Malcolm X's Organization of Afro-American Unity, and the "Black Power" organizations of the 1960s and 1970s, many African Americans believed that their survival and advancement "in the belly of the beast" could serve as a beacon of hope to colonized and oppressed people of color throughout the world struggling to obtain freedom and self-determination.[9]

Unfortunately, this black militant response has been severely undermined in the new millennium by many self-proclaimed black nationalists, particularly those who specialize in rap music, and give the younger generation the impression that to be "nationalist" and "militant' is to be anti-intellectual, male chauvinist, sexist, anti-Semitic, and homophobic. The sexist and homophobic lyrics and remarks attributed to gangsta rappers and other so-called militant black nationalists undercut the credibility of black nationalist and Afro-centric approaches to solving our problems.[10]

Those who lived through the turbulent 1960s and the sometimes painful transit from civil rights protests to Black Power demands should be able to relate their personal perspectives to this characterization of the issues then under debate, but members of both the older and the younger generation must recognize the current realities: Not only have we failed to inform the young people that they should be hotly debating their answers to the question, "Why are we here?," but we have not really prepared them to implement any of the responses they may wish to pursue. It is the older generations that have failed in its responsibility to prepare the young people for the challenges that African Americans face in the 21st century. That is why there is a critical need for a new educational organization that will assume a leadership position in preparing African American children for their future.

THE CRISIS IN LEADERSHIP

There is a critical need for the creation of a new educational organization to address the crisis for African American children because of the leadership crisis that currently exists in African American communities throughout the United States. The absence of committed, principled, and group-conscious black leaders in the post-civil rights-Black Power era would be striking if not for the general leadership crisis in the United States at large. But this situation is particularly noticeable and harmful in African American communities because the quality of independent leadership provided by preachers, professors, publishers, and even politicians, such as Harlem's Adam Clayton Powell, Jr., was impressive and often inspirational. In the post–civil rights era, however, two dominant leadership groups exist, but they have been unable to use their increased political resources and connections to corporate institutions and philanthropic foundations to address the life-threatening conditions facing African American children.

There is no need to ask these leaders to shift their priorities to focus primarily on the education of African American youth in the new millennium because they have other issues and priorities, and their search for benefactors and financial resources takes up increasing amounts of their time.[11]

The two current leadership groups—the black political establishment and the civil rights–social welfare establishment—emerged in the 1970s, but similar leadership configurations existed in the 19th and early 20th centuries.[12] The black political establishment includes black elected officials and political appointees. While they have an important role to assume in the education of African American children, this is not and should not be their primary responsibility. The civil rights–social welfare establishment includes groups such as the NAACP, the Urban League, and the Children's Defense Fund, as well as the other secular and religious organizations and foundations that assume a leadership position in defining the civil rights and social welfare objectives for African Americans. Many of these groups have taken a leadership position in defining the objectives of "schooling" for African Americans, but what is needed is a new group that will have access to "cultural capital" that will focus on the "education" of African American children in the new century.

One of the primary educational objectives for this new leadership organization would be to prepare African American children (and adults) for their leadership position in the African world. In other words, this new leadership group would be committed to closing the "responsibility gap" that currently exists between the actual position that African Americans occupy in the world and the present focus of their educational strategies, objectives, programs, and institutions for African American children. In doing so this new group would be providing a 21st century answer to a question that African Americans have been asking since we arrived on these shores, but more urgently since the end of our legal enslavement: "Why are we here?" In providing answers to this fundamental question, this new leadership group would be assisting our children in determining their own individual destinies.

THE AFRICAN AMERICAN COUNCIL ON EDUCATION

The formation of the African American Council on Education (AACE) is recommended to address these pressing issues. The main purpose of AACE would be to prepare African American children for the leadership positions they will hold among the oppressed peoples in the world in the 21st century. To accomplish this goal, AACE must remain independent of the Democratic, Republican, or any other political party. This would allow the organization to make public statements critical of both Democrats and

Republicans, black and white, and their corporate sponsors who may be involved in activities that are damaging to the physical and mental well-being of African American children.

The model for the AACE should be that of Martin Luther King's Southern Christian Leadership Conference (SCLC). But we must also learn from the mistakes in the past. Like SCLC, it should not be open to individual membership, only groups would be able to affiliate with AACE. However, unlike SCLC, AACE would not be the vehicle for a charismatic leader; rather, its policies would be determined by a revolving executive committee made up of representatives from the various organizations affiliated with the Council. Indeed, membership on this "executive committee" could be reserved for the representatives from the various professional organizations and other groups that will provide the expertise and resources for the social and educational programs sponsored by AACE. In other words, representatives of African American social work organizations, the lawyers groups, the doctors, the educators, psychologists, business groups, sororities, fraternities, athletes, social scientists, artists, musicians, historians, and urban affairs groups that are affiliated with AACE will make decisions about the organization's policies and projects. AACE would thus be in a position to provide the best professional advice and resources for dealing with the specific social, economic, and educational problems facing our children, and make recommendations and design interventions based on the latest and most thorough knowledge and research.

AACE must *not* get bogged down pursuing the myth of "black unity." Even during slavery times there were some Africans and African Americans who opposed black self-determination and any attempts to change the relationship between the oppressed and oppressors. We never have and never will achieve "unity" on any single issue or program. However, AACE will seek "solidarity" with a wide range of groups and organizations across the social and political spectrum that express a willingness to assist its membership in making a change in the lives of black children in this country.

As was the case with collective black economic enterprises in the past as documented in this volume, the AACE would be able to draw upon "cultural capital" to augment the "social capital" in African American communities to support educational activities aimed at protecting and preparing African American children for their roles and responsibilities in the 21st century. Given the social, economic, political, and cultural issues facing African American children at the beginning of the new century, AACE's objective would be to generate and use cultural capital to support the implementation of culturally salient models of schooling for African American children. There are numerous models of effective schooling for African American children and the experts associated with AACE would work with parents,

teachers, and administrators in school systems around the country to intro-
duce innovative approaches to improve academic achievement levels.[13]

While AACE would work to disseminate information about models of
effective "schooling" for African American children, the organization
would also focus its resources on their broader "education" in the home,
neighborhood, and larger community. Educational historian Lawrence A.
Cremin wrote numerous books on the education of the American people
and described the various public and private elementary, secondary, and
higher educational institutions opened in the United States. At the same
time, Cremin was also interested in telling the story of how individuals,
groups, and communities were "educated" in American society. Cremin
defined education as "the deliberate, systematic, and sustained effort to
transmit, evoke or acquire knowledge, values, attitudes, skills, or sensibili-
ties, as well as any learning that results from the effort, direct or indirect,
intended or unintended." While this definition is very broad and all-
encompassing, in his massive three-volume history of American education,
Cremin focused specifically on the "changing configurations of education
at different times in American history and the various ways in which individuals have interacted with those configurations."[14]

In my book *The Education of Black Philadelphia* (1979), I examined the
public and private schooling that was available to African Americans in the
city in the first half of the 20th century, as well as the formal and informal
educational programs sponsored by black social, political, and cultural
institutions. To use Lawrence Cremin's terminology, I attempted to
describe the "educational configurations" for the Philadelphia black community between 1890 and 1950. In some instances the educational programs offered by African American cultural institutions were organized to
inform the community about ways to deal with the problems in schooling
for African Americans in the city, such as the absence of black teachers and
principals in public secondary schools, the official practice of segregating
black students, and the absence of African American history in the elementary and secondary school curricula.[15]

The point is that there is so much more to the "education" of African
American children than what takes place in public or private schools. Thus,
while AACE would focus on the important task of improving the academic
achievement levels of African American children, the parents, educators,
and other professionals associated with the group would also make sure that
African American children become "educated" in the responsibilities that
they must assume as adults and contributing members of American society,
and as leaders among African peoples in the world. At the dawn of the 21st
century (whether we chose to acknowledge this reality or not), African
Americans in the United States are the wealthiest, best educated, and most
influential African people in the world, and African American children

must be challenged and inspired to fulfill the responsibilities that come with that leadership position. For developing the most appropriate educational strategies and programs to prepare our children for their position in the world, cultural capital becomes an important economic resource.

THE TWELVE TO TWENTY PROGRAMS

The professionals associated with AACE would be free to apply their expertise to any problems facing African American youth. At the same time, it would be an understatement to say that in most large urban areas, the social conditions for many black youths have moved beyond the control of their families, the schools, and even the police. In the battle between the streets and the community for the minds and hearts of too many of our young people, the streets have won—hands down. The fact that the vast majority of African American children are being raised by a single parent, usually the mother, who must also work to support herself and her family, helps explain why these young people are being socialized primarily by the television and the streets, and only secondarily by their families and the schools.[16]

AACE professionals would devise supplementary educational programs and strategies that could be replicated in all parts of the country for the support and training of all black children and youth throughout the "life course," but especially between 12 weeks (gestation age) and 20 years old. Working with expectant mothers, families, social service agencies, the police, and the schools, coordinated social and educational programs could be established in every community, with the objective of monitoring the social, psychological, and physical development of each black child beginning 12 weeks after conception (the first trimester). Parenting programs would be made available as well as specialized training and healthful recreation for our children until they reach adulthood. The AACE would provide the professional expertise needed to develop and implement the "Twelve to Twenty" programs.[17] These "Twelve to Twenty" supplementary education programs would allow us to monitor and intervene at the earliest possible time to guide the intellectual and spiritual development of our children in a direction that will allow them to identify their individual talents, to reach their greatest potential, and to become contributing adult members of our communities.

CONCLUSION

Cultural capital was used in the past to finance educational institutions that were important for African Americans to advance socially, economically, and culturally. What is needed is a new educational organization that will use cultural capital to provide for the education of our children in the present and the future. One of the primary objectives for this new African American Council on Education would be to prepare African American children (and adults) for their leadership position in the African world in the 21st century. In other words, this new leadership group would be committed to closing the "responsibility gap" that currently exists between the actual position that African Americans occupy in the world and the present focus of the educational strategies, objectives, programs, and institutions for African American children. This new educational group would be able to provide 21st century answers to the question: Why are we here? It would mobilize our collective resources—cultural capital—to sponsor supplementary educational programs that would work to prevent our children from falling into the clutches of the expanding penitentiary system, while at the same time preparing them for responsible roles as citizens of the United States and the world.[18]

While the capitalist economic system may be "the only game in town," we must mobilize to resist the negative effects of capitalism on our children, families, and communities. Billions and billions of dollars in profits are made annually through the exploitation of African American children in the public schools, through the media and music industries, the prison and incarceration system, and the fast food industry. The AIDS, prison, and obesity epidemics have raged throughout our communities over the last two decades and are destroying our children, who are our future. AACE's primary objectives would be to work to protect African American children from the devastating effects of economic exploitation and to prepare them for their future roles as contributing citizens and responsible adults.

Children are the least protected and most impoverished members of our communities, and African American children are presently the most vulnerable. The African American community must mobilize its resources to make the education, protection, and preparation of our children for their roles in the world in the 21st century our highest priority. In focusing our social, economic, and cultural resources on the education of our children, we will be assisting them in answering one of the most important questions in their individual lives, "Why am I here?"

NOTES

1. For discussions of the persistently high rates of HIV infection among Afri-
    can Americans under 30, see Phill Wilson, "Perspective: HIV Rates Soar
    Among Urban Gay Black Men," *HIV PLUS* 4 (April/May 2001): 8, 48;
    Lynette Clementson, "Pushing Blacks to 'Confront Our Shadows,'"*Newsweek*
    (June 11, 2001): 50–51.

2. For discussions of the reasons for the high rates of HIV infection among
    African American women, see Kai Wright, "The Great Down-Low Debate,"
    Village Voice 46 (June 12, 2001): 23–24, and Benoit Denizet-Lewis, "Double
    Lives on the Down Low," *New York Times Magazine* (August 3, 2003), 28–33.
    For a detailed report on the AIDS epidemic in Africa, see Johanna
    McGeary, "Death Stalks A Continent," *Time* 157 (February 12, 2001): 26–54.

3. For statistics on the rates of incarceration for African American males, see
    Jerome G. Miller, *Search and Destroy: African American Males in the Criminal
    Justice System* (New York, 1996), 1–30; Ellis Cose, "American's Prison Genera-
    tion," *Newsweek* (November 13, 2000): 40–45. For a detailed examination of
    the formation and operation of the "prison-industrial complex," see Joseph
    T. Hallinan, *Going up the River: Travels in a Prison Nation* (New York, 2001),
    1–10.

4. For information and statistics on the obesity epidemic," see Robert Pool,
    Fat: Fighting the Obesity Epidemic (New York, 2001). See also Judy Mazel, et al.,
    Slim and Fit Kids: Raising Healthy Children in a Fast-Food World (New York,
    1999); Jana Parizkova and Arthur P. Hills, *Childhood Obesity: Prevention and
    Treatment* (New York, 2000); Boris Draznin and Robert Rizza, eds., *Clinical
    Research in Diabetes and Obesity* (New York, 1997); and Eric Schlosser, "An
    Empire of Fat" in *Fast Food Nation: The Dark Side of the All-American Meal* (Bos-
    ton, MA, 2001), 239–249.

5. Charles T. Banner-Haley, *The Fruits of Integration: Black Middle Class Ideology
    and Culture, 1960–1990* (Jackson, MS, 1994); Rutledge Dennis, ed., *Research
    in Race and Ethnic Relations: The Black Middle Class* (San Francisco, CA, 1995).

6. For a historical background on the "collective vision" of African Americans,
    see V.P. Franklin, *Living our Stories, Telling Our Truths: Autobiography and the
    Making of the African American Intellectual Tradition* (New York, 1996).

7. Adam Fairclough, *"To Redeem the Soul of America": The Southern Christian Lead-
    ership Conference and Martin Luther King, Jr.* (Athens, GA, 1987); Bettye Col-
    lier-Thomas and V.P. Franklin, *My Soul is a Witness: A Chronology of the Civil
    Rights Era, 1954–1965* (New York, 2000).

8. See, Dinesh D'Souza, *The End of Racism* (New York: Random House, 1995;
    Orlando Patterson, *The Ordeal of Integration: Progress and Resentment in Amer-
    ica's Racial Crisis* (Washington, DC, 1997) and *Rituals of Blood: Consequences of
    Slavery in Two Centuries* (Washington, DC, 1998).

9. Tony Martin, *Race First: The Ideological and Organizational Struggles of Marcus
    Garvey and the Universal Negro Improvement Association* (Westport, CT, 1976);
    Malcolm X with Alex Haley, *The Autobiography of Malcolm X* (New York,
    1965); Joe Wood, ed., Malcolm X: *In Our Own Image* (New York, 1992); V.P.
    Franklin, *Black Self Determination: A Cultural History of African American Resis-
    tance* (Brooklyn, NY, 1992); Mattias Gardell, *In the Name of Elijah Mohamad:
    Louis Farrakhan and the Nation of Islam* (Durham, NC, 1996). For a recent

positive assessment of black nationalist ideologies, see Rod Bush, *We are Not What We Seem: Black Nationalism and Class Struggle in the American Century* (New York, 1999).

10. For critical assessments of "gangsta rap," militant black nationalism, and Afrocentrism, see Stanley Crouch, *Notes of a Hanging Judge: Essays and Reviews, 1979–1989* (New York, 1990); and *The All-American Skin Game, Or The Decoy of Race: The Long and Short of It, 1990–1994* (New York, 1997); Michael Eric Dyson, *Between God and Gangsta Rap* (New York, 1996); Adolph Reed, Jr., *Class Notes: Posing As Politics and Other Thoughts on the American Scene* (New York, 2001); Stephen Howe, *Afrocentrism: Mystical Pasts and Imagined Homes* (New York, 1998); Wilson J. Moses, *Afrotopia: The Roots of African American Popular History* (New York, 1998).

11. Robert C. Smith, *We Have No Leaders: African Americans in the Post-Civil Rights Era* (Albany, NY, 1996); Adolph Reed, Jr., *Stirrings in the Jug: Black Politics in the Post-Segregation Era* (Minneapolis, MN, 1999); Peter Noel, "The Wrongs of Mr. Civil Rights: The Decline of Jesse Jackson," *Village Voice* 46 (May 8, 2001): 41–44.

12. For background information on black leaders in the 19th and 20th centuries, see August Meier, and Leon F. Litwack, eds., *Black Leaders in the Nineteenth Century* (Urbana, IL, 1989); Howard Rabinowtiz, ed., *Southern Black Leaders of the Reconstruction Era* (Urbana, IL, 1982); and August Meier and John Hope Franklin, eds., *Black Leaders in the Twentieth Century* (Urbana, IL, 1983).

13. For discussions of models of effective schooling for African American children, see Janice E. Hale, *Black Children: Their Roots, Culture, and Learning Styles* (Baltimore, MD, 1986), and *Unbank the Fire: Visions for the Education of African American Children* (Baltimore, MD, 1994); Gloria Ladson-Billings, *The Dreamkeepers: Successful Teachers of African American Children* (San Francisco, CA, 1994); Diane Pollard, Cheryl Ajirotutu, and Edgar G. Epps, eds., *African-Centered Schooling in Theory and Practice* (Westport, CT, 2000); Carol Camp Yeakey, ed., *Edmund Gordon: Producing Knowledge, Pursuing Understanding* (Stamford, CT, 2000).

14. Lawrence A. Cremin, *American Education: The Colonial Experience, 1607–1783* (New York, 1970), xiii. See also Cremin's *American Education: The National Experience, 1783–1876* (New York, 1980); *American Education: The Metropolitan Experience, 1876–1980* (New York, 1988).

15. V.P. Franklin, *The Education of Black Philadelphia: The Social and Educational History of a Minority Community, 1900–1950* (Philadelphia, PA, 1979).

16. The literature on the history and current status of African American families is voluminous. See, for example, Robert Staples, *Black Families at the Crossroads: Challenges and Prospects* (San Francisco, CA, 1993); Andrew Billingsley, *Climbing Jacob's Ladder: The Enduring Legacy of African American Families* (New York, 1994); Robert Staples, ed., *The Black Family: Essays and Studies* (6th ed., Belmont, CA, 1998). See also Harrell R. Rodgers, *Poor Women, Poor Families: The Economic Plight of America's Female-Headed Households* (Armonk, NY, 1990).

17. Models for the type of "Twelve to Twenty" programs advocated here are discussed in William Watkins, James Lewis, and Victoria Chou, eds., *Race and Education: The Roles of History and Society in Educating African American Students* (New York, 2000); Theresa Perry and Lisa Delpit, eds., *The Real Ebonics*

Debate: Power, Language, and the Education of African American Children (Boston, MA, 1998); Janice E. Hale, *Learning While Black; Strategies for Educational Excellence for African American Children* (Baltimore, MA, 2001).

18.   Edmund Gordon and Beatrice Bridglall, eds., *Supplementary Education* (Lanham, MD, 2004).

ABOUT THE CONTRIBUTORS

V.P. Franklin is Professor of History and Education at Teachers College, Columbia University and the editor of the *Journal of African American History*. Franklin has published numerous books, chapters and articles focusing on the history of African American education, urban educational history, and student culture and activism. Among his publications are: *My Soul Is A Witness: A Chronology of the Civil Rights Era, 1954–1965* (2000), *Sisters in the Struggle: African American Women in the Civil Rights–Black Power Movement* (2001), *Living Our Stories, Telling Our Truths: Autobiography and Making of the African-American Intellectual Tradition* (1996), and *The Education of Black Philadelphia: A Social and Educational History of a Minority Community, 1900–1950* (1979).

Carter Julian Savage is the Vice President, Youth Development Services for Boys & Girls Clubs of America and an education historian. His research focuses on the history of education of African Americans in the rural South, the education of contemporary African American youth, and the theoretical framework of after school educational programs for at-risk youth. He has published articles in both scholarly and professional magazines, including the *Journal of African American History* and the *Peabody Journal of Education*. Savage received a B.A. in Mathematics, M.P.P in Public Policy, and an Ed.D. in Education Administration from Vanderbilt University.

Richard M. Breaux is Assistant Professor of Black Studies at the University of Nebraska at Omaha. He received his B.A. in English from Dartmouth College, his M.A. in African-American World Studies, and a Ph.D. in the History of Education from the University of Iowa. He has contributed to

Cultural Capital and Black Education, pages 173–175
Copyright © 2004 by Information Age Publishing
All rights of reproduction in any form reserved.

the *Encyclopedia of the Midwest* and his recently completed dissertation examines the influence of "New Negro" ideology on community-building and protest among black students at the universities of Iowa, Kansas, Minnesota and Nebraska from 1900–1940.

Peggy B. Gill is Assistant Professor of Educational Leadership and Policy Studies at the University of Texas at Tyler. She is also the Director of the Southwest Educational Research in Leadership Academy. Her research interests include the history of education, policy studies and narrative inquiry methods. Her most recent article in *World Futures* addresses issues of systemic educational change. She is currently working on a co-authored book on school restructuring.

Adah Ward Randolph is Associate Professor of Education in the Department of Educational Studies at Ohio University. Randolph has published articles in the *Journal of African American History, Urban Education, Journal of Critical Inquiry into Curriculum and Instruction,* and various books. She is currently working on a co-authored book about black principals before desegregation to be published by University of North Carolina Press.

Christopher M. Span is Assistant Professor of Education at the University of Illinois at Urbana-Champaign. He is a historian of education in the department of Educational Policy Studies. His research interests pertain to the educational history of 19th and 20th century African Americans. His most recent publications include an article on juvenile justice and African Americans in 19th Century Philadelphia and New York in the *Journal of Negro Education,* a co-authored book chapter on African American education before and after the Civil War in the Blackwell Companion to African American History, and an essay on African American education prior to the Civil War. This latter essay can be found in the volume *Surmounting All Odds,* edited by Carol Camp Yeakey and Ronald Henderson. He is completing a book-length manuscript on the educational history of African Americans in Mississippi between 1862 and 1875.

Betty Collier-Thomas is Professor of History at Temple University in Philadelphia, PA. She is the founding Executive Director of the Bethune Museum and Archives in Washington, DC, and formerly the Director of the Center for African American History and Culture at Temple University. Collier-Thomas is the author of *Daughters of Thunder: Black Women Preachers and Their Sermons, 1850–1979* (1998) and *My Soul Is a Witness: A Chronology of the Civil Rights Era, 1954–1965* (2001); editor of *African American Christmas Stories,* Volumes I & II (1999, 2000); and the co-editor of *Sisters in the Struggle: African American Women in the Civil Rights–Black Power Movement* (2001).

Monica A. White is a doctoral candidate in the Department of Curriculum and Teaching at Teachers College, Columbia University. She is currently a research assistant with the National Center for Restructuring Education, Schools, and Teaching (NCREST) and serves as a consultant in K–12 educational settings where she works with teachers and administrators, creating small learning communities.

INDEX

Cultural Capital and Black Education, pages 177–184
Copyright © 2004 by Information Age Publishing

Printed in the United States
25666LVS00003BE/2